Dr David Adam is a writer and editor at *Nature*, the world's leading scientific journal. He was previously a specialist correspondent on the *Guardian* for seven years, writing on science, medicine and the environment. He was named feature writer of the year by the Association of British Science Writers, and has reported from Antarctica, the Arctic, China and the depths of the Amazon jungle.

Praise for *The Man Who Couldn't Stop*

'A narrative that combines a scientific account of OCD from ancient times to the most recent research with passages of tenderly written memoir . . . The story of his own OCD makes a moving counterpoint to the complex and occasionally lurid history of the disorder and its treatments . . . as his book graphically demonstrates, the inside of the human mind is a stranger place than we who think of ourselves as "normal" would ever care to admit'

Sunday Telegraph

'This blew me away. Stunning' Ian Sample, *Guardian*

'[A] superb book . . . I salute Adam's courage. Coming clean on any aspect of mental ill-health is easier than it was – and yet it is not to date fully risk-free . . . For writing about that as honestly – and entertainingly – as he does, he should be congratulated . . . This account is a brave and helpful contribution to deepening our understanding of the intricate complexities of mental ill-health' *The Times*

'Adam recounts his journey with humour and detachment'
Literary Review

'*The Man Who Couldn't Stop* is quite simply book of the year, on living with OCD: just buy it now'   Adam Rutherford

'One of the best and most readable studies of a mental illness to have emerged in recent years. What makes this book compelling reading is its openness. I mean that in every sense. The author is candid not only about the inevitable limitations of any book on mental illness, when we only know so much about the brain, but also about his own experience . . . an honest and open and, yes, maybe life-changing work'   Matt Haig, *Observer*

'Adam, an award-winning science writer and editor at the journal *Nature*, is uniquely placed to examine the genetic, evolutionary, psychological, medical and "just plain unfortunate" possible causes of OCD. He does so with vigour, sharp analysis, compassion and occasional humour . . . *The Man Who Couldn't Stop* is a fundamentally important book that will bring a breath of fresh understanding to sufferers – as well as mental-health professionals, and family and friends of anyone who exhibits symptoms of OCD. I urge anyone to buy it. It will make you think again'
Sunday Times

'It has become hip these days to refer to one's quirks as "a bit OCD", as though it were a badge of cool unconventionality . . . This engaging, exhaustively researched neuro memoir, a blend of brain science and personal history, aims to debunk this popular perception of OCD and show it in its true light, as a debilitating and often life-threatening condition'   *Evening Standard*

'Adam makes an important contribution by increasing public awareness, and clarifying that OCD is not simply an exaggerated desire for hygiene and order . . . People such as Adam hold in their brains some of the most valuable contributions to the fight against neuropsychiatric diseases: blow-by-blow accounts of how their obsessions, compulsions, thoughts and emotions are linked and evolve'   *Nature*

'A captivating first-person account of how a blizzard of unwanted thoughts can become a personal nightmare. At times shocking, at times tragic, at times unbelievably funny, it is a wonderful read . . . This book will appeal to all those who are fascinated by the human mind and its unending ability to delight and to torment'   *BBC Focus*

'A lucid, humane – only intermittently autobiographical – science book. Written in the vein of Oliver Sacks or Andrew Soloman, it offers a clear history through riveting case studies and the work of key figures such as Freud, while including an overview of current research'   *Metro*

'David Adam, a successful writer, is also a sufferer of obsessive compulsive disorder, OCD. In this book he covers the history of OCD, the treatments that have been tried without success, and his experience of cognitive behavioural therapy, CBT, which was greatly helpful. A well-written, thorough account'   *Independent*

'His fascinating book will prove valuable to those afflicted by OCD but also to anyone interested in the darker recesses of the mind'   *Financial Times*

'This is a book that will challenge the way you think about what is normal, and what is mental illness'
                                          Queensland Times

'This is a remarkable book for its honesty . . . A fascinating educational read'   *Cairns Eye* (Australia)

'The dramatic behaviours of extreme OCD can make for gripping yarns. From persistent sexual or violent thoughts to obsessive daydreaming, hoarding to hair pulling, there's the risk of putting that neurological freak show on parade again. But Adam walks that line thoughtfully, because this is his experience too . . . a good-humoured, lyrically told story'   *The Age* (Australia)

DAVID ADAM

THE MAN WHO COULDN'T STOP

THE TRUTH ABOUT OCD

PICADOR

First published 2014 by Picador

First published in paperback 2015 by Picador
an imprint of Pan Macmillan, a division of Macmillan Publishers Limited
Pan Macmillan, 20 New Wharf Road, London N1 9RR
Basingstoke and Oxford
Associated companies throughout the world
www.panmacmillan.com

ISBN 978-1-4472-7768-2

The author and publisher would like to thank the Society of Authors
and Faber and Faber for their kind permission to reproduce an excerpt
from 'This Be The Verse' from *Collected Poems* by Philip Larkin.

1 3 5 7 9 8 6 4 2

A CIP catalogue record for this book is available from the British Library.

Typeset by Palimpsest Book Production Limited, Falkirk, Stirlingshire
Printed and bound by CPI Group (UK) Ltd, Croydon, CR0 4YY

Visit **www.picador.com** to read more about all our books
and to buy them. You will also find features, author interviews and
news of any author events, and you can sign up for e-newsletters
so that you're always first to hear about our new releases.

For those who deserve an explanation

Watch your thoughts, for they become words.
Watch your words, for they become actions.
Watch your actions, for they become habits.
Watch your habits, for they become character.
Watch your character, for it becomes your destiny.

Unknown

CONTENTS

ONE

Our siege mentality

An Ethiopian schoolgirl called Bira once ate a wall of her house. She didn't want to, but she found that to eat the wall was the only way to stop her thinking about it. She didn't want to think about the wall either, in fact she was greatly disturbed by the ideas and images of it that dominated her mind. The only way she could make the thoughts of the wall go away, and calm the anxiety they caused, was to follow a strange and unbearably strong urge to eat it. So she did; day after day, for year after year. By the time she was 17 years old she had eaten eight square metres of the wall – more than half a tonne of mud bricks.

Bira lived in the capital city, Addis Ababa. Her father died when she was young and she grew up with her mother. Bira had eaten mud every day for as long as she could remember, since she was a little girl. It became worse as a teenager, when she started to take it only from the wall of her home. As she did so, the images and thoughts came more vividly and more often, which only intensified her need to eat to find relief. The mud made Bira constipated and gave her severe stomach aches. Ethiopian traditional healers tried to treat her with prayers and holy water and advised her simply to stop eating the mud. But she couldn't. She couldn't stop her thoughts about the wall, and so she couldn't stop eating it.

One day, Bira couldn't cope any more. Her distended stomach throbbed with pain and her abdomen was tight with cramp. Her throat was scratched raw from the straw in the bricks and her body riddled with parasites from the soil. In tears, she walked to her local hospital. At the time, Ethiopia had eight psychiatrists for a nation of 70 million people. Bira was fortunate. She managed to see one of them. She told him that she needed help. She knew her thoughts were wrong, but she knew she couldn't stop them alone.

An average person can have four thousand thoughts a day, and not all of them are useful or rational. Mental flotsam comes in many forms. There are the irrelevant words, phrases, names and images that flash unprompted into our minds, often as we perform some mundane task. There are earworms: tunes that wedge themselves in our heads, more prosaically called stuck-song syndrome. And there are negative thoughts – 'I cannot do this,' 'I must quit' – the sworn enemy of sports psychologists everywhere.

Then there are the very strange thoughts: those occasional, random and unprompted ideas that seem to emerge from nowhere and stun because they are vile, immoral, disgusting, sickening – and just plain weird. The seductive question, 'what if'? What if I was to jump in front of that bus? What if I was to punch that woman?

These kinds of thoughts are more common than most people realize. Ask around. A friend of mine has a need to check the toilet bowl for rats before he sits. Another unplugs the iron and places it in an unusual place when he finishes with it, so he knows for certain the answer when his mind demands later: are you sure, really sure, that you turned it off? One tortured soul spent an evening unable to ignore the repetitive thought that he may have scrawled across an application form for his dream job the word cunt. Most people have these kinds of strange thoughts. Most shake them off. Some people don't.

When we cannot make our strange thoughts go away they can lead to misery and mental illness. The friends I mention above did not convert their strange thoughts in this way. But I did.

I turned mine into obsessive-compulsive disorder.

The day that the Brazilian racing driver Ayrton Senna died in a crash during a Grand Prix in Italy, I was stuck in the toilet of a Manchester swimming pool. The door was open but my thoughts blocked the way out.

It was May 1994. I was 22 and hungry. After swimming a few lengths of the pool, I lifted myself from the water and headed for the locker rooms. Down the steps – one, two, three – ouch! I had scraped the back of my heel down the sharp edge of the final step. It left a small graze, through which blood bulged into a blob that hung from my broken skin. I transferred the drop to my finger and a second swelled to take its place. I pulled a paper towel from above the sink to press to my wet heel. The blood on my finger ran with the water as it dripped down my arm. My eyes, of course, followed the blood. And the anxiety, of course, rushed back, ahead even of the memory. My shoulders sagged. My stomach tightened. It had been four weeks since the incident at the bus stop, and, as much as I told myself that it no longer bothered me, I was lying.

I had pricked my finger on a screw that stuck out from the bus shelter's corrugated metal. It was a busy Saturday afternoon and there had been lots of people around. Any one of them, I thought, could easily have injured themselves in the way I had. What if one had been HIV-positive? They could have left infected blood on the screw, which then pierced my skin. That would put the virus into my bloodstream. Oh, I knew the official line was that transmission that way was impossible. The virus couldn't survive outside the body. But I also knew that, when pressed for long enough, those in the know would weaken that to virtually impossible. They couldn't be absolutely sure. In fact, several had admitted to me there was a theoretical risk.

Stood quietly in the toilets of the changing rooms, still dripping wet, my swimming goggles in one hand and the blood-stained paper towel in the other, I ran through the sequence of events at the bus stop once again. I told myself how there hadn't been any blood on the screw when I had checked it, or at least I didn't think there had been. Oh, why hadn't I made absolutely sure?

Someone else banged through the door into the swimming pool changing rooms. They whistled. I looked at my finger. Wait a minute. WHAT THE HELL HAD I DONE? I had put a paper towel on a fresh cut. OH JESUS CHRIST. There could have been anything on that paper towel. YOU STUPID BASTARD. I looked at the paper towel, now soggy. THERE IS BLOOD ON IT. Well, of course, it's my blood. HOW CAN YOU BE SURE? Someone with Aids and a bleeding hand could have touched it before me. OH JESUS. I threw it into the bin, pulled a second from the dispenser and inspected it. No blood. That helped, a little. No blood on the next one either. BUT THEY COULD HAVE DONE. I pulled the original paper towel back from the bin. It was bloody. IF THIS IS SOMEONE ELSE'S BLOOD THEN WHY ARE YOU PICKING IT UP? I quickly washed my hands. AND WHAT IF THEY BLED INTO THE SINK TOO? DON'T TOUCH YOUR FUCKING HEEL. DON'T TOUCH YOUR FUCKING HEEL. No chance of that. WHAT IF THAT ISN'T EVEN THE PAPER TOWEL YOU THREW IN THE BIN? It could be someone else's paper towel that I was handling, someone else's blood. I looked in the bin. I couldn't see any other paper towels with blood on them. WHAT ABOUT THAT ONE?

The whistling man was ready to swim. He came to the sink, grabbed a paper towel, blew his nose and threw it into the bin. I did the same. He looked at me. I smiled. He didn't. He walked away. I didn't. He finished his swim and left. I couldn't.

Cycling home later, I was pleased with the solution I

had found. I was getting somewhere! I heard the birds and felt the spring sunshine on my face. Well, of course I couldn't have caught Aids from scratching myself on the screw at the bus stop. That was ridiculous, I could see that now. I had nothing to worry about on that score. I pulled my swimming trunks from my bag and placed them on my bedroom radiator. I rummaged in the wardrobe for my winter gloves and put them on to unfold my swimming towel and carefully retrieve the damp and blood-stained paper towel wrapped inside. I placed it on the radiator next to the trunks. It would take about ten minutes, I guessed, before it would be dry enough to check properly. Then I reached back into the bag and found the other crumpled paper towels, the ones I had lifted from the bin, and laid those out on my desk. I would check those as well, check them properly (impossible in the changing rooms), and then surely that would be that. Then I could put all this behind me. Phew! I took off the gloves and turned on the TV. The Grand Prix was about to start.

Those are my strange thoughts. That is my obsessive-compulsive disorder. I obsess about ways that I could catch Aids. I compulsively check to make sure I haven't caught HIV and I steer my behaviour to make sure I don't catch it in future. I see HIV everywhere. It lurks on toothbrushes and towels, taps and telephones. I wipe cups and bottles, hate sharing drinks and cover every scrape and graze with multiple plasters. My compulsions can demand that after a scratch from a rusty nail or a piece of glass, I return to wrap it in absorbent paper and check for drops of contaminated blood that may have been there. Dry skin between my toes can force me to walk on my heels through crowded locker rooms, in case of blood on the floor. I have checked train seats for syringes and toilet seats for just about everything.

As a journalist, I meet a lot of people and shake their hands. If I have a cut on my finger, or I notice that someone who I talk to has a bandage or a plaster over a wound, thoughts of the handshake and how to avoid it can start to crowd out everything else. My rational self knows that these fears are ridiculous. I know that I can't catch Aids in those situations. But still the thoughts and the anxiety come.

The psychiatrist who Bira saw in Addis Ababa told her she had obsessive-compulsive disorder (OCD) too. She had persistent thoughts that were inappropriate. She could not ignore or suppress these thoughts, which made her anxious. To reduce and prevent this anxiety she developed compulsive behaviour. The compulsions fuelled the obsessions. Together, the obsessions and compulsions took up so much time and caused such distress that they disrupted her life.

Most people have heard of OCD but there is much confusion about the condition. It's commonly seen as a behavioural quirk. In fact, OCD is a severe and crippling illness, and one defined as much by the mental torment of recurring strange thoughts as physical actions such as repeated handwashing. Bira was diagnosed with moderately-severe OCD. Yes, a girl who ate an entire wall of her house was thought to have it only *moderately*-severe. There are plenty of people out there who have it worse. Bira spent about two hours a day thinking about the wall and eating mud. Yet, on average, OCD patients can waste up to six hours a day on their obsessions and four hours on their compulsions. A Brazilian man called Marcus had OCD that centred on obsessive thoughts about the shape of his eye-sockets, so much so that he was compelled to touch them constantly with his fingers. Marcus prodded himself blind.

It is hard to communicate obsession – severe, clinical obsession, a true monopoly of thought. Just as the human brain struggles to comprehend the magnitude of geological time, or the speed at which electronics can operate, or even the number of times a second the wings of a hummingbird can beat, so it can seem incredible that a single notion, a unique concept, can truly dominate someone's mind for days, weeks, months, years. Here is the best description I have.

Consider a personal computer, and the various windows and separate operations that the machine can run concurrently. As I write this, there is another window open in the background that updates my email, and a separate web browser that, right now, tracks football scores. When I choose, I can toggle between these windows, make them bigger or smaller, open and close others as I see fit. That is how the mind usually handles thoughts. It shares conscious concentration between tasks, while the subconscious changes the content of each window, or draws our attention among them.

Obsession is a large window that cannot be made to shrink, move or close. Even when other tasks come to the front of the mind, the obsession window is there in the background. It grinds away and is ready to sequester attention. It acts as a constant drag on the battery and degrades the performance of other tasks. And after a while it just gets really frustrating. You can't force quit and you can't turn the machine off and on. Whenever you are awake, the window is there. And when you do manage to turn your attention elsewhere, you are aware that you deliberately do so. Soon enough, the obsession will reclaim the focus. Sometimes, usually when you wake, it is absent. The screen is blank. But push a key, move the mouse, engage the brain, and it whirrs and clicks back into place.

As recently as the 1980s, psychiatrists thought that clinical obsessions and compulsions were extremely rare. They believe now that between 2 per cent and 3 per cent of people suffer from OCD at some point in their life. That means more than a million people in Britain are affected directly, and five million more in the United States. OCD is the fourth most common mental disorder after the big three – depression, substance abuse and anxiety. OCD is twice as common as autism and schizophrenia. The World Health Organization has ranked OCD as the tenth most disabling medical condition. Its impact on quality of life has been judged more severe than diabetes. But people with OCD typically wait a decade or more before they seek help.

OCD affects men and women equally. It begins usually in early teens or late adolescence and early adulthood, though its effects can last a lifetime. It respects no cultural, ethnic, racial or geographical boundaries. OCD is a social handicap and a societal burden. Children with OCD are more likely to want friends, but less likely to make them. Adults with OCD are more likely to be unemployed and unmarried. They drag down their families. They are more likely to live with their parents. They are more likely to be celibate. If they do marry, they are less likely to have children. They are more likely to divorce. Yet many front-line doctors still fail to recognize the signs and symptoms of OCD or their significance. Few people with OCD spontaneously recover, yet two-thirds of sufferers never see a mental health professional.

The word 'obsess' first appeared in English in the early 1500s. Drawn from the Latin *obsidere*, literally 'before to sit' but more commonly defined as 'to besiege', the term has a military background. To obsess a city was to surround but not yet control it. The related *possidere*, from which we derive posses and possessed, described the subsequent stage, when a victorious army would take control of the city and conquer its people.

The drift of these words to describe troubled individuals, first in religious terms and later in clinical language, carried the same distinction. The original use of obsess reflected the belief that the strange thought – in those days attributed to an evil spirit – originated outside the victim. To be obsessed was something that happened *to* someone; a person was not obsessed with an idea – it was the idea that obsessed them. This was different from someone who was possessed, when the spirit was thought to invade and control a person from the inside.

A diagnosis of whether someone was obsessed or possessed by evil spirits often came down to whether the victim was aware of the malevolent presence; whether they recognized their thoughts as alien and so tried to resist them. Those who were obsessed were considered able to do this. Victims of possession, because they had surrendered their soul to the invading demons, were not. They remained unaware of what was happening. The distinction survives to this day. A diagnosis of OCD usually requires a degree of what psychiatrists call insight – an obsessed person must identify the strange thoughts that drive the obsession as foreign and distressing and must make efforts to reject them.

Today, obsession is a more widely used word. Because thoughts usually come and go, the head a constant swirl of involuntary emotions and sensations, it takes only a drag of coalescence of this mental stardust around a recurrent theme to form a temporary lump, a sticking point, that society calls an obsession. In this way, people say they are obsessed when they cannot get an attractive person out of their minds, or when they cannot quell thoughts about a certain food. Our minds are so fluid that any sluggish current draws our attention. We say we obsess about sport, sex, shoes, cream buns, cars and a thousand other pleasures, sometimes all at the same time. But in time, often no time at all, these so-called obsessions break away and are carried off and consumed by the mental stream. That is not the obsession we will talk about here. It would not make some-body eat a wall.

The obsessive thoughts of OCD are different and tend to cluster around a limited number of themes. Obsessions of contamination with dirt and disease are the most frequent and feature in about a third of cases. Irrational fears of harm – did I lock the back door? Is the oven switched off? – are the next most common, and affect about a quarter of people with OCD. About one in ten wrestles with an obsessive need for patterns and symmetry. Rarer, but still significant, are obsessions with the body and physical symptoms, religious and blasphemous thoughts, unwanted sexual thoughts, and thoughts of carrying out acts of violence. It's because obsessive thoughts are so often within these taboo and embarrassing subjects that so many people with OCD choose to hide them.

Obsession has no regard for rational explanation. No pathology of thought can be solved with more thought. The brilliant twentieth-century mathematician Kurt Gödel, a friend and colleague of Albert Einstein, lived his life for rationality. His incompleteness theorem used logic to explore and expose the limits of logic. Yet Gödel suffered from the wildly irrational and obsessive idea that he would accidentally be poisoned, from tainted food perhaps, or by gas that escaped from his refrigerator. He would eat no meal that his wife did not taste first. When she became ill and could not do this for him, the obsessive siege on his mind made Gödel starve himself to death.

*

Why I am writing this book? Obsession encourages attention to turn inward and drains focus from relationships with others. OCD cements the presence of an individual at the centre of their mind and their actions. And it distracts. There is always something else that you would rather think about, or not think about. I don't want to be selfish any more. I now have two children who need me. I don't want them to go through what I did. I don't want them to develop obsessions, to be held hostage by their strange thoughts, to think up a monster. And if they do, I want to be able to help them.

The best way to do that, I believe, is to investigate these strange and obsessive thoughts, to see how they work, where they come from and what we can learn from them. To question how the brain, our closest ally and biggest asset in millions of years of evolution, can turn against us so. To see what forces to the surface the obsessive Mr Hyde who lies dormant inside every Dr Jekyll – inside you – and how his betrayal can be stopped. And, as it turns out, it is a terrific story.

Strange thoughts, the seeds of obsession, are everywhere. They scatter across the population. Yet only occasionally do they take root. The first step in our journey to understand obsession is to see how this happens.

TWO

Bad thoughts

'How easy it would be for me to stick this kitchen knife into him.' Most people have thoughts like that. They are called intrusive thoughts. Most people don't talk about their intrusive thoughts.

They don't talk about them, that is, until psychologists take the trouble to ask. When they do, then survey after survey shows that about nine in ten people admit they experience intrusive thoughts that distress, bewilder, shock and perplex them. Most people have thoughts about driving their car off the road. A third of us say we have thoughts of grabbing money. More than four in ten get an urge to jump from a high place, an impulse so common that it has its own scientific name: the high-place phenomenon. Half of all women and eight out of ten men have thoughts of strangers in the nude, while half of all people cannot help but think of sex acts they consider 'disgusting'.

Intrusive thoughts are everywhere. But it took until the late 1970s for anyone to notice, when the South African-born psychologist Stanley Rachman and his Sri Lankan colleague Padmal de Silva made a stunning discovery. In trying to understand the nature of obsession, the two realized that many normal people seemed to have the same kinds of strange thoughts and impulses as patients with OCD.

Their obsessive-compulsive patients had urges to insult and physically attack people, but so, it turned out, did their friends. The patients reported impulses to push people under trains and buses, to jump from high places and to deliberately crash their car. So did their colleagues. Both groups had ideas of violence during sex, thoughts they might have committed a crime they heard about on the news and harboured irrational fears that they might have suffered some contamination, such as from radiation or asbestos.

When the psychologists wrote down the weird thoughts harvested from the minds of their OCD patients and those from their 'normal' associates on index cards, and mixed the cards up, even their most experienced clinical colleagues could not correctly distinguish which thoughts came from the damaged minds of patients considered mentally ill and which came from the highly respected people they worked and socialized with.

My OCD began with an intrusive thought, a snowflake that fell from the summer sky. 'Shall we go upstairs?' the girl had asked me. She was pretty, with long black hair that she had to push back from her eyes as we kissed. The skin on her arms was smooth and her hands, I remember, seemed so small. She was older than me, though she didn't think so. Her question: 'You're not a first year are you?' hadn't left me much room to manoeuvre. I had lied about my university course too. I knew nothing about the politics of the French revolution but it sounded of more appeal to her than chemical engineering. I knew little about chemical engineering either, but then I had only studied it for a couple of months.

I was eighteen and a happy college student. Real life was on hold and time was a string of fun nights and daytime lectures on fluid dynamics and mathematics. I had little idea what a chemical engineer did, but I didn't care. That was the future. And right now it felt good to think about only the next day.

It was November 1990 in northern England so she wore a baggy white T-shirt with a purple skirt over Doc Marten boots and black leggings. I was pleased with my newly-grown sideburns. I thought she might mention them as we stumbled through the dry sand of our early conversation. By the time we headed from the university campus and into the neighbouring maze of terraced houses I realized that she wasn't going to. We walked and we talked, about music and our friends. We reached her house and, as she invited me inside and closed the front door behind us, a new world beckoned.

It was one of those frozen Leeds nights that Yorkshire folk are so proud of. The wheezing gas fire in her kitchen generated more light than heat and the cold chased us around the room like the smoke from a wood fire. Upstairs sounded good.

'Did you have sex with that girl?' my friend Noel asked the next day.

'Yes,' I lied.

'Did you use a condom?'

'No.'

'You could have Aids.'

'Don't be daft.'

Had I had sex with that girl? No. Had we used a condom? No. Could I have caught Aids? Don't be daft. Still, I hadn't even considered the threat, despite all of the warnings. I should be more careful next time, I thought as I bought Noel a drink that night. I should have been more careful. The same thought, an echo of our conversation – you could have Aids – floated back into my mind from time to time over the next few months, but on each occasion I could muster the mental puff to blow it out. Don't be daft. Then, one hot night in the August of 1991, I couldn't.

On holiday from university as I walked back to my parents' house, with no warning the thought came again. You could have Aids. Only this time I couldn't move past the idea, or the cramps of panic it caused. 'Don't be daft' suddenly seemed an inadequate response to the scale of the threat, the possible consequences. I could have Aids. And if I did, then I was doomed. My life was over before it had truly begun. Worse, no matter what I did, no matter what anybody said, I could not change it. They could not fix it. I had lost the power over my own fate. As I tried to brush away the thought, the snowflake, it squirmed from my mental grasp and settled. Quickly it was joined by another, then another, then another. The blizzard that followed blew the snow into every corner of my mind, and laid down a blanket that muffled every surface.

I gulped for air when I opened the window in my stuffy bedroom. I heard the scratch on the ceiling of the summer insects when I turned out the light. I saw the red glow of the stereo, still switched on from when I had lay on the same bed that afternoon, which already seemed a lifetime ago. I ripped down the dog-eared posters on the wall in terror. Why me? I was so frightened that the tips of my fingers tingled. I remember I told myself that all would be fine when I woke up the next morning. That was how life was – everyone had night terrors and everyone saw things differently the next day.

The sun rose and the windows and curtains were still wide open. The thought was still there. You could have Aids. I went downstairs to the kitchen and had breakfast in the new world I would inhabit from that day, the first of the rest of my life. I watched my mum and dad gently bicker across the wooden kitchen table, and I thought how sad they would be if I did have Aids. I decided I would not tell them. I went back upstairs to my bedroom and buried my face in my pillow and wept. I could have Aids.

The obsessive thoughts of OCD are different to those that tend to dominate other types of mental anguish. Recurring and distressing thoughts are not always an obsession – at least not in the clinical sense. We can find our minds dominated by exaggerated and distressing thoughts of whether our child will survive and flourish in the world, for instance, or crippling nerves before an exam or driving test, but thoughts like that are in step with the rules and rhythms of our life. We want our child to be happy. We want to pass. We can think and worry non-stop about whether we might lose our job, but only because we know we need the money it brings to feed and clothe our family, which we feel and instinctively sense is the right thing to do.

Thoughts like that are 'ego-syntonic'. They are in harmony with our drives and motivations. Ego-syntonic thoughts can make us unhappy, but when they do it is their contents and not the thoughts themselves that are the problem. We do not question why we have them. Indeed, sometimes we resent others who do not have ego-syntonic thoughts as acutely as we do. 'I can't believe you left this to the last minute.' 'It's only been a month. Of course I still miss him.'

Taken to extremes these types of ego-syntonic thoughts can cause mental disorder, usually anxiety. But at their heart most concerns of anxiety are rational. So, usually, are the dark thoughts of depression: endless rumination on external events, regret of decisions and how life has unfolded. Severe grief, hysteria even, is based on the rational sense of loss.

Unwanted and intrusive thoughts, the raw materials of obsession, are different. They are irrational. They strike a mental discord. They are 'ego-dystonic'. They clash with how we see ourselves, and how we want others to see us. Just to think these thoughts is enough to make us question who we are. We are not dishonest, yet we could snatch the money from that open till so easily. We do not want to be the dreadful person who could think such terrible and ridiculous things. But most people are.

Winston Churchill, a one-time First Lord of the Admiralty, didn't like to travel by ship because of the ego-dystonic urge he had to jump into the water. Churchill was a well-known depressive but these, and similar thoughts he had of jumping in front of trains (he liked to stand with a pillar between himself and the edge of the platform) do not appear to have been genuinely suicidal impulses. Talking once of how he hated to sleep in a bedroom with access to a balcony from which he felt the urge to jump, he told his doctor Charles Moran:

> I don't want to go out of the world at all in such moments. I've no desire to quit this world, but thoughts, desperate thoughts, come into my head.

As Churchill observed, to have intrusive thoughts is not a sign that someone wants to act on them. A disturbing thought of sex with a child does not make someone a paedophile, just as an unwanted urge to hit someone with a hammer does not make someone a thug or a murderer. In fact the opposite is true. To consider such a thought or urge unwanted, disturbing and unwelcome – and so intrusive – is usually enough to show it is ego-dystonic and so contrary to someone's normal personality and actions.

Where do these bizarre thoughts come from? The simple, if unsatisfying, answer is that we don't know for sure. The theory used by psychologists who study OCD is that our brains have something they call a cognitive 'idea generator'. On most other occasions, this generator helps us to solve problems.

To consider all possible solutions, it's important for the mind to generate novel ideas and not immediately censor them. It's a similar principle to a corporate brainstorm exercise and how every idea to boost sales or attract customers – however stupid – gets written on its own sticky note and given a nod of approval from an overenthusiastic manager. The cognitive idea generator does not have to anchor its responses to reality. Intrusive thoughts are what happens when the mind says 'yes, and' rather than 'yes, but'.

Not all unasked-for thoughts are unwanted or un-pleasant, far from it. Mozart revelled in musical thoughts he did not command. Beethoven said something similar:

> You will ask me where I get my ideas. That I cannot say with certainty. They come unbidden, indirectly, directly. I could grasp them with my hands; in the midst of nature, in the woods, on walks, in the silence of the night, in the early morning, inspired by moods that translate them-selves into words for the poet and into tones for me, that sound, surge, roar, until at last they stand before me as notes.

Random inspirations of musical genius are all very well, if you're fortunate enough to have them. But the thoughts most likely to make the rest of us sit up and take notice are odd and unpleasant. Those are also the ones that tend to stick around. Nobody gets obsessed by thoughts that they will be too nice to people, or by urges to give all their money away to a tramp. People do not complain to psychologists of intrusive thoughts of pushing someone with the build of a heavyweight boxer under a subway train. Intrusive thoughts bother us because the usual imagined victims are the small and the weak, the puny and the vulnerable; the child and the little old lady. It's what psychologists label the Arnold Schwarzenegger effect.

This might make sense, given the theory that a mental idea generator helps us to navigate through life. We may consider it uncivilized, but there are some situations where a natural and useful reaction when one sees a stranger would indeed be to beat them over the head. The smaller the stranger is than you, and so the lower the chance that they can hurt you, the more attractive that option becomes.

According to the theory, sometimes an external cue – the rattle of a train or a dirty floor – can kick the idea generator into action, and make it churn out intrusive thoughts. At other times the trigger is internal – the result of stress or a low mood or a subconscious emotional shift, or the residue of an incomplete memory. In this case, the intrusions appear almost at random.

It's hard to test these ideas, so there is no experimental evidence to support them. All we know for sure is that intrusive thoughts pop up more in certain circumstances than others, under stress for instance, and that when they do appear, how we react is critical. A natural reaction, especially if the thoughts will not recede by themselves, is to try to force them to go away, to squash the idea, to deliberately shove the unpleasant notion behind the mental furniture or under the rug. That's a bad idea. That's when the problems can begin.

Leo Tolstoy knew well the mind's inability to repel unwanted thoughts. When he was a child, the Russian novelist would play a game with his siblings. To join a secret club called the Ant Brothers, whose members would discover wonderful things, they had only to stand in one corner of a room and try to not think of a polar bear. As hard as they tried, Tolstoy and the others could not manage it.

Fyodor Dostoyevsky, a contemporary of Tolstoy, knew of the bear conundrum too. In his 1863 book *Winter Notes on Summer Impressions* he wrote: 'Try and set yourself the task not to think of a white bear, and the cursed thing comes to mind every minute.' A century later, that Dostoyevsky quote appeared in an article in the US magazine *Playboy*, where it was read by a university psychology student called Daniel Wegner.

Wegner, who died of motor neurone disease in July 2013 just as I was finishing this book, rose to run the Mental Control Laboratory at Harvard University, but he will always be remembered as the white bear guy. His work with the bears can explain why, even though we see a hole in the road ahead, we steer our bike right into it. It shows why forbidden love offers the most thrills. It can reveal why footballers, desperate not to hit penalty kicks straight at the goalkeeper, go ahead and do just that. In 2009, he wrote an article for the prestigious journal *Science* titled 'How to think, say, or do precisely the worst thing for any occasion'. Most of all, Wegner's research shows why unwanted intrusive thoughts can hang around; why some people find them so difficult to brush off. It shows how we can turn them into obsessions.

In the 1980s at Trinity University in San Antonio, Texas, just a quick gallop from the Alamo and one of the last places on Earth that anyone would associate with a polar bear, Wegner asked some of his students to repeat the Tolstoy trial under scientific conditions. He asked them to try to not think of a white bear.

Students told not to think of the bears found it difficult. And students told to do the opposite and to encourage thoughts of white bears, of course, thought of more. (Wegner kept track by asking them to ring a bell.) Most surprising was what happened next, when Wegner reversed the tasks so those students previously told to think of the bears were now asked not to, and vice versa. Those students who had originally tried to keep away the white bears now found their minds flooded with them – more so than the students instructed to think about them originally.

It's an experiment that has been repeated many times since with similar results. It is hard, if not impossible, to suppress unwanted thoughts. And to try leads to an increase in the thoughts later on, after someone has stopped attempting to suppress them. The latter effect appears in psychology textbooks as the rebound effect of thought suppression. Most psychologists call it the white bear effect – try to make an unwanted thought go away and it will bounce back, harder and stronger than before.

Anyone who, to borrow a phrase from Oscar Wilde, can resist everything except temptation will recognize just how hard thought suppression is; everyone who has tried to give up cigarettes, or to stick to a calorie-controlled diet. That feeling, the urge and craving, is the sound of the white bear as it paws at the door.

This ironic effect – that a suppressed thought comes back stronger – could underpin a range of unusual human behaviours. It could explain, for instance, why those smokers who are the most motivated to quit also seem to find it the hardest to give up. The brain could interpret intrusive thoughts about a substance as a craving for it. The more smokers try to push away the thoughts of a cigarette, the more they amplify their craving. Studies show those people who had tried and failed to quit cigarettes are indeed more likely to suppress thoughts. A similar effect has been seen in obese people who overeat: they are more likely to suppress thoughts about chocolate and chips, and so increase the craving for them. Suppressing a thought before sleep can even make it resurface in a dream.

What's going on? According to theories of how the mind works, the white bear effect is down to two mental processes. First, people who try not to think of the white bear must choose to think of something else, and so they introduce and employ a conscious distraction; thinking about what they had for breakfast, for instance. But before we can introduce a distraction, we must know there is a target to distract ourselves from. So, before we can suppress a thought, we must scan our conscious mind to see if it is there. And to do this, we must think of what we want to look for – the white bear – which is the target that we don't want to think of.

Second, a separate process begins to make sure that the target, the unwanted thought of a white bear, is not present. While this second, monitoring, task is automatic, an unconscious routine that takes little work, the same is not true for the distraction, the thought suppression. That takes real effort, and so cannot last. If the monitoring process lingers after the distraction process has ended, and psychologists think it does, then our minds will continue to search for it. And this means we will find the unwanted thought more frequently than if we had never tried to suppress it in the first place.

That's not to say that intrusive thoughts can't be banished, at least in the short term. Distraction – to keep the mind busy – is a pretty effective way to do that. But it's difficult to keep up for too long. Markus Wasmeier could manage it for barely three minutes – just long enough for the German skier to write his name into the record books.

Stood at the top of a mountain in the early 1990s, Wasmeier's teammate Hansjorg Tauscher was given the strangest piece of advice of his career. He was fast, no doubt about that – he had astonished the winter-sports world when he tamed the fearsome downhill run at Beaver Creek in Colorado to win the 1989 world championships – but his coach had noticed a possible flaw. 'You think too much.' Tauscher was quick in the turns, but he stiffened on the fast glide sections that linked them together. And while the groomed icy runs that Alpine racers hurtle down at speeds near 90mph may look smooth, up close they are a strength-sapping series of bumps and lumps.

As they crouch and let gravity propel them down the mountain the mind of an Alpine skier in a glide can start to wander. Most do not wander too far. They start to think about how they could go even faster and as they do so they usually try too hard to control the actions of their feet and legs. The result: they tighten, hit the bumps harder and drag themselves that crucial fraction of a second down the leader board.

Juergen Beckmann, the coach, thought he had the solution. A former downhill racer himself, until a high speed crash almost broke his neck, Beckmann knew the mental problems of the glide well. Watching Tauscher practise, he decided to try an unorthodox control technique that he had picked up from research carried out in the 1960s on short-term memory. To keep the thoughts from his idle mind, Beckmann said that day, Tauscher should count backwards. When he started to glide, he should start at 999 and descend in threes. His mind and his thoughts occupied, the theory went, his legs would be more flexible and his run faster. Tauscher was sceptical, but he gave it a go. He disappeared down the mountain, mumbling under his breath '999, 996, 993 . . .'

Today, Beckmann works as a sports psychologist at the Technical University of Munich. His research to help athletes perform under pressure is world famous. But it was his work with the German Alpine ski team from 1991 to 1994 that arguably brought the greatest success. As Tauscher started to ski and count backwards, his times improved. Pretty soon, the former world champion was convinced, and Beckmann, emboldened with his apparent success, shared the secret with the rest of the team.

That was when Beckmann began to work closely with Wasmeier, another former world champion, this time of the giant slalom event back in 1985. The skier was widely considered past his best and even Beckmann's mother said her son's work with him was a waste of time. Yet, at the 1994 Winter Olympics in Norway, Markus Wasmeier won two gold medals for Germany – in the giant slalom and the super-giant slalom. Against all expectations, he earned the unlikely title of the greatest German skier of all time and was named the country's sportsman of the year. He then retired, to spend more time with his thoughts.

Beckmann's backwards count was a form of ritual, which is one way to keep unwanted thoughts from the mind. Rituals are common, and not only among skiers. Just as most people have intrusive thoughts, so too about half of the people in the general population surveyed by psychologists will admit they perform odd and meaningless rituals.

Some check the cooker is switched off when they know already that it is. They might give in to urges to tap a wall or count silently, or, if they touch somebody on the left shoulder, feel the need to touch them also on the right. These are not superstitions, which are typically a response to an external cue, such as a salute to a magpie. They are compulsions – an irresistible internal urge to act in a way that is irrational. People don't tend to talk about their compulsions either.*

Most people seem able to cope with their day-to-day rituals and compulsions – or at least they do not seek medical help for them. But, like obsessions, for some people their compulsions can cause real difficulties. These problems, and the subsequent calls for help, usually come when obsessions and compulsions start to work in tandem. The combination can produce OCD. Put simply, most people with OCD develop their compulsions as a way to make their intrusive thoughts go away.

The most obvious way to employ a compulsion to drive away an intrusive thought is to use it to answer a question. If the thought that comes to your mind time and time again is about whether you locked the back door or not, then a compulsive and reassuring check on the door should

---

* Compulsions were recorded long before psychologists got involved. Folklore from Eastern Europe tells how vampires are compelled to count scattered objects. Frightened people would sprinkle grain and seeds around graveyards to keep the undead busy. The television show *Sesame Street* features a vampire puppet called Count von Count who likes to, well, you get the idea.

settle the matter. More indirectly, some people use compulsions as a way to stop the thoughts coming in the first place. A 14-year-old girl with obsessive intrusive thoughts that worms would enter her body, for example, avoided the threat by refusing to open her mouth to speak for ten months.

Sometimes the nature of the compulsions seems to bear no relation to the subject of the obsessions at all. People with OCD can be compelled to tap surfaces or count or say secret words to themselves to 'undo' the imagined consequences of an intrusive thought, for example that their best friend will die. That might sound unhelpful, but then does counting backwards from 999 make someone a technically better skier?

Compulsions can make obsessive thoughts go away, but only for a short while. One of the many cruel ironies of OCD is that the compulsions, the weapon that obsessed people reach for, make the situation worse. Compulsions act in the same way as thought suppression. An intrusive thought silenced with a compulsive act comes back. It comes back hard.

Mental health professionals refer to OCD as a secret disease and a silent epidemic. The number of people who report obsessions and compulsions to doctors is routinely much lower than the studies of their prevalence would suggest. A lot of people with OCD choose to suffer in silence. Their thoughts are their dirty little secret. They believe they are freaks, and their silence has allowed compulsive actions to come to define their condition.

Compulsions, a need to wash hands, check the back door is locked or to turn a light switch on and off a dozen times, are visible in a way that obsessions – dark intrusive thoughts best kept secret – are not. Like the shape of the letter C in OCD, compulsions are open to the world; they offer a handle on the condition. And like the shape of the letter O, obsessions are sealed off.

While most people recoil from thoughts of unacceptable, distasteful and downright savage behaviour, not everybody does. Some people experience unpleasant thoughts in a different way; they do not find the idea of hurting someone ego-dystonic, it does not clash with their instincts and motivation. Some of these people, unfortunately, go on to act their thoughts out. We know this because some become sexual offenders.

Deviant intrusive sexual thoughts, which shock most who have them, do not seem to trouble such people. As ridiculous as it may seem, part of this is because they believe their crimes cause no harm. Some men who abuse children believe that a child can be interested in sex with an adult; some rapists believe that women enjoy it; some exhibitionists think their actions are harmless and even give pleasure because they do not touch their victims. Yet even people such as these, whose moral compasses are so severely skewed, can be troubled by their thoughts. Even these people have intrusive thoughts that they find unwanted, and in fact can cause them great distress.

Eddie was one of these. Eddie was 32, married with a

child, and he was also a persistent exhibitionist. He would drive to a strange town and wait in a park until a woman walked by. Then he would expose himself. He believed his routine – which also involved parking some distance from the scene of his crime – would make it harder for him to be caught. He did it dozens of times. Yet despite the lengths to which Eddie went to avoid detection, afterwards his mind would flood with intrusive, recurrent – and irrational – thoughts that he would be identified. After Eddie exposed himself the first time, he had repeated thoughts that he would be arrested in front of his wife and child, and be named in the local paper as a sex offender. They occupied almost every moment and persisted for nearly a month.

Eddie was not unusual. Psychologists have investigated how intrusive thoughts occur in other sexual offenders, including child molesters and rapists. Frequently, especially at first, these people report persistent and intense thoughts of the consequences if they were caught. And it is not prison that they fear the most. It is humiliation and loss of status. They know full well that, even though they see their behaviours as normal, the rest of society views sexual offenders as monsters. This challenges their view of their place in the world. The thoughts about being caught threaten their own sense of themselves as a good person. They experience them as ego-dystonic. And as such they find them unwanted and intrusive.

Unwanted thoughts can centre on the most innocuous of situations. Plenty of people, for instance, report intrusive thoughts about the flaws of partners – boyfriends, girl-friends, wives and husbands. Now, nobody is perfect and a little tension is usual in all relationships from time to time, but in recent years psychologists have started to report a bizarre manifestation of obsessive-compulsive symptoms along these lines.

Here's Mike, a 28-year-old married man:

> I am constantly preoccupied with my wife's emotional imbalance. She overreacts to every minor conflict or challenge she encounters at work. Every time it happens I think to myself 'what kind of mother is she going to be' . . . It really distresses me. I know all of her good qualities and I know she loves me. I know I am over-reacting but I just can't let it rest.

And Jennifer, a 25-year-old businesswoman:

> I can't stop thinking he is a loser and it just won't work. Then I start obsessing about who will provide for me and the children . . . I love him and I think he will make an excellent father, and when I think about it rationally I don't think it's an issue.

In 2012, scientists in Israel produced a way to probe these symptoms. Called the partner-related obsessive-compulsive symptoms inventory, it asks people in a relationship to agree or disagree with questions such as 'I feel an uncomfortable urge to compare my partner's physical flaws with those of other men/women' and 'I am troubled by thoughts about my partner's social skills' and 'I find it hard to dismiss the thought that my partner is mentally unbalanced.' It's easy to smile, but when such thoughts can't be turned off then the consequences can cause just as much distress as obsessive thoughts of violence and disease.

Jack, aged 40, who had been with his partner for four years, was disturbed by intrusive thoughts about their relationship.

> I check whether I feel love or not. Is this the same feeling as the movies? I try to imagine how life would be by her side in the next twenty years. I imagine how it might be with someone else. I fear I will be stuck with these doubts for ever and won't be able to take it anymore.

Is this OCD? Certainly, Jack complains of thoughts that he doesn't want, that recur, cause him distress and force him to seek constant reassurance. But it's hard to see how many people, especially women, would have much sympathy. Does everybody who marries not have similar doubts at some stage? Isn't this just a classic case of a man who fears commitment? If it is OCD, could and should it be fixed?

Psychiatrists are clear: OCD is not simply an exaggerated form of everyday worries. And it is a mistake to think that the apparently trivial subjects of some intrusive and obsessive thoughts mean they cannot bring serious problems. Bira thought only of a mud wall, and the consequences came to dominate her life. Mike, Jack and Jennifer all sought help for their obsessive thoughts about their relationships and the negative impact these thoughts had on their life. Their thoughts caused them persistent distress for several hours each day. That's the OCD.

There will be some people who, if they have read this far, will have turned each page of this book with a shake of their head. Ideas to hurt children? Urges to drive my car off the road? *I* don't have thoughts like *that*.

That's certainly possible. Even the best conducted surveys that use trained and face-to-face interviewers come up against a stubborn 5 per cent or so of people who deny they have, or ever have had, unwanted intrusive thoughts. Some are probably lying, though psychologists won't say so. There is a different explanation. If you are absolutely certain that you don't have intrusive thoughts then don't feel too smug just yet. Some people do have these thoughts, the urges to commit murder or to torture animals, *but they simply do not recognize and report them as unwanted.* To these people, such thoughts could feel as normal as to ponder what to buy a child for their birthday. There is a name for such individuals: psychopaths.

In 2008, psychologists in Canada published the results of an experiment that aimed to test whether psychopaths would report fewer unwanted intrusive thoughts. Psychopaths are broadly defined as people who behave in a way that breaches social expectations and norms, but who feel no remorse or shame when they do so. They lie, cheat and steal and can inflict great cruelty with no care that others consider what they do is wrong.

In search of psychopaths, the Canadian psychologists quizzed inmates of the Nanaimo Correctional Centre, a medium-security facility on the south shore of Brannen Lake in Vancouver Island, a local beauty spot and one popular with holidaymakers. One prisoner there told them he had thoughts about throwing a baby off a bridge, just to see the reaction of people, and another had an urge to perform his martial arts on someone for no reason. But almost three-quarters of the prisoners questioned said they did not have intrusive thoughts.

Were these convicts who denied intrusive thoughts psychopaths? The scientists asked them to answer a set of 60 questions, designed to probe people for psychopathic traits. It's a self-report version of the so-called psychopath test. Sure enough, those prisoners with the highest scores on this psychopath test were also those who were less likely to report intrusive thoughts. If they experienced the intrusions and the impulses at all, they seemed less troubled by them. They did not find them repugnant, perhaps because they did not find the contents disturbing.

It's possible that the prisoners were not psychopaths, just liars. Perhaps, even under the controlled conditions of an anonymous study, they were reluctant to admit their most bizarre and unwanted thoughts. Maybe they worried their darkest thoughts would be recorded and used against them. As we'll see, they often are.

THREE

The mademoiselle and the
Rat Man

I do not fear HIV as it is now understood – a fragile and
hard-to-catch virus that leads to an infection that is largely
managed with drugs, at least by those who can get them.
Obsession closed around my thoughts as they were in 1991
and keeps them in that state today. So the HIV I focus on
is the disease of the late 1980s, a devastating and life-ending
consequence of lack of control, of a moment's thoughtless-
ness. A threat so severe that in 1986 it demanded the UK
government beam into our houses shocking television
adverts with crashing gravestones and the catchphrase
'AIDS: Don't Die of Ignorance'.

Not surprisingly, HIV and Aids quickly replaced the
Cold War nuclear threat – of the Frankie Goes to Hollywood
song 'Two Tribes' and Raymond Briggs' book *When the
Wind Blows* – as the Great Fear of popular culture, and
soaked through to the manners of day-to-day life. 'A man
round the corner in Boundary Lane has Aids,' my mother,
not known for her mealtime jokes, announced to us one
night in the late 1980s. 'Yes, he's got one in each ear.'

Australia had it even worse. The government there screened a frankly horrific advert that showed HIV as a grim reaper who knocked down people – including a sobbing schoolgirl and a mother with baby – with bowling balls, and had their bodies dragged away as garbage.*

A generation was traumatized – as early as 1983, just a couple of years after HIV was identified, the first cases of what was then called Aids-phobia were reported – two men in their thirties, both with underlying mental conditions, who tested negative for HIV but were crippled by their fear of the disease. By 1987, so concerned that irrational obsessions with HIV were spreading faster than the virus itself, experts convened a special workshop in Munich to discuss ways to tackle the problem.

This reaction to the threat of HIV is an example of how obsessions can closely mirror society's fears and anxieties. In the 1920s, doctors in the US reported a surge in what they called syphilis-phobia, which coincided with a campaign to highlight the dangers of the disease. In the 1960s and 1970s there was a spike in irrational fears of asbestos, just as the dangers of the material had come to popular attention. By the 1980s and 1990s it was HIV. The US psychiatrist Judith Rapoport wrote in her book *The Boy Who Couldn't Stop Washing* – which introduced many people to OCD – that by 1989 a third of her obsessive-compulsive patients focused on HIV and Aids. The disease,

---

* Both the Australian and UK adverts were on YouTube last time I checked.

she wrote, appeared 'so terrifying, so irrational that it could have been the creation of an obsessive-compulsive's worst fantasy'.

In this new century, society has a new topic to obsess it. In 2012 Australian scientists reported the first cases of obsessive-compulsive patients who fixate on thoughts about climate change – a bogeyman for the new millennium and one that, similar to Aids in the 1980s, poses an uncertain, universal threat, depicted in lurid detail by the mass media.* Some of these people fear that increased temperatures will evaporate the water they leave out for their pet cats and dogs, and so they check the bowls time and time again. Others repeatedly make sure that taps, heaters and cooker are not left on, not because they fear the consequences for themselves, but because of the perceived impact of their negligence on water resources and greenhouse gas emissions, and so on the fate of the planet. One was obsessed with the idea that global warming would make his house fall down. He compulsively checked the skirting boards, pipes and roof for cracks, and repeatedly opened and closed its wooden doors to make sure that climate change had not brought a plague of termites.

Psychiatrists have traditionally viewed OCD as an anxiety disorder, along with conditions like phobia. Certainly, obsessions can appear similar to phobias, which are likewise

---

* Full disclosure: I used to write these stories.

exaggerated and often irrational fears. The anxiety caused by OCD and phobia are the same, and so is the sense of helplessness and impotence, and the awareness on some level that it's all a bit silly. But people with phobias have one escape that those with OCD do not: they can usually avoid the stimulus that provokes their fear. Someone with an acute fear of heights can refuse to stand near the edge of a high bridge, or to walk along cliffs. Arachnophobia is only a problem for arachnophobes when they are in the presence of spiders. Someone with paraskevidekatriaphobia, a fear of Friday the 13th, is truly a paraskevidekatriaphobe for only a couple of days or so a year. In phobias, the feared stimulus is external. But in OCD it comes from within, from our own thoughts.

Obsessions and phobia can, however, focus on the same fear. Andy Warhol had a persistent dread of HIV in the 1980s, which the artist called the 'magic disease'. He refused to eat sandwiches prepared by another gay man and when his partner Jon Gould developed pneumonia in 1984, Warhol told his housekeepers to wash their clothes and dishes separately. Given what was known and not known about Aids at the time, it's hard to see Warhol's fear as completely irrational. He certainly didn't think it was. He didn't fight the thoughts. And that means that he probably didn't have OCD.

Overlap between phobia and OCD exists for a more primitive terror. In the early 1960s, clinical psychologists at a mental hospital in Warrington near Liverpool treated a middle-aged American woman obsessed with a fear she would be buried alive. To stop this from happening, the woman wrote detailed instructions of how her body should be cut up after her death and left several copies of these notes around her house so they would be discovered if she died. Each night she had to compulsively check these instructions were in place before she could sleep. Sometimes she would spend so long on these pre-sleep checks that she never went to bed at all.

Was her fear irrational? Like Warhol, the woman could have argued not. Her obsessions and compulsions began when she read a newspaper story of a man closed up in his coffin while he was still alive. Tales of premature burial were common in the past, and inventors fitted coffins with bells and whistles and other ways for the revived deceased to draw attention from underground. Many countries in Europe passed burial laws in the eighteenth and nineteenth centuries to ensure that corpses were kept above ground for enough time to give the not-really-dead time to come round.

George Washington and Frederic Chopin shared this fear of being buried alive – formally known as taphephobia – and it was common for people to include in their will requests for candles and mirrors to be held to their dead mouth to detect breathing, while others asked to be decapitated or stabbed through the heart before they were placed inside their coffin. The famous will of Alfred Nobel, the Swedish inventor of dynamite who pledged his fortune to set up the academic prizes that bear his name, ends with the words:

> Finally, it is my express wish that following my death my veins shall be opened, and when this has been done and competent doctors have confirmed clear signs of death, my remains shall be cremated in a so-called crematorium.

Crematorium owners did well from taphephobia.

As well as being an obsessive-compulsive, the woman in Warrington was claustrophobic. She could not ride in an elevator or an underground train or sit in a locked room. The psychologists thought they could treat her compulsions if they eased her phobia. If she was not frightened of small and enclosed spaces, they reasoned, she would not need her grisly instructions and her nightly checks on them. They were wrong. Months of treatment at Winwick hospital, now a housing estate that overlooks the M62 motorway, cured her of the claustrophobia, so much so that she could sit inside a closed cupboard. But she never lost her obsessive-compulsive fear of an early grave, and could never sleep until she had made sure she would not wake up in one.

Given cases like these, it's perhaps tempting to see obsessions and compulsions as a modern complaint, yet another manufactured condition of the pampered and self-indulgent postwar generations with little more serious to concern them than whether they left the gas on. But OCD, or something like it, seems to have troubled people for centuries.

For as long as people have claimed religious, scientific or medical authority, others have sought their help for distress caused by intrusive thoughts they cannot make go away. Yet in return religion, science and medicine have traditionally offered little comfort. If not burnt at the stake for witchcraft or forced into an exorcism to drive away controlling demons, people who reported odd thoughts have been locked up, declared mad, given huge doses of hallucinogenic drugs, shunned or had their brains blasted with electricity. Their intrusive thoughts were considered beyond the pale – they were the products of an impure soul, the work of the devil, the output of an evil heart or the function of a diseased mind. They were freakish, and those who had them were freaks.

Sigmund Freud had a different idea. Freud said that OCD was down to repressed guilt about childhood masturbation. Thanks Sigmund.

Freud owes much of his fame and reputation to his work on OCD, or what we would today call OCD. He preferred the term obsessional neurosis, and even he, no stranger to the weird ways of the human mind, found the condition bizarre. He once wrote:

> This is a mad disease, surely . . . I don't think the wildest psychiatric fantasy could have invented anything like it, and if we did not see it every day with our own eyes we could hardly bring ourselves to believe in it.

Freud saw the mind as a fluid and interconnected bundle of experiences and motivations, some of which were apparent to the individual, and some not. Mental conflict – the suppression of sexual and toilet instincts in childhood, usually – would fester in the darkest corners of the subconscious. Psychological problems later in life were echoes of this original disturbance, he reckoned, the mental pings of a distress beacon buried somewhere inside the mind – even if they manifested themselves in quite different ways. To treat such a neurotic patient, Freud concluded, a doctor must locate, expose and disarm the buried trauma through psychoanalysis. They must talk to the patient about their childhood, their sexual experiences and their parents to ease the buried trauma to the surface. It has become the classic help of a psychiatrist's couch.

On 1 October 1907, Freud put onto his couch a 29-year-old Austrian lawyer and reserve soldier in the Imperial Army. The man was short and knock-kneed, with black hair, brown eyes, a sharp nose and an oval chin. He lived in Vienna and his name was Dr Ernst Lanzer. Lanzer's case became a sensation, yet the world would not know his identity for almost eighty years. Instead he was known by the dark alter ego that Freud's colleagues gave him, a name that scientists still use today and one that only hints at the swirling intrusive thoughts that drew him into the world of OCD and the waiting room of Sigmund Freud. Ernst Lanzer was the Rat Man. And the Rat Man, sadly, was a mess.

Lanzer told Freud how he was consumed by ridiculous ideas. He constantly worried that he would, without reason or intention, take a blade and cut his own throat. He feared terrible things could happen to his (already dead) father. Most disturbingly, his mind was filled with a sadistic vision that caged rats would be tied to the buttocks of his loved ones, and forced to gnaw through into their anuses.

Lanzer had become obsessed with thoughts of the rats while on a military exercise in Galicia that summer when a fellow officer described a grotesque Oriental torture technique. Historians have traced the story's origin to a popular book at the time, *The Torture Garden*, by Octave Mirbeau. In the book, a Chinese professional torturer describes his favourite technique:

> You take a young man, as young and strong as possible, whose muscles are quite resistant . . . you undress him . . . you make him kneel, his back bent on the earth, where you fasten him with chains riveted to iron collars which bind his neck, his wrists, his calves and ankles.
>
> Then in a big pot, whose bottom is pierced with a little hole, you place a very fat rat whom it's wise to have deprived of nourishment for a couple of days to excite its ferocity. And to this pot inhabited by this rat you apply hermetically like an enormous cupping glass to the back of the condemned by means of stout thongs attached to a leather girdle around the loins . . . You introduce an iron rod, heated red hot at the fire of a forge. The rat tries to escape the burning of the rod and its dazzling light.

In halting and emotional words, Lanzer told Freud that he could not dispel intrusive thoughts that the torture would be carried out on his girlfriend and his (dead) father. He would counter the obsessive thought with a compulsive response, always the same: he would say to himself 'but' and then perform what Freud called a 'gesture of repudiation' and then say 'whatever are you thinking of'. Only in this way, he said, could he prevent the feared situation from happening. The thoughts of torture, he assured Freud, were foreign and repugnant to him.

The subsequent psychodynamic analysis that Freud performed – probes of the young Lanzer's sexual experiences and his awkward relationship with his father – seemed to help, at least according to Freud, who would later claim that he was able to completely restore Lanzer's personality by explaining to him the symbolic meaning of his obsessions with rats. These included associations between the rodents and money, his father's gambling, marriage and a childhood incident when Lanzer had bitten someone and been punished. The Rat Man, Freud concluded, was angry with his father and so unconsciously fantasized about having anal intercourse with him. Repression of this idea caused the obsession, Freud said. Making Lanzer aware of this, the doctor claimed, made the obsession go away.

By 1908 Lanzer had a stable job with a law firm, in 1910 he was married and in 1913, after the required six-year apprenticeship, he qualified as an attorney. Despite these successes, Lanzer's story has no happy ending. Called up to fight on the outbreak of war in August 1914, he lasted just three months. On 21 November he was captured by the Russians. Four days later he was dead.

By then, Freud was on the up. In the spring of 1908, he had caused a sensation when he presented Lanzer's case, and a story of how he had cured him, in a marathon lecture that opened the First Psychoanalytic Congress in Salzburg. Ernest Jones, a British psychologist who was at the meeting, later wrote:

> [Freud] described the analysis of an obsessional case, one which afterwards we used to refer to as that of 'The Man with the Rats'. He sat at the end of a long table along the sides of which we were gathered and spoke in his usual low but distinct conversational tone. He began at the Continental hour of eight in the morning and we listened with rapt attention. At eleven he broke off, suggesting that we had had enough. But we were so absorbed that we insisted on his continuing, which he did until nearly one o'clock.

Historians have since questioned the truth of Freud's account of his success with Lanzer (it is the only case for which the famous doctor's original notes survive). Frank Sulloway, a psychologist at the University of California, Berkeley, who has revisited much of Freud's work, has concluded that: 'The Rat Man – cured or not – was clearly intended to be a show-piece for Freud's nascent psychoanalytical movement.' Certainly there are discrepancies between Freud's notes and his subsequent write-up. Lanzer's treatment seems to have lasted for a few months, rather than the full year that Freud claimed in his reports. And there are doubts about whether Lanzer was helped as fully as Freud insisted – doubts that are impossible to investigate given that Lanzer's death prevented any long-term follow-up, by Freud or anyone else.

Freud was far from the first medic to record irrational and obsessional thoughts and behaviours. Others before him were interested in these unusual states of mind and their reports had already started to converge on common symptoms. The first medical case study of this new age – the patient zero of OCD – was not the Rat Man, but a young French woman from the early nineteenth century known as Mademoiselle F.

She was, the mademoiselle remembered, about 18 years old when her curious behaviours began. It is doubtful that anybody around her noticed at the time. Her odd action was nothing more noteworthy than to take one of her regular visits to the house of her aunt without her apron. She did not forget it. She had always worn her apron on such visits before, but on that day she chose quite deliberately to leave it at home.

Her curious thoughts had started some time earlier, on her previous visit to the same house. This time, we can be certain that nobody else noticed, for she was already on her way home when the idea struck her with no warning and no provocation. What if she had stolen something from her aunt? What if the loot was somehow concealed in the folds of her apron? The solution, she later recalled, was obvious. She would not wear the apron again.

The curious thoughts, and the curious behaviours, continued. The mademoiselle, a tall woman with auburn hair and blue eyes, worked as an accountant. She was honest and worked hard, but she began to fear that she would somehow wrong her clients. She took longer to prepare accounts and invoices as she was forced to check her sums and her records. Her concerns grew more intense and made her reluctant to handle money, in case she retained some in her fingers. And what if her fingertips could somehow drain value from the coins and notes that passed through them? Was that not another way for her to cheat those who trusted her? It was an irrational worry, she knew, but she decided that the most sensible course was to give up her business.

By now, the thoughts that plagued the mademoiselle were not a secret. Her friends protested. If she stole some money, they said, she would know about it. And the contact of her fingers could not alter its value. That is true, the mademoiselle would reply, my preoccupation is absurd and ridiculous. But I cannot prevent it. Without work, the concern broke beyond its boundaries and flooded into her everyday life. She cut the hems from her dresses and wore her shoes so tight that the skin from her swollen feet gathered in bunches above, to keep her from placing stolen items inside. She held her clothes when she walked in hesitant steps so they did not brush against doors and furniture. And she scrutinized the keys, knobs and handles of windows and wardrobes with forensic duty; all to prevent the transfer to her of anything of value.

Years passed. Frustration and exasperation took root as she exhausted the inadequate advice of her friends and relatives, as well as her own reason. Her fears, and the behaviours she followed to ease them, sometimes faded, but they always returned. Some sixteen years after she first laid aside her apron, the mademoiselle, exhausted and bewildered, headed for Paris in 1834 and committed herself to the care of the renowned psychiatrist Jean Etienne Dominique Esquirol.

Esquirol was director of the Charenton lunatic asylum, a centuries-old institution on the banks of the Seine that previously held the writer and libertine Marquis de Sade. From a wealthy background in Toulouse, Esquirol had studied at the influential Salpêtrière hospital in central Paris, where he went on to launch and teach a course in mental disorder, set up in the hospital's dining hall. As well as his position at Charenton, Esquirol ran a private clinic – a *maison de santé* – in the nearby village of Ivry, where affluent patients would pay 10 or 15 francs a day for care. 'To see madhouses risen to such extraordinary prices,' a Paris newspaper said of Esquirol's clinic in 1827, 'One would be tempted to believe that insanity is a privilege and that, without being a bureaucrat or a capitalist, it is inadvisable to rave.'

Mademoiselle F had stayed with Esquirol for two years by the time he wrote of her case. She was, he said:

> . . . never irrational; is aware of her condition; perceives the ridiculous nature of her apprehensions and the

absurdity of her precautions; and weeps at and makes sport of them. She also laments, and sometimes weeps in view of them.

Even in the *maison de santé*, the mademoiselle still guarded against her feared thieving. 'Before leaving her bed,' Esquirol wrote,

. . . she rubs her feet for ten minutes, in order to remove whatever may have insinuated itself between the toes or beneath the nails. She afterwards turns and re-turns her slippers, shakes them, and hands them to her chamber-maid, in order that she, after having carefully examined them, may assure her that they conceal nothing of value. The comb is passed through the hair a great number of times, with the same intent. Every article of her apparel is examined successively, a great number of times, inspected in every way, in all the folds and wrinkles, and rigorously shaken. After all these precautions, the hands are powerfully shaken in turn, and the fingers of either hand rubbed by each other. This rubbing of the fingers is performed with extreme rapidity, and repeated until the number of rubbings, which is enumerated in a loud voice, is sufficient to convince her, that nothing remains upon them. The close attention and uneasiness of the patient are such, during this minute exploration that she perspires and is almost exhausted by the fatigue of it. If, from any cause, these precautions are not taken, she is restless during the whole day.

The woman went to the theatre and on trips home to see her family. She ate and slept well. In many ways she was the life and soul of the residential clinic. Each night she would join others in the drawing room, and her conversation was 'gay, humorous and sometimes mischievous'. The only outward sign of her inner torment came if she was forced to switch seats, or if she inadvertently touched her head or dress, or the chair of another. Then she would rub and shake her fingers.*

Esquirol said her condition was a form of monomania, or partial insanity – a concept he developed and promoted, which argued the mind could be unbalanced by a single train of thought. Someone with monomania was mad, at least partly mad, but they were aware of it. Only a part of their brain and so a specific function was affected, the rest was normal.

The concept of monomania, framed as the obsessive pursuit of an idea, caught the public imagination – as shown by its prevalence in literature written at the time. The memorably dark characters Heathcliff in Emily Brontë's *Wuthering Heights* (1847) and Raskolnikov in Dostoyevsky's *Crime and Punishment* (1866) are both described as monomaniacs. Perhaps the most famous depiction of monomania was Herman Melville's Captain Ahab, who was consumed by a single-minded madness to kill the great white whale in *Moby-Dick* (1851).

---

* We don't know if the mademoiselle recovered. Esquirol didn't report what happened to her.

Monomania had many types, which Esquirol and his followers used to explain a range of unusual, antisocial and illegal behaviours. They made the biggest impact in the field of law. Denied the status in society they felt they deserved, Esquirol and his cronies used monomania to gain control of the medico-legal process used to assess the sanity of defendants in the French courts – which at the time often came down to a friend or neighbour who would turn up and say that a murder suspect who claimed insanity had always seemed fine to them.

With monomania as their lever, French psychiatrists forced their way into public discussion of several grisly murder cases that captivated Paris in the early nineteenth century. In 1828, for instance, a servant girl called Henriette Cornier went on trial for the sudden and inexplicable murder of her employers' small child. Cornier, said one medic called by the defence, was a monomaniac propelled to kill, and so should be considered legally insane.

The debate crossed the channel to London with a young French man called Louis Bordier, who was convicted of the murder of his girlfriend and sentenced to hang at Horsemonger Lane gaol in October 1867. At the time, Britain still executed some condemned prisoners in public, and the gallows at Horsemonger Lane were more public than most, set up on the roof of the gatehouse at the front of the gaol. Charles Dickens had been so horrified at the scenes at one such execution of a husband and wife there in 1849 – watched by a claimed crowd of 30,000 people

– that he wrote a famous letter of protest at the death penalty to *The Times*.

With Bordier just days from his date with the noose, Dr Harrington Tuke, the honorary secretary to the British Medico-Psychological Association, wrote an emotional plea for clemency in the *Lancet* medical journal. Bordier, he said, was a monomaniac.

> If he be hung the cruel absurdity will be committed of inflicting capital punishment upon a lunatic, and fixing upon his kindred the unjust stigma of relationship to a responsible and cold-blooded assassin.

To support his case, Tuke pointed out that Bordier had listened to the jury's guilty verdict and to the judge deliver the death sentence with 'stolid indifference' and deaf to the wailings of his two little girls, had walked unconcerned from the dock.

The appeal made no difference: Bordier was hanged the following week – the final execution held in public at Horsemonger Lane. His death did not finish the arguments over his state of mind. A response to Tuke's letter from the surgeon of Newgate gaol, just across the River Thames, who had examined Bordier – and whom Tuke had criticized – appeared a fortnight later. Bordier's conduct in the trial, the surgeon said, did not support the claim of madness, even partial madness:

When his eldest little girl was placed in the witness box, he bent his head so low as completely to hide his face from the observation of any one in court, as if he could not bear the glance of his own child, or bear to look upon her.

The glance of a child would one day prove pivotal in my life too.

When I found that I could not make my irrational thoughts of HIV go away, I spent a lot of time on the phone to the National Aids Helpline. I would ring them from the phone box at the side of the busy road opposite the house into which six of us had moved at the start of the second academic year. I would call to tell them how the fears that I had of the virus had spread, and about all of the extra ways my thoughts now told me that I could have caught the disease. It felt good to say those things out loud. It was a relief to free them from my head and expose them to the light. Was there, say, a risk when I played football and scraped my knee along the abrasive Astroturf? Someone else could have done the same after all, and left a smear of infected blood at that exact spot. No, they would respond, no need to worry. The risk was very low.

Thanks, I would say as I blew out my cheeks – that's reassured me. I might even have believed it, for just as long as it took to replace the handset and turn to leave the phone box. But, wait, very low? The risk was very low, so there was a risk? Shit, what if I hadn't explained what happened exactly right. They might have misunderstood. The risk could be higher if they realized what really had happened. I should call back, just to confirm. I would dial the number dozens of times a day. Sometimes I would hang up before they answered. I couldn't understand why my mind would circle round, why the sense that everything would be all right was so fleeting.

The National Aids Helpline, I quickly worked out, was staffed by about half a dozen people at any one time. I learned their voices, and was encouraged when someone new picked up the phone – surely they would be the one to convince me. After a while, they started to recognize my voice too, and my feared situations. That was bad. They would tell me that they had already given me an answer and that I needed to accept it. I didn't want that. I wanted the hit. Tell me I am not infected. So I invented new scenarios, just similar enough to real ones to bring that familiar flicker of comfort when they were dismissed. And, sorry National Aids Helpline workers circa 1991 and 1992, but I disguised my voice. I even put on different regional accents. I'm sure you knew. Not that it did any good. Reassurance, like offence, is taken not given. And my mind would not take it.

Every night HIV was the last thing I thought about before I went to sleep. And it was the first thing I thought of every morning. And it was pretty much all I thought of in between. I have few memories from that time of anything else. I lost interest in the stuff that had seemed important just a few months previously; music, books and films no longer held my attention. I no longer cared how other people's stories ended, for I could no longer identify with anyone else's trivial concerns. What did it matter, really, if this man in a hospital drama had hurt his leg? If I had HIV and I broke my leg, then I would still have HIV when they fixed it. I had a rival narrative in my head in which the stakes just seemed so much higher than anything that went on in life outside.

I decided to donate blood. They would test for HIV. My anxiety spiked as they pierced my skin with the needle but then, as I watched the thick red fluid pour from my arm, a plastic cup of orange squash waiting on the shelf, I felt not fear but a surge of exhilaration – oh, I should have done this ages ago! Of course there was nothing in my blood; no virus was slowly eating away at my cells, my promise and my future. They would tell me I was all right and I would believe them.

The nurse took away the plastic bag taut with my blood and she gave me a biscuit. I heard the rain outside batter against the windows and I saw the world again as it had been before that first obsessive thought. I saw the opportunities and the hopes, I looked beyond the horizon and I smiled. The relief was so strong. And then, on the way out, I picked up the leaflet. Why did I pick up the leaflet?

The leaflet, one of a number in a plastic rack by the blood centre door, said their tests looked not for HIV, but the antibodies the immune system raised against it. And those antibodies could take three months to show up. Three months in which I could catch Aids and nobody could tell me that I hadn't. As I read the words I loathed them. Whatever anybody said, they could not be sure. The thoughts and the terror and the desolation flooded back across my senses. The dam I had just built to hold them back collapsed. Unwilling to go forwards and unable to go back, I dropped the half-eaten biscuit onto the pavement and watched it swim with the rain.

FOUR

An emerging obsession

Is OCD truly a mental illness? Some experts say yes, some say no and some say it doesn't matter. They're probably all correct; this area is a mass of vague terms and a mess of overlapping meanings. It's always been that way, dating back to the eighteenth century and the Scottish physician William Cullen, who introduced the term neuroses, a broad notion that stemmed from his idea that madness reflected damage to the nervous system. By the middle of the nineteenth century, the Austrian medic and poet Baron Ernst von Feuchtersleben argued that more severe afflictions of the mind such as delusion should be promoted into a different tier, which he called the psychoses. The division stuck, despite the obvious problem that plenty of people with neuroses seemed to have a worse time than those who had the supposedly more serious psychoses. Those terms aren't used in medicine to classify patients any more, but the replacements aren't any clearer.

'Mental illness' is a catch-all but many people don't want to be called 'mentally ill'. OCD is not an 'illness' anyway, psychologists say, it is an 'abnormality'. Some people with OCD reject the label 'abnormal' and prefer 'disorder'. But 'disorder' and 'illness', according to psychiatrists, mean the same thing. It's clear that schizophrenia is a mental illness. Yet the UK government says that one in four of its citizens will develop a 'mental illness' during their lifetime. That's more than fifteen million people and to get the figures that high they have to include the big three – substance abuse, anxiety and depression – as well as OCD. Is anxiety a mental illness? Is an alcoholic mentally ill? It's not hard to see why most charities who work in this area prefer to call it 'mental health'.

The best representation, though still flawed, is probably to divide mental illness from severe mental illness, with this second group made up of people who lose touch with reality. That's close to where we were more than a century ago, with neuroses and psychoses. In this book, I use the terms disorder, illness, abnormality, condition and syndrome as synonyms, because it introduces variation and because, as we've seen, it's hard to organize them into any hierarchy. I mean none of them to be pejorative.

Whatever we call it, it took me a long time to recognize my problem. OCD was that thing those people did when they washed their hands a lot, wasn't it? People talked about Monica Geller from the television show *Friends* as having OCD because she was so uptight about cleaning and crumbs in the bed and that stuff. I didn't think like that. I wasn't a perfectionist. I wasn't bothered by crumbs in the bed; I was scared that I would catch a terrible disease, which was very different. So I found it hard to accept that I had OCD and that I could be helped, even after the people on the other end of the National Aids Helpline gently suggested I should talk to a psychiatrist rather than them.

The persistent and common belief that OCD is simply an exaggerated desire for hygiene and order is not the fault of the doctors and scientists, who have been telling people it is wrong for decades. Psychologists found convincing evidence that people with OCD do not think and behave in that way in 1960, when they looked at the records of people referred to the Tavistock Clinic, a drop-in centre in London that diagnosed and treated various psychological problems. Each patient to the clinic had to answer nearly nine hundred questions on their attitudes and behaviours, and the scientists looked at the responses to those that related to obsessive and compulsive character traits, such as 'I tend to brood for a long time over a single idea' and 'I take pride in having neat and tidy handwriting'. The patients had to grade them as true or false.

With a statistical technique called factor analysis, the psychologists bundled together the answers that seemed to associate with each other – to produce a picture of how someone who answered true to one question would be most likely to answer the others.

They found two separate and distinct patterns, which they labelled the A-type and the B-type. The A-type was a person more likely to fold their clothes carefully, to be thorough in everything they did and to be punctual. The

B-type was someone who checked things, had bad thoughts and memorized numbers.

The B-type – described as a person whose daily life is disturbed by the intrusion of unwanted thoughts and is compelled to do things they know are unnecessary – we can recognize now as OCD. The A-type – an exceedingly systematic and methodical person, who pays much attention to detail and has a strong dislike of dirt – psychologists identify as a person with the similar-sounding, but quite different, problem of obsessive-compulsive personality disorder (OCPD).

The two are not completely separate – traits and symptoms from one can appear in someone with the other. And some people with OCPD can develop OCD – in fact, for many years it was thought that only people with obsessive personalities could develop OCD. But there is a clear difference between a person with OCPD and one with OCD. While OCD is defined by harrowing ego-dystonic ideas that clash with our sense of the sort of person we are, the thoughts of OCPD tend to be ego-syntonic – in line with one's desires and needs – and so much easier to accept. Put another way, OCD is hell for the sufferer but, while OCPD may be hell for those close to them, the person with OCPD is usually happy to clean and tidy and takes pride in doing so.

Visit the home of someone with OCPD and not a chair or rug will be out of place. Yet people with OCD whose compulsions demand that they clean often restrict the practice to a specific room. OCD patients can have spotless toilets that sparkle with bleach next to a filthy kitchen caked with months-old food. An OCD washer who cleans his hands 200-odd times a day can wear the same underwear for weeks.

In many ways OCPD is what people mean when they use the term anal personality. Indeed, the phrase anal (usually short for anally retentive) personality grew from Freud's work on obsessions. Of course it did. Freud thought that children went through an 'anal' phase when their chief interest was their bowel movements. Unfortunately for the child, this phase coincided with the parents also taking an interest in the child's bowel movements, and getting the child not to deposit them in their pants.

Mental conflict during this phase – sometimes just the very act of the parent interfering with how and when the child could go to the toilet – could lead to turmoil in the child's mind, Freud said, which would resurface as personality traits that mirrored the child's efforts to exercise power over their excrement: orderliness, stubbornness and a need for control. These were the features of Freud's classic anal personality type; anally retentive described when these behaviour traits lingered into adulthood.

When people hear of OCD they frequently think of anal personalities and OCPD. They see towel folding and books arranged on a shelf by genre, size, or alphabetical order. In September 2011 the London department store Selfridges was selling what it called an obsessive-compulsive disorder chopping board, etched with ruled lines and a protractor for perfectly sized portions. When I talked to publishers about the idea of writing this book, one suggested we put a bar of soap on the cover. People with OCD are believed to live in spotless houses and to freak out when someone sneezes on them. The cover of the book *Obsessive-Compulsive Disorder for Dummies* does feature a line of neatly ironed identical white shirts on their hangers. True, OCD can show itself in these ways. But it's a selective and self-selecting picture, and one that cannot account for the intrusive thoughts that drive the behaviour.

The close similarities, at least superficially, between the way that OCD and OCPD can manifest themselves, tied with the reluctance of many people with OCD to talk about their obsessive thoughts, is one reason why even severe cases of OCD are sometimes misdiagnosed, or not diagnosed at all. Another is that OCD can be masked by other mental disorders, which frequently co-exist in the same patient – depression, anxiety and eating disorders among them.

In recent years, experts in OCD have tried to educate their fellow health-care workers to this problem: some patients who report to dermatologists with constantly chapped hands, for instance, could have OCD. But, unless they are asked the correct questions, this will not be spotted. The questions are not complex. Joseph Zohar, an OCD expert in Israel, has produced a list of five that he says should help doctors and nurses screen for clinical obsessions: Do you wash or clean a lot? Do you check things a lot? Is there any thought that keeps bothering you that you would like to get rid of but can't? Do your daily activities take a long time to finish? And are you concerned about orderliness or symmetry? To answer yes to any of these questions does not mean that someone has OCD but it should prompt further questions – along similar lines to these but with a range of possible answers to indicate the severity of symptoms.

The most common of these more advanced diagnostic tools is called the Yale-Brown obsessive-compulsive scale – five questions about obsessions and five similar questions about compulsions. Each is answered on a scale of 0 to 4. Question three, for instance, asks how much distress obsessions cause, with 0 = none and 4 = near-constant and disabling. Question six asks how much time each day is spent on compulsions (0 = none, 1 = less than an hour, 2 = one to three hours, 3 = between three and eight hours, 4 = more than eight hours a day).

From a total score of 40, a tally of above 32 is taken to indicate extreme OCD. But at the other end of the scale, it's possible to score seven and be in the normal range. So, in principle, someone who spends an hour a day thinking obsessive thoughts, and up to three hours a day engaging in compulsive behaviours is considered normal, so long as they are not particularly disturbed by either, and they find they can, more or less, carry on with their lives.

That's the way that psychiatry works. It's the way that medics diagnose mental illness. A condition – OCD, depression, bi-polar, whatever – is either present or it's not. Officially, it is no more possible to be a little bit OCD than it is to be a little bit pregnant or a little bit dead. Someone has OCD or they are normal. That distinction is drawn for valid reasons, mainly to monitor disease trends and to decide who is eligible for treatment. But in the real world, it's not that simple. In fact it's a lot more complicated. What we can call sub-clinical OCD is everywhere. The people of Dunedin, for one, are riddled with it.

Perched on the coast of the South Island of New Zealand, Dunedin was the country's largest city until 1900, but has done little to trouble the editors of *Wikipedia* since. Fame briefly visited in the 1980s, when a series of highly rated sixties-influenced guitar bands emerged, and notoriety beckoned when a clumsy marketing slogan to promote a 2008 cricket match, 'it's all white here' – based on the colour of the players' clothing – went down badly with the visiting team from the West Indies. The local television news handled the row with the sensitivity and nuance of a British tabloid newspaper and illustrated its report with archive footage of the Ku Klux Klan.

Yet the people of Dunedin are special. From the mid-1970s to the present day, the health of more than a thousand Dunediners, all born between 1 April 1972 and 31 March 1973, has been regularly assessed: these people have been tested, prodded, jabbed, measured, checked, questioned and, most importantly, recorded. The Dunedin generation comprises one of the best so-called cohort studies in the world – long-running surveys of the health of a group of people, how it changes and how it is influenced. Cohort studies are pretty common, but what sets the Dunedin work apart is the effort the study organizers make to keep it going. On assessment day, which comes every few years, they bring participants back to Dunedin from wherever in the world they live. Some 96 per cent of all living participants were included in the round of check-ups when they were aged 32. That's unprecedented for such a study, which typically sees at least a third of the original subjects drop out by that stage.

The Dunedin data set is valuable to scientists interested in the real-time study of human health and development. Another of its attractions is that it probes the mental as well as physical health of its volunteers, with a psychiatric assessment part of its battery of tests. The Dunedin dataset has been used, for example, to assess the role that teenage use of cannabis could have in people who go on to develop psychosis. And it's been used to probe the levels of OCD in people who, according to the official cut-off line set by psychiatrists, don't have OCD at all.

When scientists looked at the results for two of these Dunedin assessments – performed when the participants were aged 26 and 32 – they found that up to a quarter of the cohort had reported some form of recurring obsessive thought or compulsive behaviour in the previous twelve months. And when the scientists published these findings in 2009, they raised an argument in the academic community. This wasn't because of the results, which were in line with those from other studies. A 2010 survey of almost three thousand people across Belgium, France, Italy, the Netherlands, Spain and Germany, for instance, found that

13 per cent of the subjects admitted to a period of two weeks or longer when they experienced unpleasant recurring thoughts or felt compelled to perform repeated actions at some point in their life. And a similar exercise in the United States reported the same year that 28 per cent of Americans had experienced such a two-week spell.

No, the controversy came because the scientists said the results of the Dunedin psychiatric assessments held some important implications for society. In the official write-up of the study's findings, the researchers suggested that doctors screen the 'normal' population to identify – and treat – these sub-clinical obsessive and compulsive symptoms. This might lower the risk of some people going on to develop 'full-blown' OCD, and other mental health problems, they said, which would reduce distress and costs in the long run. They concluded:

> Cost-effectiveness analyses will be required to decide whether these cases should be treated, but such calculations should take into account that treatment of mild cases might prevent a substantial proportion of future serious cases.

Not so fast, said Murray Stein, a psychiatrist at the University of California San Diego. In an editorial published in the same issue of the *American Journal of Psychiatry* as the Dunedin study's results, Stein cautioned against any assumption that people with symptoms of OCD need help if they have not asked for it. 'We must consider,' he said, 'the very real possibility that the reason so many people with obsessive-compulsive symptoms fail to get treatment is that they manage quite well.' He continued:

> As mental health professionals, we should do everything we can to promote awareness about and accessibility to mental health interventions. As clinicians we have an obligation to help reduce the suffering and improve the functioning of the patients who come to us for help. But, lest we forget, most people with obsessive-compulsive symptoms in the community, whether diagnosable or subthreshold or anywhere in between, are not patients. To suggest that we do more to identify and treat such individuals implies that we know better than they whether and when they need our help.

Who needs help? I did, but I didn't accept that I did, at least at first. One problem with OCD is that this 'at first' stage can last for years. That's down to a mental paradox. On the one hand, the thoughts and fears of OCD blended so seamlessly with the rest of my cognition, they felt so embedded and so real that it was hard to believe they could be taken away. On the other hand, I knew the thoughts were silly. And just like almost everybody, I had other types of silly thoughts too. I felt the urge to jump from a high place. I had random ideas that I had written the wrong name on a birthday card the moment I sealed it inside the envelope. I checked the back door was locked even though I just turned the key. And these intrusive thoughts went away. They went away by themselves. So I thought my thoughts of HIV would also go away by themselves.

I knew that I couldn't catch Aids from someone else using my toothbrush, or from dried blood on the ice rink where someone had burst their nose, or from blood that might be contained in water dripping from an upstairs window that landed in my eye when I looked up. I knew that if I had sat on a drug user's syringe I would have felt it. I knew that my mum's towels were safe, even though she had to have a blood transfusion one Christmas. And so I thought that one morning, hopefully tomorrow morning, I would wake up and leave behind the silly thoughts that made me worried about all of those things. Unfortunately, that's not how OCD works. My intrusive thoughts did go away, but there was a catch. One went away just as soon as another came along to take its place.

It was the US psychologist William James in 1892 who first described thoughts as a stream of consciousness. The term was subsequently popularized by a writing style in which undirected words seem to flow from an author's head onto the page – *Ulysses* by James Joyce is perhaps the best-known example. Like all streams, this mental flow is uneven – there are fast and slow sections, eddies and currents, pools and falls. Some thoughts relate to current tasks, or those we have just finished or are about to start. Some are triggered by other thoughts or by actions, or as a clear response to external events. Intrusive and obsessive thoughts are different. They seem to bob up from nowhere.

I was a serial monogamist when it came to OCD. My

stream of consciousness had a taut net strung across it, a net just big enough to trap one misshapen irrational thought at a time. The only way to free a trapped thought was for another to knock it out, send it on its way, and for it to settle there instead. Some intrusive thoughts would remain for days or weeks, others would last for just a few minutes. But the net was always full. And the content of the net, the thought that was in residence at the time, was always on my mind.

Not everybody experiences OCD in the same way. For some people with OCD the mental hijack of their attention is the only apparent symptom of the disorder. They don't carry out overt compulsions. They don't feel the need to convert their mental anguish into physical form. They say they suffer from a form of OCD called pure-O.

Most of these people, scientists think, do still carry out compulsions – but they are mental compulsions. They might try to 'undo' the impact of an intrusive thought by deliberately thinking of something else to neutralize it. Or they might start to predict the kind of situations that are likely to trigger the unwanted obsessive thoughts, and then seek to avoid them. Both of those mental routines are compulsions. When someone with OCD uses them to suppress or push away the thought, they reinforce it as surely as if they had performed a physical act like touching a wall or checking for blood on a rusty nail. Their response legitimizes the thought and gives it significance.

For most people, the intrusive thoughts are what bother

them and the compulsions are a relief, albeit a temporary one. The intrusive thoughts come first. But some people with OCD describe what sounds like a reversed flow of this cause and effect. The behaviour, the compulsion, is more like a tic. It comes first. They can't explain why they need to tap their hand on their leg a set number of times. They are not doing it as a way to drive something from their mind. They just feel they need to do it, and if they resist the urge to do so then they get anxious.

In these cases the intrusive thoughts follow the resisted compulsion – if these people don't tap their leg then they worry something awful will happen, perhaps their parents will die in a car accident. That's a form of OCD known as the just-not-right experience.

It's pretty difficult to track the true course of events in OCD, the sequence of obsession-compulsion-obsession and where it begins and ends. After all, a circle, even a vicious one, has no beginning or end. But there is evidence that some people with OCD find the unwanted compulsive behaviour distressing, rather than the unwanted obsessive thoughts. Other psychologists have taken this idea further. They have suggested that, even in cases where the compulsions appear to follow intrusive thoughts, it could be the behaviour and not the cognition that triggers the OCD event. The thought appears only as a way to justify the odd behaviour.

The high-place phenomenon – the common urge to jump from a window or bridge – has been explained like this: Say you are standing near the edge of a cliff and enjoying the view. There is no safety barrier and part of your brain, the part that watches for hazards and instinctively avoids them, gets nervous and instructs the legs to take a step back, to minimize the risk. A different part of the brain registers this order to mobilize the legs and seeks to explain it, by comparing the imagined threat to the real threat. Yet there is no immediate threat. You are standing still. So why step back? What's the problem? The brain – the intrusive thought generator – throws up an (irrational) suggestion: the problem must have been that you wanted to jump.

That all happens in milliseconds, and the strongest signal, the one that breaks through from all of this subconscious activity, is the conclusion that comes as an intrusive thought: I want to jump.

OCD dissolves perspective. It magnifies small risks, warps probabilities and takes statistical chance as a prediction, not a sign of how unlikely things are. Example – someone once told me that to catch HIV from a kiss was a one in a million chance. But there are seven billion people in the world, right? And if they all kiss someone at some point in their life, then more than 7,000 of them are at risk. If we assume that only about one in 3,500 kissed people have HIV, then that still leaves two people who will catch the virus that way. Why shouldn't one of them be me?

That's risk assessment by homeopathy. The hazard is so dilute that it is no longer present. Yet as Jim Carrey's character in the film *Dumb and Dumber* replies with excitement when a woman says the odds of her agreeing to join him on a date are one in a million: 'So, you're telling me there's a chance!' Even when I accepted that it was OCD that made me feel this way, which took a while, there is still the fear of an ironic twist, that someone with an obsessive fear that they will catch HIV in a spectacularly unlikely way could be one of the unfortunate individuals who falls foul of the numbers, and actually does. People *have* contracted HIV in unusual circumstances – from their dentist, for example.

That helps to explain why people with OCD perform the same checks, again and again. We see the one in a million event and not the nine hundred-and-ninety-nine thousand nine hundred-and-ninety-nine non-events that we should do. If I touched a door handle with a scratch or a scab on my finger then my mind instantly told me to check there was no blood there. Many times it told me to check before I touched the handle in the first place. At the time, it makes sense. No blood, no risk. To check, I thought, would make my life easier. Each time, I believed that one more, one last, check would give me the certainty I craved. But one check was never enough. Afterwards, each time, I doubted how thoroughly I had completed the check. So I would do it again.

I once stared for an hour at a photograph of me and some friends in a youth hostel in France to try to convince myself that our toothbrushes were different colours, so I would know no-one else would have used mine. You could just make out the toothbrushes held in a cup that the photograph showed on the shelf behind us. Well, you needed a magnifying glass really, so I bought one. Each time I put down the picture, the urge to pick it up and look again returned.

For a while, psychologists thought that the repeated checks of OCD might be down to poor memory, and the prior checks simply not remembered. But if there is a memory deficit, then it's a very specific one: people with OCD may not be able to remember clearly if they locked the front door, but they can tell you what they had for breakfast before they left the house. The answer seems more subtle. It is not the accuracy of recall that matters in OCD, but a loss of confidence that those memories are true. People who carry out compulsive checks seem to trust their memory less, and the more they check, the more this distrust grows. It is another vicious cycle: memory uncertainty provokes the need to check, and to check increases memory uncertainty.

Here's an example of that in practice, one that features one of the dullest experiments in the history of science. Psychologists at Concordia University in Montreal asked students to turn on an electric stove, turn it off again, and then check it was off. Others were asked to turn a tap on and off. All were told to repeat their task again and again and again until they had done it nineteen times. Before and after the repetitive tasks, the volunteers (including those allocated to the taps) were each asked to turn off three knobs on the stove – and then to check they were off. Immediately after each test, they were asked to recall which they had turned off.

All of the students could recall the details of the first

test. They remembered how they had turned off the stove switches. But, for the second test, the one performed after the repetitive checks, the scientists found some important differences. Those students who had spent all of their time with the stove remembered the second test check differently from the first. They had less confidence that their memory was accurate, and their recall was hazy – not as detailed or vivid. The study showed that repeated checks of the cooker – but not of the taps – introduced doubt in the mind of the checker. Other scientists have repeated the experiment and found the same effect on memory. It can start after just two checks.

The results suggest that the more someone checks that a cooker is off, or that there is no blood on a tissue, then the more that scene becomes familiar. The brain remembers familiar events differently, it tends to focus on meaning rather than colour and shape, which are easier to recall. This makes recall of familiar events less detailed. In OCD this means, the more that we do something, the less sure we can be that we did.

The problem goes deeper. Some people with OCD can stare at a light switch, and still not convince themselves it is off, or look carefully at their scrubbed hands and not believe they are clean. That cannot be down to changes in memory. It is altered perception, and there is some evidence that, just as to check damages confidence in memory, so to stare, even for just a few seconds, reduces confidence in the information collected by the eyes. To re-read names, addresses and documents, as people with OCD often must do, could render their meaning less clear – just as to say a word over and over again seems to make it lose its meaning, a well-documented effect known as semantic satiation.

I knew my OCD was bad when I decided to write a poem about it. I don't have the poem any more, and I wouldn't include it if I did. Some things are just too awful to share. The gist of it was that I was a stone and that my friends were fish. They sprouted legs and walked on the land. They grew up. They changed. They evolved. I stayed as a stone. Self-pity is rarely attractive, but even so.

FIVE

The OCD family

New York City fire fighters call a death-trap dwelling a Collyers Mansion. The nickname comes from the Harlem brownstone house of Homer and Langley Collyer, two brothers who were found dead there in 1947, surrounded by 140 tonnes of collected items and rubbish, including prams, rusted bicycles, old food, potato peelers, guns, glass chandeliers, bowling balls, camera equipment, dressmaker dummies, a canoe, the folding top of a horse-drawn carriage, rusty bed springs, pickled human organs and a two-headed baby in jars, eight live cats, broken Christmas trees, the chassis of a Model T Ford car, fourteen pianos and pots of their own urine and excrement. The brothers were compulsive hoarders. Like most hoarders, they did not see the problem.

Intelligent and well-educated, both brothers had attended nearby Columbia University; Homer was a lawyer and Langley an engineer. But after their mother died in 1929 they became recluses and hid in the house at 2078 Fifth Avenue behind windows they boarded up and booby traps they set to deter intruders. Homer lost his sight in 1934 and his brother became his keeper. Their father had been a doctor – he would paddle the canoe to work along the Harlem River – and, surrounded by his medical books, Langley saw no need for outside assistance. Doctors, he feared, would remove his brother's optic nerve, and so leave no hope of recovery. Instead, Langley fed Homer a diet of oranges, more than a hundred each week. The piles and piles of newspapers, he said, were for his brother to read when he recovered.

Their parents had been wealthy property owners and the brothers were rich, but they hated to waste money, Langley especially. Rather than pay for the subway, he would walk the New York streets as far as Brooklyn, and drag a box behind to scavenge junk. The last time the brothers were seen outside the house together was when they carried a fallen tree through Manhattan. After thieves broke into their home, they never left the house unattended again. The rooms were so full of their stuff that during an attempt to evict them, a locksmith managed to penetrate just two feet into their house in three hours.

In recent years, television programmes have profiled hoarders, some of whom have become minor celebrities. Homer and Langley were genuine stars. After a society reporter called Helen Worden introduced them to a captivated city in 1938, for years everything they did was news – along with some of the things they didn't. When neither brother showed his face after a nearby property caught fire, the city newspaper *The Sun* ran the headline: 'Recluses

Calm Despite Blaze: Collyer Brothers Show No Interest In Fire Next Door'. Their secretive nature only magnified interest, together with wild stories of the treasure they sat on. Yet burglars who did break into the house found no swag worthy of the crime.

Langley was sometimes accompanied by journalists on his nightly excursions. One time, a reporter showed him around the *Herald Tribune* office on West 41st Street, where the supposed hermit was fascinated by the presses, had his photograph taken and lectured staff there on the principles of printing. He dismissed the stories that swirled about him and his brother. The windows were boarded, he said, because local children smashed them otherwise. He and Homer, he said, just wanted to live their lives their own way. His old and shabby clothes were a defence. 'Dressed like this, no one ever molests me.' Dropped back at his house by the reporter in a taxi, Langley stopped to pick up scraps of paper and broken glass on his way into the house. 'It's the same every night. Rubbish in the yard.' The paper wrote this of them: 'Two brothers – indrawn, sufficient unto each other, leading the life they choose, following a rationality all their own.'

On 21 March 1947, police received an anonymous call about a dead body in the house. Patrolman William Barker broke in through an upstairs window and crawled for two hours through wall-to-wall clutter, including cardboard boxes and umbrellas tied together, until he found Homer Collyer, dead in a tatty blue and white bathrobe, his head resting on his knees. Some speculated that Langley had murdered his brother and scarpered – sightings of him were reported in nine states. But the police continued to search the house, pulling out box after box of stuff the brothers had held onto – old phone books, an early X-ray machine, a cavalry sabre, thirteen ornate mantel clocks, two pipe organs, five violins, their mother's unfinished knitting and a horse's jawbone. Outside, efforts to clear away the brothers' stuff and so gain access to the house produced a growing pile of bric-a-brac and collected rubbish on the sidewalk. That and the stench from the house drew a crowd of 600 people.

Langley's body was discovered by a workman on 8 April – more than two weeks after that of his brother, yet just a few feet away, partially decomposed and gnawed by rats, covered in three large bundles of newspapers. He was wearing a red bathrobe over four pairs of trousers but no underwear. Bringing food to his older brother, by then paralysed with rheumatism, Langley had been caught and crushed by an avalanche of junk from one of his own booby traps. Homer starved to death a few days later. Both were buried with their parents in the family plot at Brooklyn's Cypress Hill cemetery.

The city tore their house down and the site is now a park that bears their name. After learning about their lives, I visited to pay my respects in February 2013. It's a scruffy rectangle of grass and trees with a plaque that explains its past life mounted on the railings that separate it from the street. Just three blocks from the colourful chaos of 125th Street, the cultural artery of Harlem, it's difficult to imagine

Homer inside the house, helpless and calling to his trapped brother with increased desperation, unable even to lift his arms to pull at the mounds of their precious belongings that became their prison.

Local officials have tried to rename the park. The Collyer brothers, they say, are a poor advert for modern Harlem; terrible role models for the city's new generation. Feared and misunderstood in life, Homer and Langley are scorned even in death, for following a rationality all of their own.

Hoarding is one of twenty or so separate conditions that scientists link to OCD. Just as autism is now considered a spectrum of related syndromes, so OCD is believed to sit on its own spectrum, alongside other conditions linked either by the presence of intrusive thoughts or by seemingly compulsive behaviours. In fact, some psychologists suggest that autism itself is an OCD spectrum disorder. Autism can feature a need to observe rigid routines and rituals, and some autistic patients report both obsessions and compulsions.

Some conditions on this OCD spectrum are neuro-logical disorders. These tend not to feature the distressing thoughts of OCD, but they do show enough superficial similarities – repetitive and unwanted behaviour for example – for scientists to look at how they might be related. Tourette's syndrome is one of these.

Contrary to the way it's usually portrayed, only about a tenth of the people with Tourette's syndrome compulsively shout out swear words. Mostly it is a condition of tics

– persistent and involuntary physical jerks, twitches and repetition of noises and phrases. It's been known about for almost two centuries and today is found in about one in every hundred children. The tics don't come from out of nowhere – they are described by those who have them as similar to the urges we all get to sneeze and yawn. We might resist them for a while, but the feeling builds until some form of release is inevitable. To carry out the tic then brings great, but temporary, relief.

Some scientists put Parkinson's disease on the OCD spectrum. Parkinson's is not a form of OCD. It is well characterized as a neurodegenerative disorder that shows itself with tremors and rigidity. But some patients with Parkinson's do show symptoms intriguingly similar to compulsions. Some Parkinson's patients can find it impossible to resist unwanted urges to line up pebbles, or to repeatedly dismantle and assemble door knobs. Others develop impulsive behaviour, usually after treatment with drugs. A 68-year-old Argentine woman who was treated for Parkinson's developed both compulsive shopping and kleptomania. She began a teleshopping habit and had what she described as an uncontrollable fascination to shoplift cosmetics and beauty products. Other Parkinson's patients develop compulsive gambling habits.

Impulsive behaviours sit on the OCD spectrum too. There's an important difference between compulsive and impulsive acts: motivation. While compulsions are the repetitive performance of apparently senseless actions, impulses are better viewed as a tendency to act quickly and without regard for the consequences. They often bring some kind of pleasure or reward, at least at first. Sex is often impulsive, and plenty of psychologists treat problematic sexual behaviour as an impulse-control disorder.

Marie was a sexsomniac. It started one night in France when Marie's husband Lee woke at 2 a.m. to find her violently beating and manipulating his penis. He described her mental state during the attack as confused, though probably not as confused as Lee's. In the morning, Marie couldn't remember a thing. It worsened. She tried to push marbles into his anus and Lee woke in intense pain to find three padlocks placed around his penis and testicles. One night, Marie produced bits of a mincing machine. After several years, the couple, who had three children, went for help to a hospital in Dijon – she with feelings of shame, despair and guilt and he, not unreasonably, with feelings of worry.

Sexsomnia is considered a type of parasomnia, or unusual behaviour in sleep. It's very much on the fringe of the conditions linked to OCD, but it's similar to other types of uncontrolled and impulsive sexual behaviour, which are more relevant. Some experts see common ground between OCD and incessant use of Internet pornography, for instance, or regular encounters with prostitutes. We might roll our eyes when a movie star exposed as a serial philanderer tearfully says he will seek help for his problem, but the psychological issue of sex addiction is widely recognized. It's one of a number of nonparaphilic sexual behaviours. These tend to be unrestrained forms of culturally and legally acceptable practices, usually consensual sex and masturbation.*

Matt was a 48-year-old pastor at a small suburban church in the United States. Married with a child, Matt would masturbate to online pornography up to three times a day. Church members noticed Matt was not around. He missed board meetings and racked up huge bills on pornographic websites. He would get up late at night and head for his study after his wife, Karen, had gone to sleep. One night, Karen, who had noticed mysterious charges on their credit card statement, walked in on him. Matt went for help the next day.

There has been little research on nonparaphilic sexual behaviours, but, as Matt's case shows, there is one important difference from OCD – and one related to the difference between impulsive and compulsive acts. Matt was aroused by his impulses and went out of his way to encourage them. That he didn't fight his thoughts meant that he didn't have OCD.

Other sexual thoughts, however arousing, can be resisted, and those do sometimes lead to OCD. Robert worked in a bank and had been happily married for seventeen years. Yet when an attractive female customer walked in, Robert could not help but think of her naked. Robert didn't like it. He found the thoughts immoral and inconsistent with the love he felt for his wife. He interpreted

---

* Paraphilic sexual behaviour is considered deviant – exhibitionism, necrophilia and worse.

them as signs that he was an unfaithful husband and, to keep them away, he would avoid shopping malls and other places where he might see women. In the end, he told his wife – so she would stop him if he began to act upon his thoughts.

Faulty impulse control can also drive conditions such as pathological gambling and pyromania. Jean Esquirol, the nineteenth-century French psychiatrist who saw Mademoiselle F. and promoted monomania, was interested in these phenomena too. Together with his student Charles Marc, Esquirol reported the case of a woman who compulsively stole from Paris shops. Esquirol and Marc called her a kleptomaniac, and though they are generally credited with inventing the term, reports of apparently compulsive theft go back to 1816 and the Swiss physician Andre Mathey, who wrote of patients with a 'unique madness characterized by the tendency to steal without motive and without necessity'. Today, kleptomania is much rarer than OCD. Kleptomaniacs are typically older than conventional shoplifters, who usually steal for personal gain, and – just like people with Tourette's – they report a rise in tension before the theft, and a sense of relief afterwards. Similar is compulsive shopping, or compulsive buying as psychologists prefer to call it. It briefly appeared in psychiatric textbooks a century or so ago under the term oniomania (onios is Greek for 'for sale').

A particularly distressing impulse control disorder is trichotillomania, which makes people pull out their own hair, frequently to the point where it produces visible bald spots that they cover with a wig. They usually remove hair from their head, but some people pluck out their eyelashes and tug at their pubic region. They are not always aware of what they do – one man treated for severe hair-pulling looked down while he drove and was astonished to see the dashboard covered in his own hair. Some eat the hair; one 34-year-old woman in Turkey did so for more than a decade, until surgeons were forced to remove a hair ball that completely filled her stomach. When trichotillomania produces hair balls that extend beyond the stomach and loop down into the intestinal tract, doctors call it Rapunzel syndrome. It takes its name from a fairy tale, but Rapunzel syndrome can kill.

Then there is skin-picking disorder, which sees people compulsively scratch at spots, scabs and other bumps and blemishes, sometimes for several hours a day and even while they sleep. A third of skin pickers chew and swallow the bits they pull away. Some use tools – needles, pins, razor blades and staple removers. The results can be near-fatal. A man in the eastern United States once had to rush his skin-picking middle-aged wife to hospital because he thought she had been shot. He came home to find her with what looked like a gaping bloody bullet hole in her neck.

His wife had become obsessed with what she described as a pimple on her neck and would scratch at it with her fingernails. On that day she picked at it with tweezers and worked her way through the skin. She continued, and dug her way through the tissue underneath, until she reached muscle. A tweezers-grab of flesh at a time, she went on until she exposed and nearly pierced her carotid artery. Had she done so, she almost certainly would have bled to death.

The woman was an intelligent, articulate accountant and normal in every way, bar one. She was utterly delusional when it came to the appearance of her skin. She had started to pick at it when she was 44, and was frustrated because every doctor she saw failed to understand she did it not to self-harm but to improve herself, to remove defects. She would point at normal patches of her face and insist they were unusual. She refused to acknowledge even the possibility that her perception of blemishes was exaggerated. In reality, the only imperfections were the scars from her picking that dotted her legs, arms and face.

Probably the most debilitating of the OCD spectrum conditions is body dysmorphic disorder. BDD plagues people with intrusive thoughts on a specific theme – defects in physical appearances, usually their own, but sometimes those of family or friends (when it is known as BDD by proxy). It affects men and women roughly equally. Most are concerned with perceived flaws on their face or head, such as small wrinkles they see as hideous abnormalities. People with BDD can spend hours each day on compulsive rituals; they examine themselves in the mirror and camouflage their skin with layers of make up. Sufferers usually believe that their imagined defect will provoke horror in others, so some rarely leave the house, and when they do they wear a wig, hat or sunglasses, or hold themselves in a certain position. Some find it difficult to walk past shop windows or cars without stopping to check their appearance; others cover all the mirrors in their house with towels. Most seek repeated reassurance that they look normal. About a quarter of patients with BDD attempt suicide.

It's not new. In 1891, Italian psychiatrist Enrico Morselli wrote of a patient who, 'in the midst of his daily affairs, in conversations, while reading, at table, in fact anywhere and at any hour of the day, is suddenly overcome by the fear of some deformity'. It is thought to affect between 1 per cent and 2 per cent of the population today, but, like OCD, a combination of shame among patients and poor awareness among doctors leaves it under-diagnosed. Many patients with BDD keep their thoughts to themselves because they worry others will dismiss them as vain and narcissistic. When they do seek help, they often claim instead to suffer from depression or anxiety, which they think carry lower stigma. Patients with BDD are more likely considered delusional than those with OCD, because fewer recognize the absurdity of their thoughts and actions.

Sometimes confused with BDD is a different condition called Body Integrity Identity Disorder – which sees otherwise healthy people believe they have too many arms and legs. They ask surgeons to amputate their healthy limbs – which places the surgeon in an awkward position. If they refuse, and some do, then the person may go away and attempt to do it themselves with an axe or kitchen knife or homemade guillotine, and some do.

When the intrusive thoughts that bother someone concern not their appearance, but their health, the result can be hypochondriasis. Just like 'a little bit OCD', the term hypochondriac has become detached from its clinical definition. Hypochondriacs, we say, are those who complain frequently of sniffles and coughs, who worry that a headache is a sure sign they have a brain tumour.

That sounds mild – a little silly even – but true clinical hypochondriacs experience life in a similar way to someone with OCD; they convert intrusive thoughts of illness into obsessions, and then develop lengthy compulsive rituals to address them. They take their own temperature, pulse rate and even blood pressure. They compulsively check they can swallow, keep a close eye on their urine and excrement and feel for cancerous lumps. In some cases, these constant prods and pokes bring on the bodily changes and discomfort they fear in the first place. They almost always ask others for reassurance – family, friends, doctors, specialists, hospital phone lines, and experts and non-experts on the Internet. Unlike OCD, which comes from thoughts, people with hypochondriasis tend to fixate on genuine physical sensations and exaggerate their impact.

Eating disorders such as anorexia nervosa and bulimia nervosa show some striking similarities to OCD. Repetitive and strongly held thoughts force people to carry out rituals and patterns of behaviour to reduce anxiety – refusal to eat or inability to stop – followed immediately by compulsions to make themselves vomit or over-exercise. Thought suppression seems to play an important role – with those who try and fail to squash negative thoughts about their eating habits more likely to show symptoms of bulimia.

People with anorexia can show obsessions and compulsions unrelated to food or weight, including an irrational desire to arrange things in symmetrical patterns.

One of the newest additions to the list of abnormalities that could relate to obsessive-compulsive symptoms is maladaptive daydreaming. Freud said to daydream was infantile and neurotic, but these days psychologists and neuroscientists see daydreaming – sometimes called undirected thought or mind wandering – as a normal and probably useful part of human cognition. It might help us to solve problems, and we can usually snap out of it when we need to. Some people turn their daydreams into something more serious. They do it compulsively; they find it hard – if not impossible – to not daydream and the behaviour has a negative effect on the rest of their lives. Rachel was one of the first people identified with this problem.

As a child in the United States of the 1970s, Rachel would spend much of her time in a self-created fantasy world. She would imagine herself in her favourite television shows and run episodes inside her head. As a teenager, Rachel started to lose control of what she and her parents had always considered a harmless hobby. She recalls how the daydreams took over until she was no longer in charge of her thoughts and her life – vividly similar to the language people with OCD use to describe their obsessions.

Rachel, later a successful lawyer, sought and received treatment, eventually taking medicine commonly given to tackle OCD. She is far from alone. *Wild Minds*, a web forum for maladaptive daydreamers, has some 2,200 members from across the world. In 2011, scientists in New York reported the first academic survey of the condition. They questioned by email 90 people – 75 women and 15 men – who described themselves as excessive or maladaptive fantasizers. These people did not know each other, but they reported a tight set of thoughts and behaviours.

The level of detail was striking – 'I have spun tons of plot lines in this world spanning multiple generations of characters,' one said.

> The parts of my daydreams I obsess over are the most intense emotional scenes . . . a character's parents or best friend dies, a character is injured, abused, tortured or raped, or even just has a terrible argument with a loved one . . . Characters fall in love, get married, have and raise children, develop deep and strong friendships.

The people who responded to the survey said they would spend, on average, more than half their time in daydreams.

Only one in five of the daydreamers saw daydreaming as harmless – the rest had tried to stop. A quarter described the activity as addiction, obsession or compulsion. 'I have tried to limit my daydreaming in the past,' one said.

> I tried hard to just focus on what was around me and keep in mind only real people, things and events that were happening in the here and now. It was a battle. Me against my daydreams. They won.

There's more. Do you check your partner's underwear to find traces of his/her sexual intercourse? Do you check up on his/her way of dressing up if he/she goes out on his/her own? Those are questions 29 and 30 of a 'Questionnaire of Jealousy' prepared by scientists at the University of Pisa. It aims to probe a mental syndrome called obsessional jealousy; others have labelled it non-delusional pathological jealousy, and have framed it as an obsessive-compulsive spectrum disorder. People with non-delusional patho-logical jealousy show similar behaviours to OCD. They respond to intrusive thoughts with excessive checks and requests for reassurance. And they avoid situations that might provoke the thoughts – for example, they can keep their partner in the house so they can't meet potential suitors.

When you add that lot up then OCD doesn't seem quite so rare and unusual. You almost certainly know someone affected. Yet people with these OCD spectrum disorders have something else in common besides their thoughts and urges. They don't tend to bring their problems up in conver-sation. Their conditions are socially unacceptable because they often centre on shameful and taboo subjects. Sufferers assume their dark, intrusive thoughts reveal their true nature: someone who thinks such things must be mad, bad and dangerous to know. That phrase is over-familiar through repetition, but look again at the power of the individual adjectives.

I tried often to talk about my fear of HIV with friends.

I didn't admit my worries that I had caught it from, say, a mix-up of our toothbrushes in our shared bathroom, I kept the details vague. But I thought it might help to bring up the subject more generally: 'So what about that Aids stuff then, that's all a bit scary eh?' The usual response was a nudge and a wink and a knowing smile. 'So, who was she?' Even today when I tell people I have had a persistent fear of HIV since my teenage years they assume it was because I was promiscuous. Hardly. My OCD was something of a passion killer.

People talk about the stigma of mental illness, and they are right to do so. While it is considered fine, encouraged even, for those with a bad cold or an upset stomach to offer details of their ailment in great detail, to bring up the subject of mental health is often not just a passion killer, it's a conversation killer. Awkward silences and awkward glances tend to follow. I have hidden it when I have applied for jobs. Do you have a mental illness? Well, which box would you tick?

The stigma is less now for some mental disorders, such as depression. People sometimes talk about how anxious they are as if it's the inevitable cost of a busy and enviable life. We are encouraged to discuss schizophrenia and bi-polar disorder in less suspicious tones. But we have some way to go with OCD. As we've seen, most people don't talk about even their most fleeting intrusive thoughts, because they fear they might be labelled as violent or perverted. So how does one begin to tell the neighbours that one is obsessed that one will sodomize their pet rabbit? Or confess to school friends one's obsessive thoughts that one will turn into a rat, and so one checks compulsively for signs of a tail? Those are both genuine cases of people who sought help for OCD. Which box would you tick?

SIX

Cruel to be kind

In his book on depression *The Noonday Demon*, Andrew Solomon describes how he was taken to hospital with a dislocated shoulder and how he was terrified that the pain would trigger a mental breakdown, as it had done before. He knew his mind, its weak spots and vulnerabilities, and he pleaded with the emergency room staff for the chance to talk to a psychiatrist, to head off the psychological impact that he believed would follow the physical trauma. They didn't understand. They told him to relax. They told him to picture he was on a warm beach and to imagine how it felt when he wiggled his toes in the sand. Solomon's shoulder was fixed, but within days his depression returned with a vengeance.

When I first went for help with my intrusive thoughts of HIV, I was told to wiggle my toes in imaginary sand too. I had gone to a drop-in centre run by a mental health charity on the edge of the university campus, and they had made an appointment with a counsellor. This was outside the medical system and that was deliberate. I didn't want to see a psychiatrist because that was for crazy people. I didn't want to talk to a doctor, because I didn't want anything written down. Stories in the newspapers at the time warned that those who asked their doctors about HIV and requested tests were being denied health and life insurance.

The counselling was useless.* We performed relaxation exercises and I pulled imaginary golden thread from my nose. Neither stopped the intrusive thoughts. And we talked about my childhood, my parents and my relationship with them. That's classic psychodynamic analysis – the technique developed by Freud. That didn't help me either, but then, despite the claims of Freud and those who followed him, there is zero evidence that psychodynamics works with OCD. In fact, it could probably make things worse.

In the mid-1960s, psychiatrists in London encountered a middle-aged woman with OCD who had been treated for ten years with Freud's methods. The woman had become obsessed with blasphemous intrusive thoughts when she was a child that became increasingly sexual when she was a teenager, such as thoughts about sex with the Holy Ghost. She carried out repetitive acts to reduce the anxiety – she dressed and undressed time and again and walked up and down stairs. Taught by Freudian therapists about the importance of sexual symbolization, she then found it traumatic to close drawers, insert plugs, clean tall glasses, enter trains and eat bananas.

---

* The counsellor, however, did her best.

Much of Freud's take on the causes and treatment of OCD now looks ridiculous, yet it dominated approaches to the disorder for decades after his death. That's not because he was right, it's because his sky-high profile ensured his work on obsession was translated into English, which became the most widely used language of the new field of psychiatry in the twentieth century. This translation process created a problem. Freud, who spoke German, used the term *zwangsneurose* (obsessional neurosis). The word *zwang* was translated as 'obsession' in London, but 'compulsion' in New York. Faced with confusion, scientists introduced the hybrid term obsessive-compulsive, a label subsequently given to millions of people, as a compromise.

The popularity of Freud's suggestion that internal conflict generated obsession only started to wane in the 1960s, when a new breed of scientists muscled in on the field of OCD. They were called behavioural psychologists, or simply behaviourists. The behaviourists had their own firm belief. All behaviour was learned, even abnormal behaviour. And as such it could be unlearned. To treat obsession, they just needed to find the right trigger.

The use of behavioural psychology to treat OCD comes directly from the famous experiments of the Russian physiologist Ivan Pavlov, who reported how dogs learned to associate food with a bell rung to announce mealtimes, so much so that they would drool at the sound of the bell even if no food appeared. Pavlov's lab called the reaction of the dogs reflex at a distance, but other scientists preferred the term conditioning, and they thought it could explain phobias and the irrational fears of OCD. The causes of irrational fear were not in someone's sexual history, they said, but in their environment. Someone with obsessions of catching a disease from a public toilet, for example, had probably once become severely ill after a visit to a particularly unhygienic washroom. This 'classical conditioning' gave birth to the irrational fear, which was maintained and nurtured by a related process called 'operant conditioning'. The person, the theory went, would start to avoid toilets to reduce stress and because this action would work, it would negatively reinforce the behaviour.

In one bizarre case of conditioning, a man found that he was impotent when he tried to have sex with his wife – but only when the couple were at home. In therapy he described how he had previously been discovered in bed with another man's wife and how the cheated husband had thrashed him. The man remembered how his assailant's wallpaper, by unlikely coincidence, was the same as that on the walls of his and his wife's own bedroom. The beating had made him classically conditioned to associate sexual desire and the wallpaper with the fear of violence. One redecoration later, the problem went away.

Conditioning had a flip side. If someone could deliberately be made to associate undesired behaviour with an unpleasant experience, the behaviourists thought, then the drive to carry out that undesirable behaviour should cease. This spawned the era of what became known as aversion therapy. It saw compulsive gamblers play fruit machines

CRUEL TO BE KIND

wired up to deliver electric shocks, alcoholics given a drink together with drugs to make them vomit, and over-eaters forced to watch a doughnut cooked in front of them while they sniffed at pure and rotten skunk oil.

Most shamefully, psychologists in the 1960s and 1970s used aversion therapy to try to reverse homosexuality. Gay men were shown photographs of naked men and women, and if they looked at the man for too long, their therapist would shock them with electricity. Success of the treatment was judged by how many women each homosexual managed to sleep with over the year or so that followed, and the relative size of their erections when shown straight and gay pornography. Those who failed to convert were coached on how to chat up a woman and how to read her body language.

There is some evidence that a form of aversion therapy was tried in ancient times. Roman citizens who drank too much alcohol would be forced to swallow an eel from a wine glass. And early Buddhist texts describe an over-talkative chaplain who was cured of his habit by a cripple who hid behind a curtain and used a pea shooter to fire pellets of goat dung into the chaplain's mouth whenever he opened it to speak.

Aversion therapy was used to treat OCD. A 49-year-old obsessive-compulsive patient was equipped by a psychologist at a Birmingham, UK hospital in the early 1970s with a device that strapped electrodes to his fingers and auto-matically delivered an electric shock if he washed his hands too often (the water completed the circuit). Frank Kenny, a psychologist at the Memorial University of Newfoundland, went further with aversion therapy for obsession. He thought he could use it to turn off not just the compulsions but the intrusive thoughts themselves.

Kenny would ask his patients to form an image relevant to their obsession, or to say a repetitive phrase, and then he would blast them with painful electricity. He did it thirty or forty times in each session, for up to five sessions a week. It could produce 'lasting change' he reported.

It must have been quite a sight. Mrs D, a 33-year-old housewife and one of Kenny's first subjects, for example, would say out loud her intrusive thought: 'I am going to have sex with my dog' and then raise her finger. Kenny, sat behind, would take this as his cue to shock her and Mrs D would react to the pain, wait thirty seconds and repeat 'I am going to have sex with my dog.' Zap. 'I am going to have sex with my dog.' Zap. Kenny grandly called the treatment Faradic Disruption (Michael Faraday being the scientist who invented the electric motor).

Aversion therapy was controversial among scientists, and dynamite in the media. Anthony Burgess' 1962 novella *A Clockwork Orange* graphically describes a (fictional) aversion method called the Ludovico technique, in which the book's antihero Alex has his eyes pinned open and is forced to watch violent scenes and listen to his favourite classical music, while under the effect of a drug that induces nausea. Alex subsequently tries to kill himself.

By the time the film of the book was withdrawn from British cinemas in 1972, a full-scale backlash was under way against aversion therapy, which some critics claimed was being used to brainwash people in the style of Aldous Huxley's *Brave New World*. Opponents in the US labelled behavioural psychologists Rockefeller Nazis and said (with a confused take on politics) that they bred communists. One prominent behavioural psychologist at the time, Jim McConnell at the University of Michigan, was later targeted by the terrorist known as the Unabomber.

I had a mild brush with aversion therapy. After several years of denying that I needed to, I eventually went to see a psychiatrist. I was still in Leeds, by now studying for a postgraduate degree, and a psychiatrist came to the university's medical centre once a fortnight. He gave me a red rubber band and told me to wear it on my wrist and snap it against my skin whenever I had an intrusive thought about HIV or Aids. That was treatment for OCD in the mid-1990s. It was called thought-stopping, and it was another idea of the behaviourists. My band lasted a few hours. The next one survived a day. I went to a budget stationery shop and asked for the biggest bag of rubber bands they had.

Thought-stopping, scientists now accept, does not help people with OCD, any more than relaxation techniques or Freudian psychodynamics do. Still, my trip to the psychiatrist was not wasted. It showed me that I was not alone. The psychiatrist had asked me if I wanted to join one of his group sessions for OCD. I didn't. I wasn't keen to hang out with hand-washers because I didn't see how it would help. My problem was different I said, and I doubted anyone with OCD would truly get it. 'David,' he replied, 'I am seeing three other people at this university with OCD and they have the same irrational fear of HIV that you have.' I felt a strange sensation; I now realize it was hope.

He also told me the way to beat OCD. It sounds easier than it is. He told me that the compulsions, in my case the urge to make sure I had not exposed myself to HIV by checking and seeking reassurance, fuelled the obsessions. He explained the vicious circle that I was trapped inside. The way to stop the ride and get off, he said, was to resist the compulsions.

To beat OCD was as simple as that, just as scoring a hole-in-one on the golf course is as simple as hitting the ball directly from the tee into the hole. I played a lot of golf at that stage of my life. The odds that a regular golfer like me will score a hole-in-one have been worked out as twelve thousand to one. Before I was able to properly resist any of the compulsions of my OCD, I managed to score two.

I never smoked but I imagine that to resist the compulsions of OCD is what it must be like to try to quit cigarettes. Like sticking to a diet, to stop the compulsive checks ultimately comes down to willpower. But what must be resisted in OCD is not a physical craving, but the mental pull of your own consciousness. In the grip of a compulsive urge there is nowhere to hide and nothing to reason with. To resist a compulsion with willpower alone is to hold back an avalanche by melting the snow with a candle. It just keeps coming and coming and coming. The obsessions and compulsions of OCD are linked by a force of nature so strong that to break the connection demands almost supernatural effort. When I was in the grip of the worst of OCD, if you had asked me not to investigate suspicious red stains on a communal towel, you may as well have ordered me to fly or to shoot thunderbolts from my fingers.

Some days I had more supernatural willpower than others. Some checks seemed more harmless than others. I learned which situations would prompt the thoughts and the urges, and worked out ways to avoid them. If I was unsure whether someone else had drunk from my glass, I didn't finish it. If an opponent on the Astroturf football pitch shredded his knee, I would avoid him. In that way I muddled through. I had good days and I had bad days. I had lots more bad days. When things became especially bad, when a thought just would not budge, then I would force myself back to donate blood. The blood donor service would take it only every sixteen weeks. I would count down the days in a diary.

It's not that OCD meant I could not function, and that I couldn't think of or do anything else – I did well in exams, I had friends and girlfriends, furious arguments and fun conversations, and I held down some decent jobs. It's just that I was thinking about something else at the time. I was thinking about HIV and how I might have caught it when I learned that my grandmother had died, when I found out that Princess Diana had been killed, when I saw *Pulp*

Fiction at the cinema and when I watched rower Steve Redgrave claim his fifth Olympic gold medal on television. I was thinking about HIV and Aids in the days before I got married – I had met a climate scientist at a conference the previous week with a sore on his lip and I couldn't be sure that we hadn't mixed up our drinks. OCD stole something from me at that stage of my life; it took away my attention.

There is a great line in a book about famous hypochondriacs by Brian Dillon. It's called *Tormented Hope* and it talks about a point in the life of a hypochondriac when things change. They begin to secretly date everything back to the moment they first realized something was wrong. Life previous to that point, he writes, looks idyllic and elusive. In a similar way, I am a world expert on the events of 1991, or more precisely whether they happened before or after the summer, before and after my first obsessive thoughts. Those before, I participated in. Those after, I watched. Obsession meant that I navigated much of life after the summer of 1991 on autopilot. I was up front and central. I looked the part and smiled at the passengers, but something else was flying the plane.

Then there was Stoke City. As I write this book in 2013, Stoke City is a football club that plays in the English Premier League. As you read it, I hope it still does. I'm not one for the over-intellectualization of football, but Stoke City helped me through my years with OCD.

I used to go and watch Stoke play before the summer of 1991, so it offered a bridge that could connect me with those idyllic and elusive days. And then there was the impact when Stoke City scored a goal. It's tragic, I agree, but at my grandmother's funeral, my younger brother and I stood awkwardly next to each other, we barely said a word. Yet just a few weeks later, when Peter Thorne scored for Stoke City in a match against Cambridge United, we hugged and yelled at each other at the top of our voices. A Stoke City goal, a mixture of elation, release, celebration, relief and usually, quite frankly, surprise, would penetrate. I felt it. OCD put a shock absorber on most of my emotions, especially those that I could see coming. But it couldn't buffer the feeling of a Stoke goal.* I know, like I said, tragic. Worse, even. When you rely on goals from Stoke City to get you through life, you know you truly are fucked.

That was my way to live with OCD. And as most people with OCD never get help, and those who do take, on average, seventeen years to see the right person, most do have to live with it. In fact, we can be pretty confident that people have lived with intrusive thoughts, obsessions and compulsions for centuries. This is not the first book to describe the impact of irrational and recurring weird thoughts. Not by some six hundred years.

Margery Kempe was born around 1373 and some experts consider her book, published in 1436, the first

---

* See 'Kevin Keen goal vs Derby County RRPNG4' on YouTube. I was behind the goal and thinking how contaminated blood might have got onto my razor before that went in. That's me in the red and white shirt.

autobiography written in English. A clergyman took her dictation and wrote the account of her life – still in print – in the third person. Kempe fought against intrusive thoughts of erect penises. 'She was shriven [granted absolution], and did all that she might,' the book says. 'But she found no release, until she was near at despair.'

One of the most detailed historical accounts of the impact of intrusive thoughts was recorded by John Woodward, an early eighteenth-century fellow of the Royal Society and professor at Gresham College, London. He wrote about Mrs Holmes, a 26-year-old woman from London Bridge who became obsessed with thoughts of a porpoise that she saw in May 1716 in the River Thames:

> She never awaked but this Thought first came into her Mind; and continued till she went to Sleep again . . . She frequently endeavoured to cast that Thought out; and to introduce another, that might be more pleasing to her; in which she sometimes succeeded; but the new Thought, however pleasant at first, became, in a little time, as troublesome and disturbing as that of the Porpoise.

An apothecary advised Mrs Holmes to 'be cheerful and brisk' – the eighteenth-century equivalent of 'pull yourself together'. Woodward was not impressed with this advice, lamenting that it was the common response of 'those who are not Judges of these things, and who do not know, that People in this Case are subject to the Fury of a Morbid Principle, and wholly under the Government of it'.

There are historical accounts of what can seem compulsive behaviour too, though we should interpret them with caution. Repetitive actions, even those that seem obsessive and irrational, say little that is precise about a person's state of mind. Some stories of the history of OCD, for instance, include a tale from the ancient days of the Buddha, some 2,500 years ago, and an apparently obsessed monk who felt compelled to sweep the floor of the monastery continuously. That may look like OCD, but other accounts from the time describe how the Buddha told one of his disciples, Suddhipanthaka, to deliberately sweep the floor non-stop to reach enlightenment. We might say today that Suddhipanthaka was 'a little bit OCD' with his sweeping. But he wasn't.

One prominent person in the past who did seem to suffer from genuinely compulsive behaviour was Samuel Johnson, the eighteenth-century English writer and dictionary compiler. His biographer James Boswell noted how Johnson would count his steps and make sure that he always started on the same foot. Often, he would stop, count again and then head back to try again, even while his companion would carry on down the street.

Many historical accounts of obsessive behaviour detail not just the presence of intrusive thoughts, but the folly of trying to suppress them. These writers may never have seen a white bear, but they knew of the effect. Martin Luther, the sixteenth-century German priest who inspired the Protestant reformation and suffered from obsessive thoughts, gave the advice:

Grit your teeth in the face of your thoughts and for God's sake be more obstinate, head strong and wilful than the most stubborn peasant or shrew. Indeed, be harder than an anvil . . . If necessary speak coarsely and disrespect- fully like this: Dear devil, if you can't do better than that, kiss my toe.

'Kiss my toe, OCD', that's what I should have said. But I wasn't ready. Not yet.

SEVEN

The God obsession

If almost everybody experiences intrusive thoughts, and intrusive thoughts are the raw materials for obsessions, then why does almost everybody not develop OCD?

The mind is a thought factory. Every day it processes a conveyor belt of thousands of thoughts, good and bad, happy and sad, useful and intrusive. The factory must decide how to act on them and then issue instructions to respond. We each do this differently, based on our unique combinations of early experience, environment and biology; our biases, preconceptions and knowledge. The thought factory must work fast. The conveyor belt always rolls and new thoughts arrive in a constant stream. Something always comes in and something always goes out.

Chemical engineers call a system like that a continuous process. It's the opposite of a batch system, in which they dump all the ingredients in a pot and leave them largely undisturbed to do their thing. Continuous processes are more efficient because you don't have to turn them off and start again to change the quality and the quantity of product. Turn up the temperature, increase the pressure, slow down the flow and you can tweak how the process converts the raw materials into something useful. Our thought factory does that too. In different circumstances, under pressure or stress, when we are tired or angry, we alter the way we process our thoughts.

The thought factory works pretty well. But it has a flaw. No chemical engineer would design a continuous system in which the inward flow of raw materials could not be turned off. That is a recipe for disaster. It can turn a minor problem into a full-scale catastrophe.

To understand OCD we must look at the conditions inside the thought factory, prising off the lid to see how two different minds can process the same thought in radically different ways. This was a task beyond the behavioural psychologists. In fact it was a concept that the behaviourists firmly rejected. They had no interest in what went on between the ears, only in how it showed itself as action. The mind was a black box and the thought processes inside, they claimed, unimportant.

It took until the 1980s for a new group of scientists, cognitive psychologists, to challenge that view. They argued that thoughts and how they were processed were crucial, not just to understand mental disorder but to treat it. They were ready to lift the lid on OCD. And when they did, one of the first places they looked for an answer was religion.

I'm an atheist but I have no specific axe to grind with religion. That's important to say because what follows could easily be construed as an attack. For the record, I'm not saying that religion is a mental illness, or that OCD and religious beliefs are the same thing. I'm not saying that OCD makes people religious, or that religion causes OCD.

Religion does not cause OCD, but, as we've seen, attempted suppression of intrusive thoughts probably does. Unrealistic demand for pure thoughts probably does. And to be told that if you think certain things then you will forever burn in Hell probably doesn't help.

In 2002, psychologists risked their eternal souls for science and deliberately misled dozens of Catholic friars and nuns, scattered across the convents and nunneries of northern Italy. The psychologists wrote to religious institutions and asked for volunteers to help with a study. The scientists wanted to look at the link between religious belief and obsessive symptoms, but they didn't admit that at first. They said only that they were interested in how people think. They kept the information intentionally vague, they said, to avoid a 'defensive attitude' from the pious.

Dozens of the nuns and friars came forward to help and the scientists sent them questionnaires to assess their personalities and to judge how obsessive-compulsive they were. They repeated the exercise with two other groups: citizens actively involved in church activities, and university students who said they had no interest in religion. The psychologists found that the friars and the nuns, together with the regular churchgoers, were more likely to report thoughts and behaviours consistent with OCD.

OCD and religion have walked hand in hand through

the centuries. The initial spiritual interpretation of obsessions and compulsive behaviours means that most early accounts of what would now be considered medical problems are set in a religious context. Plus, it was the clergy to whom most people turned with their concerns. Obsessive thoughts of sin – that one had committed a sin or that one was perpetually tempted to sin – have long plagued the devoted. As far back as the sixth century a Mount Sinai monk called John Climacus wrote of intrusive, blasphemous thoughts, which would invade an individual's mind against their will and which proved almost impossible to evict: 'This deceiver, this destroyer of souls, has often caused men to go mad.'

By the fifteenth century, intrusive thoughts of sin were called religious melancholy, or scrupulosity. The latter term was popularized by Antoninus, an archbishop of Florence. A scruple, he said, was a state of fear and indecision, which arose from mental questions that were impossible to answer and doubts that could never be settled. It comes from the Latin word *scrupulum*, which means a small sharp stone. The church compared the stubborn moral doubt of scrupulosity to the feeling of a pebble in your shoe. No matter how often you stopped to remove it, when you next took a step it was still there. Say what you like about medieval Italian religious leaders and their contribution to science, they knew a good analogy when they saw one.

One reason we can be confident that religion does not cause OCD is that obsessions and compulsions crop up with similar frequency in both secular and strictly religious countries. But, although the total number of people with OCD is unaffected by a country's religious leanings, the more religious a place, the more the clinical obsessions of these people centre on religious issues. Religion might not provoke obsessions, but it does provide an outlet for them.

Various studies over the last few decades display this trend. Just 5 per cent of OCD cases in England feature obsessions and compulsions that relate to religion, 10 per cent in the United States, 11 per cent in India and 7 per cent in both Singapore and Japan. Numbers shoot up in the Middle East: 60 per cent of people with OCD in Egypt report religious obsessions, 50 per cent in Saudi Arabia and Israel, and 40 per cent in Bahrain. In Turkey, a secular country with pockets of intense religiosity, the burden of religious OCD shadows the geographical influence of Muslim culture and increases as you travel from west to east.

Psychologists who have studied this link between OCD and religion say it could come down to ways of thinking called dysfunctional beliefs. Most people have dysfunctional beliefs, which we usually pick up in childhood. They are not mental disorders, they are lenses placed across our cognition. They distort the way we perceive the world and can help explain why different people interpret identical situations in different ways. Some people are more likely than others, for example, to focus on the negative outcomes of their actions, and to exaggerate the way these outcomes damage themselves and others. That's a dysfunctional belief called catastrophizing. It makes people more likely to be anxious.

Psychologists have identified three types of dysfunctional belief important in the development of OCD. The first is an inflated sense of threat and personal responsibility. The second is perfectionism and intolerance of uncertainty. The third is a belief in the over-importance of thoughts and the need to control them. To be clear, to have one of these dysfunctional beliefs is not to have OCD, but it does increase the chance that someone will develop OCD, because they will then incorrectly process the intrusive thoughts that are common to most people. What's more, the strength of the dysfunctional belief – how hard people with OCD cling to it in the face of contrary evidence – might influence the degree of insight they have into their condition.

The different types of dysfunctional beliefs could explain the range of symptoms seen in OCD. Perfectionism could underpin a compulsive need for symmetry, while inflated responsibility and overestimation of threat could combine to promote checking obsessions about dirt and disease. And beliefs about the over-importance of thoughts – bad thoughts lead to bad deeds – could drive obsessive thoughts of dangerous or inappropriate behaviour.

Dysfunctional belief about the over-importance of thoughts is sometimes called thought-action fusion, because it implies to someone that a thought is the moral or the physical equivalent of an action. Thought-action fusion, for example, can make people believe that to 'think' about having sex with someone – a married man or a child – is as bad as actually doing it. Does that sound familiar?

'I say to you that everyone who looks on a woman to lust for her has already committed adultery in his heart.' According to the Gospel of Matthew, Jesus Christ says that to his followers during the Sermon on the Mount. It's a good description of thought-action fusion. Thoughts, in other words, are equivalent to actions. The tenth commandment goes further and forbids people to want (covet) property owned by somebody else. Just to think an impure thought is itself a sin.

Psychologists say that thought-action fusion could explain the way OCD shows itself among religious people. Some Christians, for instance, are often distressed to discover they can even conceive of sin. Their impure thoughts, they believe, must show they are not as devout as they hoped. Thought-action fusion makes these people believe that their thoughts – their thoughts alone – represent moral failure that makes them more likely to face God's punishment. These distressing sinful thoughts are, of course, ego-dystonic, they run contrary to the individual's faith. This makes the person more likely to try to suppress the thoughts, and so for the thoughts to return.

This link between religious belief and thought-action fusion can be tested. In 2012, psychologists asked dozens of senior figures in the Lutheran church how they would respond if one of their parishioners sought their help for scrupulosity. The scientists created a hypothetical worshipper, who they said was worried that she was going crazy because she could not get unwanted thoughts of cursing God out of her mind. She no longer read the scriptures, they said, because of the intrusive urges she felt to desecrate the pages. The thoughts caused her great anxiety and she prayed for up to eight hours a day for forgiveness.

Most of the spiritual leaders were sympathetic. They said they would reassure the woman that God was merciful and forgiving and that He understands the difference between involuntary and deliberately sinful thoughts. But significant numbers said they would also recommend action that, however well intentioned, we know (from the white bear effect of how suppressed thoughts return harder), would just make the situation worse.

They said they would tell the woman to pray harder, and attempt to replace her sinful ideas with more acceptable thoughts. Some said they would warn her that God expects purity in thought and deed, while a few would go as far to point out that to think sinful thoughts risk God's punishment. The church elders who themselves showed the most signs of thought-action fusion were the most likely to offer this unhelpful advice.

There are different forms of OCD and so too, of course, are there different forms of religion. What's of interest to scientists is how the demands of each faith seem to influence the way obsessions and compulsions develop among the devout. Protestant Christianity places strong significance on thoughts: beliefs, intentions and motivations. Sure enough, studies of protestant Christians show that the more religious they are, the more likely they are to report the signs of thought-action fusion. Islam puts great emphasis on ritual. Muslims are expected to wash in a set manner and perform repetitive prayer routines several times each day. Obsessive and intrusive thoughts that interfere with these are called *waswaas*, or whispers of Shaytaan. They can force people to doubt whether they performed prayers properly, and so make worshippers repeat, or start actions again. The Islamic text *Sahih al-Muslim* addresses intrusive doubts a Muslim may have about the number of performed prayers:

> If any of you doubts during his prayer and he does not know how many he has prayed, whether it is three or four, then he should discard and cast away his doubt. He is to continue upon what one is sure of [the lesser] then perform two prostrations before making tasleem.

Scrupulosity in Catholic Christians often includes a mix of thoughts about impure beliefs – an urge to worship Satan – and behavioural doubts, such as obsessive thoughts they will drop the Eucharist in communion. Contamination fears are common in religious OCD, but again, the specific nature of the contamination depends on the demands of the religion. Jewish people can develop OCD centred on thoughts that they cannot avoid non-kosher food.

Religious or not, most people can hold several dysfunctional beliefs at the same time. Inside our thought factories, these various cognitive biases spin our thoughts in different directions to clash, collide and bounce off each other. If the combined effect is to make people more likely to react badly to an intrusive thought, then the result can be OCD.

Joan reacted badly to an intrusive thought. A 43-year-old, Joan had worked as a training officer with a large company in the south of England when a young man who worked under her was fired for misconduct. Joan already suffered from obsessions and compulsions. She had to retrace journeys to make sure she had not hurt anyone. Now, she started to think that she had telephoned the sacked man's parents, and told them about an embarrassing incident. She worried that the phone call would lead to him being severely punished, and that he would be driven to suicide. Joan was married with three children. She had made no such phone call. But the obsessive guilt she felt about it was so strong and so real that she tried to kill herself.

Joan is a good example of thought-action fusion. She believed that to think something was morally the same as to do it. And she believed that to think about an event made it more likely to happen. So though she made no phone call, just the act of thinking that she might have done was enough to trouble her. Joan had another type of dysfunctional belief relevant to obsessions too. She had an over-developed sense of responsibility.

Inflated responsibility is probably the most important dysfunctional belief in OCD. Obsessive-compulsives often feel responsible both for having thoughts and for the negative consequences of their thoughts on themselves or others – and for not acting to prevent those consequences. They believe that if they have any influence over an outcome, then they are responsible for it. This triggers a cascade of twisted secondary ideas – 'having this thought means I want to do it' or 'if I fail to prevent harm then it is as bad as directly causing harm'. Some people with OCD are compelled to pick up pieces of broken glass from the street. They worry that, if they don't, then someone else might cut themselves on the glass. If the person with OCD fails to prevent that happening, they think, well I may as well have walked up to the stranger and deliberately hurt them. So they take the glass home. And then they are forced to keep it. To throw it out with the rubbish could see the refuse collectors hurt themselves. That's why some people with OCD have a collection of broken glass in their house. Others gather banana skins for the same reason.

Cognitive psychologists use dysfunctional beliefs to construct theories of how minds can misfire. In the mid-1980s, a psychologist called Paul Salkovskis, then at Oxford University, built on the concept of inflated responsibility to suggest the first modern cognitive model of OCD. The model has proven very influential. It marked the beginning of the end for the dominance of the behaviourists when it came to the psychology of OCD, and it led to a whole new set of treatments. Best of all, it can be demonstrated with a famous scene from a Woody Allen movie.

*

Christopher Walken had just turned 34 when the film *Annie Hall* was released to worldwide acclaim in April 1977. Walken played Duane Hall, Annie's brother, who, sat in his bedroom, memorably asked Allen's character Alvy if he could confess something. Driving at night, Duane said, he sometimes had an impulse to steer his car into the oncoming traffic. He could anticipate the explosion, he said, the sound of shattering glass and the flames from the spilt gasoline. Allen's unsympathetic reply is that he's due back on planet Earth. But Duane has the last laugh when he is instructed by his father to drive the couple to the airport that evening, which he does at speed while Alvy looks nervously on from the passenger seat.*

The cognitive theory of OCD says it is not important that Duane has such thoughts – as we know, they are common. What matters is how Duane reacts to them, how he appraises and interprets them. If Duane could brush them away, think them a nuisance and dismiss or simply ignore them, then the intrusive thoughts should pass as quickly and easily as the headlights of the oncoming cars. But if he instead decided that the urges were important and that they deserved attention, then that is a danger sign. If Duane interpreted the thoughts as having serious consequences, for which he was personally responsible, then he could turn them into a clinical obsession. He could start to think that he was a dangerous driver who must take

---

* If you haven't seen it, search YouTube for 'Walken in Annie Hall'.

extra care not to lose control. He might start to avoid driving; he would be distressed by his thoughts and might try to suppress them. And so the intrusive thought would return, harder and stronger and more difficult to ignore.

Unlike many ideas about the causes of OCD, this cognitive theory of obsession can be tested. It is a fairly straightforward job for a scientist to make a volunteer feel responsible for a situation. Imagine, for instance, that you are asked to sort 200 mixed pills (twenty each of ten different colours) from a glass jar quickly into semi-transparent bottles, each of which must contain a different colour. Psychologists at Laval University in Quebec reported the results of such a test in 1995. One set of volunteers were told it was just a practice exercise and that the results would not be counted. Another set was told that lives could be at stake: a pharmaceutical company planned to use the pills to fight a virus in Asia and needed to know how easily the different colours could be identified. The second group, of course, took longer and performed more checks, and also reported more anxiety, doubt and preoccupation with error.

Or imagine that you are an undergraduate psychology student and, in reward for credit towards your degree, you agree to join a study to look at fear of snakes. Your tutor removes a live snake from its cage to show you, and wants you to fill in some questionnaires. After the tutor returns the snake, he beckons you into a separate room to speak your thoughts aloud for five minutes so that your stream of consciousness can be recorded and analysed – oh, but first just close the cage door, will you?

Next door the tutor finds a form supposed to measure your anxiety while you looked at the snake. Whoops, let's go back to the other room and do that first. 'Look at the snake and then rate your anxiety on this scale,' he says. But the cage is empty. Uh-oh. 'OK, you go ahead with the stream of consciousness exercise and I'll go look for the snake.' How do you feel? A snake is loose – and it's your fault.

Psychologists at the University of Maine reported this experiment in 2008, carried out with a hundred of their female students and one harmless snake bought from a local pet shop. The students were not really responsible for the snake's escape – while they shuffled between rooms, someone else stole in and removed the reptile from the cage. But the students weren't to know that – or that they were involved in a trial not of snake phobia, but of the link between responsibility and intrusive thoughts.

To test the role of responsibility, the psychologists repeated the charade with a parallel group of students, with one exception: this time the tutor closed the cage door himself. The snake was still missing when the students returned to the room, but the escape was now his fault and not theirs. Sure enough, when the psychologists listened to the stream of consciousness tapes, they found that the students fooled to take responsibility for the escape reported more intrusive thoughts of snakes.

The Maine psychologists tested another feature of the

OCD cognitive model, a prediction that intrusive thoughts are more likely to form if they are salient – that is, if they relate to current concerns. They sub-divided the student groups according to how much they said they were afraid of snakes and described this fear as a measure of salience. Again, the results supported the theory. The more afraid of snakes they were, the more intrusive thoughts appeared. Together, the psychologists said that their study backed an important part of the OCD cognitive theory. If a person feels responsible for an event that they judge as personally relevant, they will experience increases in related intrusive thoughts. With great responsibility, comes great power.

And great fear. In April 2013, the Israeli military admitted that one of its soldiers had developed OCD because she was given the job of guarding state secrets. Her air force commanders repeatedly warned her not to disclose the classified information, and told her she would have to pass lie detector tests. The soldier began to compulsively ensure her locker was secure, checked classrooms for discarded pages and would pick up scraps of paper she found around the base in case any of her colleagues had dropped restricted documents.

Nothing, perhaps, can bring on a sense of responsibility more than having a child. Most new parents will check their sleeping baby is breathing, and then go back to check again. That's normal. Some new parents take it too far. They turn their new sense of responsibility into OCD.

Sara had a five-month-old son called Justin. Sara had

dreadful thoughts that she would strangle or drown him. But Sara loved Justin, she was responsible for him and she would never hurt him. Sara forced herself to seek help. She told a psychiatrist about her thoughts, about the images she saw of Justin's coffin and of herself in jail; about how sometimes Justin would survive her imagined attempts to murder him. She told how she could not put Justin in his bath, or be alone with him, because she could not trust herself not to kill him – especially when he was asleep and would not realize that she had put her hands around his throat. Sara told the psychiatrist that she would kiss Justin's head to try to make the thoughts go away.

When Sara told these terrible things to her psychiatrist, Sara was sectioned. She was involuntarily committed, locked away in a hospital to keep her away from Justin. But Sara was no risk to Justin. Sara had postnatal OCD. You've never heard of postnatal OCD? No, neither had Sara's psychiatrist.

Postnatal depression is now recognized as a serious problem and mothers-to-be know that they may struggle through the first few months. But postnatal OCD is almost unheard of outside the pages of scientific and medical journals. Yet it is common. As many as one in ten new mothers develop signs of it. Childbirth can worsen OCD in women who already have the condition, and it can bring it on for the first time in others

The obsessions that strike new parents who develop postnatal OCD take a particularly distressing form. Mums and dads (and it does affect men too) take their baby home, thank friends for the cards and neighbours for the good wishes, and close the door to gaze into the sleepy eyes of their child, who utterly depends upon them. Then, from nowhere, they feel a powerful urge to throw the fragile infant into the fire, or cook it in the microwave, or hurl it down the stairs, or push their thumbs into its eyes, or squeeze it until its bones snap, or plunge a knife into its chest, or, against all of their instincts and good sense, despite them straining every neuron to shake the idea, to sexually molest their own newborn baby.

Outside their heads, none of this happens. As we saw earlier, people with OCD do not act on their intrusive thoughts. But the new parents who develop OCD don't know that. And lots of them simply don't want to take the chance. That's why hysterical new mothers with OCD can refuse to hold their babies, even though they want to do so more than anything else. And it's why new dads who develop OCD refuse to enter their child's bedroom with a pair of scissors. It's why Sara would kiss Justin, to try to undo the evil in her head. It's why she went to see the psychiatrist. And it's why the psychiatrist locked her up.

Sara's psychiatrist was no doubt concerned because one or two mums in a thousand experience urges to hurt their babies as part of genuine psychosis that emerges after they give birth. There is a big difference. Postnatal psychosis features delusions, 'the Devil is out to get my baby', and hallucinations, 'I saw smoke and fire come out of the baby's ears.' But, most importantly, if the parents recognize and report the thoughts as unwanted and if they resist them, then, as with all forms of OCD, they show they are alien to their personality and so unlikely to be carried out.

Don't take my word for it. Stanley Rachman, the psychologist who performed the first survey of intrusive thoughts in the general population, probably knows more about OCD than anyone else on the planet. He has treated hundreds of people since the 1960s. And he has never had a single OCD patient who complained to him about intrusive thoughts – and he has heard the lot – go on to hurt a child. Not one.

My baby daughter was six months old when I noticed the blood on her leg. It was summer 2010 and she wore a pair of shorts and there, above the knee, was a dull smear of red. Out of my bag came the nappies, the spare clothes, the raincoat, the various creams and wipes, the jumper, the hat, the spare hat, another nappy and a plastic box that rattled with snacks as I hunted for the sticking plasters. Strange, there was no obvious cut or graze, and she wasn't in a position to damage herself anyway – crawling was months away, let alone walking. Had she been bitten by an insect, or had I scraped her leg as I lifted her in and out of the playground swing? She would have cried out, wouldn't she? If it was blood, I realized, then it probably wasn't her blood.

I was the obvious source of the blood, and sure enough, when I looked carefully, I saw a scratch on the back of one of my fingers, probably from the spiky bushes that guarded the gate to the playground. There was a similar smudge on my finger. I must have brushed her leg against my scratched finger as I lifted her. Click. My idea generator delivered another scenario. It could be someone else's blood. And it could be HIV-positive. She could have rubbed it into her eyes.

My baby daughter enjoyed our return trips to the playground that day, and only complained about me lifting her in and out of the swing on about the eleventh time. Yes, the stained part of her leg did seem to touch part of the metal guard as I pulled her out, well, more or less. But, did she put her hand there as she swung? Once more for Daddy? I couldn't see any blood on the swing, and I couldn't see any blood on the grass underneath, any of the times I looked. I still couldn't see any when I came back with a torch to have another search that evening. I was 38. It was almost nineteen years to the day since that first summer night when I discovered that I could not ignore my intrusive thought. You could have Aids. She could have Aids.

Before that day with my daughter, I had settled for a life with OCD. I knew people with depression, anxiety, anorexia, bi-polar disorder and ADHD; others had died of cancer or in accidents. One killed herself. I had started to accept that OCD was my thing. There is a useful cliché on mental health – don't compare your insides with other people's outsides. From the outside, I probably appeared happy. A little withdrawn, distracted or quiet in some situations perhaps, but happy. Most people, I figured, would also have had a moment in their lives that they secretly dated events against. I would just have to accept mine. I would have to live with my OCD.

I reversed that decision the day I made my baby daughter an accomplice. I telephoned my local doctor the next morning to make an appointment. It stopped here. It stopped with me.

EIGHT

Animals and other relatives

We think humans have free will. It's one thing that separates us from animals. We are masters of our biology, not the other way around. Yet there is something animal about OCD, something atavistic and primitive.

Videos surface from time to time on the Internet of people engaged in compulsive behaviour: postmen dip in and out of a box to check for letters with the same jerky repetitive movements that a wading bird uses when it ducks for fish.* Drivers who return to check they locked their cars patrol the doors in the way that a bear lumbers around the perimeter of its territory. Just like humans, animals show common patterns of behaviour and ritual. They stop at the same places to eat, bathe and sleep. Some of this behaviour can appear compulsive.

In 1952, the Nobel prize-winning Austrian zoologist Konrad Lorenz described how water shrews would travel

---

* Search for 'OCD mailman' on YouTube.

along set paths 'strictly bound to them as a railway engine to its tracks'. He saw how the shrews would jump over a stone that blocked their way, and how, when the stone was removed, they continued to jump. The animals, Lorenz said, would 'disbelieve their senses' if those senses reported a need to change their behaviour. Of course we don't know what the shrews were thinking at the time, and because of this, some scientists in the OCD arena are sniffy about reading too much into animal behaviour. Repetitive actions are not necessarily compulsions, they insist. Compulsions are a response to an obsessive thought. There are some eerie similarities between rituals and compulsions, though. There is something very OCD about some animal behaviour.

The Japan Dog Festival is the country's largest and most prestigious show. Run by the Japan Kennel Club, it's a celebration of the pedigree of the nation's finest dogs and an excuse to watch them slalom through bendy poles and scamper around an obstacle course. The 2008 show was held at the Big Sight International Exhibition Centre in Odaiba in the run up to Christmas, and owners who attended had more to worry about than how their pets would fare in the festival's Agility Cup and the Champion of Champions event. A team of veterinary scientists from the University of Tokyo was there to ask how many of their dogs chased their own tails.

In the comics and cartoons of childhood, all dogs chase their own tails. Next to an appetite for slippers, it's a defining feature of the species. In the real world, while most tail-chasing is harmless, some dogs take it too far. They do it several times a day, and when they catch their tails they bite repeatedly until they make them bleed. Some scientists think such behaviour is the OCD of the dog world. They call it canine compulsive disorder.

Other animal rituals resemble the behaviours of OCD. One is compulsive grooming. Birds pick out their own feathers, mice and cats pull away their hair and dogs chew their fur. Dogs lick their paws until they are raw and inflamed. Horses show a damaging compulsive behaviour called cribbing, when they grip a fence or post with their teeth and pull their head back sharply, time and time again. Mice hoard marbles and other useless objects.

In animals, these routines are known as fixed action patterns – innate behaviour sequences triggered by specific circumstances and seen across a species, even in animals raised in isolation. They often emerge when the animal is under stress. Humans are not generally considered to exhibit fixed action patterns. But some of our behavioural rituals seem compulsive too. Look at the routines of sports stars under pressure: how tennis players must bounce the ball the same number of times before they serve, and golfers waggle the club as part of a familiar pre-shot routine before they swing to hit the ball. People in the shower often wash themselves in a set pattern. And just like Lorenz's water shrews, people heading from A to B like to stick to preferred paths.

Lorenz himself noted:

I once suddenly realized that when driving a car in Vienna I regularly used two different routes when approaching and leaving a certain place in the city. Rebelling against the creature of habit in myself, I tried using my customary return route for the outward journey and vice versa. The astonishing result of this experiment was an undeniable feeling of anxiety so unpleasant that when I came to return I reverted to the habitual route.

These are rituals, not compulsive behaviours. But they show that, just like animals, our motor response to some stimuli can be repetitive and patterned – just like the kinds of behaviour that can emerge in OCD.

Scientists think the behavioural rigidity of ritual is useful. It could help animals, and perhaps humans, to perform certain tasks with less mental effort, so allowing them to save precious energy to direct towards something else. In times of stress, that could help them survive. Here's a question – could OCD be what happens when this primitive process goes wrong? When it is deployed at the wrong time? When I put my baby daughter in and out of the swing, to check she had not caught HIV, was I responding to some ancient survival mechanism with ritual?

The link between OCD and rituals intrigues scientists. Some human cultures certainly show behaviours that in another place and time would look like pathological compulsions. Nepalese Sherpas place 100 miniature clay shrines, 100 food cakes, 100 butter lamps and 100 dough effigies in a symmetrical pattern; the Gujars of Uttar Pradesh bathe and then make twelve offerings of red and white substances to twelve deities; the Moose of Burkina Faso sacrifice red, black or white chickens, depending on the situation; the Zuni native Americans make offerings at six points around their village while others take six puffs of special cigarettes and wave towards the six points of the Zuni compass. Apache Indians burn all clothes worn during the dressing and burying of a corpse, as a way to keep away intrusive ideas, images or words associated with the dead person.

One of the most detailed comparisons of human ritual and OCD was performed in 1994, when anthropologists published an exhaustive analysis of the complex initiation rite of the Bimin-Kuskusmin cannibals of Papua New Guinea. Highlights of the ritual see the boys told they are contaminated with female sexual fluids, before they have their heads covered in yellow mud and are told they will be killed or that something terrible will happen to them. They are sealed inside a house, coloured pigment smeared on their heads and faces and they are made to eat and vomit up specific foods that the tribe associates with women. More face smearing – sow blood this time – follows, and further taunting of contamination, of breast milk from infancy. The boys are cut and the blood applied to their penises. They are told this will destroy their penises, while their nasal septum is pierced. Hot marsupial fat is dripped onto their arms. The pus from their burns and blisters is collected and placed onto fruit being worn by their tormentors, who then chant sacred words, during which the boys are told not to swallow their saliva. When the chants finish, the boys must eat salt and pus, are painted again, and have their septum pierced again. They are cut twice more, with their blood placed this time onto the penises of the others. Almost done, the boys now eat five 'male' foods, are painted again and anointed with fat, oil and boar blood. When they are not being cut, painted, pierced, burnt, insulted, force-fed or chanted at, each boy is locked away for days on end in a windowless hut with his own faeces, urine, blood and pus.

Looking at written accounts of the boys' ordeal, the anthropologists identified eleven separate OCD-like rituals, most of which occurred multiple times. They found concern with dirt, actions to remove contaminants, disgust at bodily secretions, numbers of special significance, fear of terrible events, repetitive actions and violent images – all of which are common features of obsessions and compulsions. One of the most regular ritualistic themes was a fear that something terrible will happen, specifically that someone would cause harm to themselves or others. In other words, most of the rituals in this ceremony reflected the theme of responsibility.

This research does not show that cultural rituals are a form of pathology, just as it does not suggest that OCD patients perform culturally significant rituals. Instead, the anthropologists suggest, humans may have a specific biological capacity for ritual, just as we do for language. In a few people this universal (and culturally acceptable) ability might malfunction, and lead them to construct meaningless and idiosyncratic (culturally unacceptable) rituals on their own. That would be OCD.

Other scientists have taken this idea further. OCD, they suggest, could be more than a basic capacity gone wrong. OCD might have once been useful. OCD might be a feature. The disorder might have evolved.

It's certainly tempting to see the main elements of OCD – wash, clean, check – reflected in ancient strategies that might have helped early humans or even earlier mammals to survive. Grooming strengthens social ties and could protect against disease, while checks on offspring, mates, territory and supplies would boost security. Those individuals who were the most aware of risk would be those least likely to succumb to hazards, and an ordered, symmetric environment is one easier to scrutinize for predators. If these traits were adaptive, if they once conferred a benefit that encouraged survival, then they would be more likely to spread through future generations. Anxiety is generally agreed to have evolved like this; the fight-or-flight response would have helped our ancestors to better respond to threat. The anxious man who runs away after he spots a lion in the distance lives to be anxious another day.

The problem with attempts to connect modern human behaviour to ancient scenarios and evolutionary processes in this way is that the link is very difficult to test – at least to the standards of proof demanded by those who protect the notion of evolution from what they see as abuse. The field – known as evolutionary psychology – hardly helps itself when it throws up headline examples that many choose to interpret as old excuses for modern bad behaviour: claims that men evolved to rape, for instance.

It's difficult to test the evolutionary basis for human behaviour, but it can be done. In 2005, scientists in London worked out a way to examine the evolutionary platform for anxiety. They looked at the details of a post-war UK birth cohort, 4,070 men and women born in 1946, and picked out two pieces of information about the participants: whether they were judged as anxious or neurotic as teen-agers, and if they had died in an accident. The researchers found the least anxious adolescents were the more likely to die in an accident before they reached 25. High anxiety was associated with reduced accidents. The study concluded that anxiety protected young people, presumably because they were more reluctant to take risks.

The work was published in 2006 in the journal *Psychological Medicine*, and has a confounding – though so far unreported – postscript. William Lee, the psychiatrist who led the research, has repeated the study several times since with data from different birth cohorts, from people born in Aberdeen in the 1950s to Norway in the 1990s. None showed the same protective effect for anxiety. Lee struggles to explain the contradiction – perhaps the original study was a fluke, or maybe, because the number of fatal injuries in society has fallen, the effect is now too small to detect.

There are no comparable experimental studies to test if OCD traits improve the chances of survival, and it's hard to see how such studies could be done. But there has been plenty written about a possible evolutionary basis for OCD. Explanations like this in evolutionary psychology with no experimental back-up are typically labelled 'Just So' stories

– a reference originally to the tales of Rudyard Kipling that explained, for example, how the leopard got its spots, but a term more recently used to criticize misleadingly simple explanations. When it comes to the possible link between evolution and OCD, the psychiatrists, psychologists and anthropologists who have discussed it are generally up-front about the speculative nature of their ideas. With that in mind, let's take a look.

While anxiety is a response to a clear and present danger – the approach of a lion, say – the possible contribution of obsessive and compulsive traits to survival is more subtle. OCD is usually about threats that may occur in future – I wonder if there is a lion behind that rock? Still, this type of harm-avoidance might increase survival and so be passed on through evolution.

Some psychiatrists say OCD could have evolved as a psychological immune system. An individual with involuntary and repetitive thoughts about a concealed lion would experience fear and so develop a way to avoid the perceived threat, even if there was no lion there. In this way, obsessions could be ways to practise the response to threats without the risks of exposure to real-life danger. This advance preparation would give a clear advantage over others when the imagined threat became real. In this model, obsessions are akin to the antibodies generated by the physical immune system, a first line of defence prepared to counter a future threat. Compulsions are the behaviours learned to avoid or minimize the threat.

These obsessions may have been useful to early humans but, like all biological traits, they would not have been distributed evenly across the population. Just as the physical immune system can go haywire and attack the body's own cells, so some individuals could experience obsessions and compulsions in extreme forms that do more harm than good. In this way, OCD could be as much a dysfunctional by-product of (useful and adaptive) obsession, as generalized anxiety disorder today is a dysfunctional product of the (useful and adaptive) flight-or-fight response.

Psychiatrists have suggested another way that OCD could have evolved in humans: through a process called group selection – individuals who should perish because they carry traits that have a negative effect on them, but who get a free ride from evolution because those same traits benefit a wider social network. Group selection is controversial too – it seems to go against the every-gene-for-itself principle of the survival of the fittest – but there are some proposed examples, food sharing and cooperation between ants and honeybees among them.

To combine group selection and evolutionary psychology puts an idea on the slenderest of scientific thin ice, but psychiatrists in Canada have speculated that OCD represents an ancient form of behavioural specialization – a form of group selection suggested for insects that live in complex social structures stratified into distinct groups such as workers and drones. The majority of human compulsions – checking, washing, counting, hoarding and requiring precision – the psychiatrists say, could have benefited ancient human societies, especially hunter-gatherer communities, even if they had a negative impact on the individual.

Take checking. In his 1960 book, *Pygmies of the Ituri Forest*, the Harvard University anthropologist Patrick Putman wrote of Congo people who did not know how to make fire. They placed great importance on the need to keep several fires alight across the countryside so one group could always borrow fire from another. 'While on the march,' Putman wrote, 'the pygmies carry glowing embers with them; they can keep a brand lighted for ten miles during a rainstorm.' In this scenario, someone with a compulsive urge to check, to make sure their fire or carried embers was still alight, could be useful. The compulsion could give them and their wider group a tiny edge in the race to survive, and, repeated often enough, that could be enough to see it passed on.

Compulsive washing could be beneficial too. People with obsessive-compulsive demands for more rigorous hygiene could have influenced the behaviour and so the survival of entire tribes. The Waica people, for example, an isolated jungle tribe who live along the border of Brazil and Venezuela, will only drink water brought from upstream of any fords. That makes sense now, given what we know about infectious bacteria, and any hiker who has scooped to drink from a babbling mountain brook knows the sickening feeling when they discover upstream the rotten carcass of an animal. But how could the Waica's ancestors have known about this risk? People who get ill from contaminated water do not typically show symptoms straight away, and this makes it difficult to associate one with the other. Could the practice instead have started with an irrational obsessive-compulsive action that stuck because it happened to benefit the tribe in the long run?

The actions of a small number of obsessive-compulsive people in such societies, the Canadian psychiatrists suggest, could have spread and raised sanitary standards, and so improved the health and survival chances of the entire group. It's a long shot, but can we rule it out? It would certainly be a mistake to assume that OCD could not present itself in this way, even in such a primitive people. Charles Seligman made such an assumption, and history will not let him forget it.

Seligman was a British anthropologist who visited the islands of Melanesia at the start of the twentieth century, and famously declared its native people free of mental disorders, except where there was obvious pressure from Europeans. Later work overturned his claim, and found that schizophrenia, for one, was as common there as everywhere else. Seligman, it was widely assumed, had falsely attributed the weird behaviour of mental illness, which he must have seen, to eccentric local custom. In anthropological circles a tendency to confuse the signs of mental problems in foreign parts with bizarre and alien cultural behaviour is now known as Seligman's error.

In the search for a possible evolutionary explanation for OCD, in recent years scientists have focused on another primitive drive, an emotion we share with animals and one that could misfire to produce obsessions and compulsions: disgust. Disgust probably evolved as a way to stir nausea and so protect us from illness and disease – picture your favourite delicacy rotten and covered with maggots and see if you feel like eating.

This 'core' disgust extends to other sources of dirt and possible infection too: rats, for instance, and an unflushed toilet. There are two other disgust domains. One is animal-reminder disgust – revulsion at objects and acts that show us our mortality and animal origins, including aversion to mutilation, injury and some sexual acts: incest, perhaps, or even just a man in his twenties who has sex with an 80-year-old woman. People tend to describe that as 'disgusting' rather than 'unusual' or 'not for me, thanks'. The third disgust domain is contamination, the fear we could catch an infectious disease from another person. Think how you feel when someone coughs over you.

All three types of disgust are powerful sensations and strong drivers of behaviour. When authorities in Ghana wanted to improve public hygiene, they broadcast television and radio adverts that graphically highlighted the way faecal material could stick to people's hands after they had been to the toilet – and how they could then transfer it to food eaten by children. The campaign provoked a 13 per cent rise in the number of people in Ghana who said they washed their hands with soap after they used the toilet. The number who did so before they ate shot up by 41 per cent.

The link between disgust and hand-washing intrigues OCD researchers, and several have suggested that obsessions and compulsions linked to fear of contamination by germs could be down to an excessive disgust response. Results from a few small studies support this link. Volunteers who report the most obsessive-compulsive thoughts and behaviours, for example, can be the most likely to experience more severe disgust when they see images of filthy toilets or gross injuries.

Of particular relevance is the mental impact: how a thought can bring on disgust, with physical consequences. Someone who has spent the night vomiting because they ate some dodgy shellfish need only think of a prawn sandwich the next day to set them off again. Charles Darwin, who was interested in the emotions – as well as the origins – of people and animals, noted this effect. He reported 'how readily and instantly retching or actual vomiting is induced in some person by the mere idea of having partaken of any unusual food'. That sounds like thought-action fusion.

Perhaps the most famous case of contamination OCD relates to the bloodthirsty murder of a king and his guards, plotted and executed by a husband and wife. The man takes over as king, but after his wife handles the bloody murder weapon she is plagued by obsession. She feels compelled to wash her hands time and time again, yet she cannot scrub away the vision of the blood she sees there. It does not end well for either of them: she kills herself and he has his head cut off by a rival dressed as a tree. But then, that's what happens when you take career advice from strange women you meet on a Scottish moor.

Lady Macbeth, of Shakespeare's play and of course the woman mentioned above, might today be told she suffered from mental pollution: a sense of internal dirtiness that persists despite the absence of external dirt. Psychiatrists see mental pollution a lot with women who have suffered sexual abuse. No matter how often they shower and wash, the women still feel dirty, contaminated. In the last few years it has become clear that mental pollution can play an important role in OCD.

Andy suffered from severe OCD that was traced to mental pollution. A civil servant in London, Andy developed his condition in the 1990s after his wife left him for another man and Andy was pursued by the authorities for child maintenance payments. He became obsessed with thoughts of the brown envelopes they used to send their demands. He felt the envelopes could contaminate him. Andy would react to his feelings of contamination by washing his hands, up to 80 or 90 times a day. He had to sleep in gloves to protect his brittle skin.

Assuming that Andy was behaving in a similar way to OCD patients who fear physical contamination, germs from doorknobs for example, psychologists tried to help him with the same techniques they used for those patients. We'll come to exposure therapies in a later chapter, but here's a teaser: as part of the treatment, Andy would spend whole days covered in brown envelopes, from head to toe, in an attempt to make him less sensitive to them and their perceived physical threat.

But there was no perceived physical threat. It was not

the physical envelopes that made Andy feel dirty, but the feelings associated with his thoughts of them. He did not even need to see one. He could conjure an image of the envelope in his mind that brought on such intense disgust that he would need to wash his hands. Just like Lady Macbeth, Andy's washing was futile, because the source of the sense of contamination was internal.

Mental contamination is closely tied to disgust. Imagine a stranger with bad breath and crumbs at the side of their mouth who grabs you unawares and presses their mouth against yours for a sloppy kiss. As you picture the scene, can you feel as your own mouth curls and your nose wrinkles in that familiar shape of disgust? Now, would you like a drink of water? In experiments with female students, after such an exercise a significant number said they wanted to rinse out their mouth or to wash their hands. Disgust caused by the thought of the dirty kiss – the thought alone – had made them feel dirty inside. They were mentally contaminated. Out, damned spot. Out.

If OCD is a product of shared evolutionary history, or the overreach of a natural capacity for ritual or disgust, then that might explain one of the most noticeable features of the disorder: consistency. It would mean that the condition does not crop up spontaneously in individuals, but rather as a shared biological response to some external or internal primer. We see this on the ground. Time and time again, different types of people with the same types of OCD report the same forms of obsessions and respond with almost identical rituals, even though they are separated by thousands of miles.

The nature of these shared obsessions and compulsions seems stable over time – case reports from centuries ago feature identical thoughts and behaviours to patients who report them now. And they are consistent across the world – identical forms of OCD have been found just about everywhere scientists have looked for them, from western Europe, the United States and Canada, to Latin America, the Middle East, China, India and Australia. In these cases, different cultures and experiences seem to make no difference.

A few years before I developed my OCD, Claire, a 10-year-old girl from Texas, came down with exactly the same obsession. When a schoolteacher told her class about the threat of Aids, she could not get thoughts of the disease out of her head. She would not eat in a restaurant in case someone had picked up food with bloody fingers, refused to kiss or hug anyone outside her immediate family, and had asked the school nurse about fears she would catch Aids from snot thrown in the classroom, a wet bus seat and a soiled book. When a boy in her class said: 'Have sex with me. I hope you get Aids,' she found she had to repeat the phrase. Only if she then added a silent 'just kidding' six times at the end of the sentence, she said, could she prevent harm to her six family members – herself, her mum, dad, brother, dog and fish. Claire developed other compulsive behaviour, and would feel urges to spit, hop and touch walls in sequences of six – all as a way to ward off the intrusive thoughts of HIV.

When Claire started to refuse to go to school because of her fears, her mother tried to help by explaining the sexual transmission of Aids. Claire responded by stopping the family dog from sleeping on her bed, because it was a boy. At this point, her parents took her for help. She was hospitalized but was helped to make a recovery. She will be in her thirties now.

Like Claire, I was lucky. Help for mental health in the UK is patchy, but after I saw my local doctor and told him my story it emerged that we were in the catchment area for a specialist outpatient OCD service based at a mental health unit at a hospital a few miles away. It was the same hospital where my daughter had been born. The doctor passed me along to them. This time, there would be no elastic bands. And this time, for my daughter's sake as much as mine, I was determined to make it work.

NINE

Man hands on misery to man

By the time my case worked its way through the health service to reach the specialist OCD unit, my obsessions about HIV had spread to the many different ways I thought I could pass the virus to my baby daughter, who by then was about eight months old. If I cut myself shaving, or in clumsy attempts at home improvement, I was compelled to wash my hands repeatedly before I touched her, in my mind to remove any risk that I could pass her contaminated blood. I was distraught. I had become a hand-washer. My fingers were always chapped and dry. I told people it was because I had to clean and sterilize her milk bottles so often.

One night I showed her my electric toothbrush and woke with a start the next morning to intrusive thoughts that I had flicked my blood from its bristles into her eyes. I was compelled to check if I could have done. I locked myself in the bathroom, drew a face on the mirror with shaving foam and held the buzzing wet toothbrush at various distances to analyse where the water sprayed. It didn't help.

It wasn't just HIV by then. When I discovered that some of the old paint I had enthusiastically stripped and burned from the cupboard doors in our bedroom contained lead, I became convinced I had poisoned her. No matter how many times I cleaned the carpet, if I dropped one of her toys or her milk bottle I considered it contaminated. More blood tests – this time my wife and I for lead (both normal). My wife drew the line at tests on the baby, as my OCD wanted, because that required a needle to be stabbed into her young head. I even found a national lead paint hotline to call. On my third enquiry to them inside twenty-four hours, afraid they would recognize my voice and refer me to the answers they had offered previously, I convinced my wife to ask my questions for me.

I was concerned not just that I would pass HIV to my daughter, but also that I would act in a way that would make her more likely to develop obsessions and compulsions herself. On that score, I was right to worry. Studies since the 1930s have shown that OCD seems to run in families. Relatives of those with OCD are themselves more likely to show symptoms than the general population. So, here's another question, is OCD genetic? Do I carry it in my DNA?

There is no single obsession gene, just as there is no gay gene, or intelligence gene. To start with, there just aren't enough genes to go around, to map one-to-one onto the entire spectrum of human attitudes, behaviours and physical attributes. All genes work alongside other genes. A few of our traits (wet or dry earwax) and a few diseases (cystic fibrosis) have been traced to the impact of a solitary gene, but they really are a few. Even eye colour, for years a classic textbook example of single gene control, is now known to be under the control of many different genes that act together.

This helps to explain why, despite recent technological progress, most of the promised medical reward of human genetics remains on hold. The more scientists explore, the more murky and complicated the picture becomes. That means that when it comes to the genetic causes of OCD, unfortunately we don't have much to go on. There are some clues, but they are pretty abstract clues. One of these came in summer 2012, when scientists in the US looked at the genes of five generations of an obsessive family.

OCD was rife in the family. Great-great-grandpa and great-great-grandma had two children, both of whom had OCD. Four of their eight grandchildren had OCD too and so did eleven of their eighteen great-grandchildren. Of the eleven great-great-grandchildren born by the time of the study, five were judged to have OCD. None of the family had married anyone with OCD, so if there was a genetic link, and there surely was, then scientists could have expected this family, and others in the same study, to reveal it.

Detective work followed. With little more than a processed blood sample, lab researchers can automatically screen a person's DNA for more than half a million specific and common genetic variations. Nobody has every one of the half million possible variants – such a person would be very ill and very odd indeed. Instead, they are sprinkled across the population, and the different ways they appear in individuals act as flags, which draw attention to regions that might carry genetic risks. When scientists compare these genotype maps, and the symptoms in the people where the maps look similar, they can start to narrow the focus for a genetic cause for illness, down from the entire genome to a few flagged regions. That's an essential step if targets for treatment are ever to emerge.

In the US family study, when the scientists looked for patterns shared across the generations, the strongest linked OCD to specific genetic changes at the tip of chromosome one. It was far from a smoking gun though. The association with OCD wasn't clear-cut, and other regions of other chromosomes were implicated too, just with even less certainty.

A parallel study that looked for patterns in the genotypes of 1,465 unrelated people with OCD from across the world produced equally weak results. In that research, a technique called a genome-wide association study, the scientists fingered a different genetic region, this time on chromosome 20. Genome-wide association studies often produce graphs of results named Manhattan plots after the famous pointy skyline of New York City. Each prominent skyscraper on the plot corresponds to a possible genetic cause, and so a possible step towards a treatment. In this case, the output of the OCD study looked more like the skyline of Washington, DC, which is universally flat because planners allow no building much taller than the distance across the street it stands on.

No skyscrapers in the OCD Manhattan plot indicates no clear genetic causes. That doesn't rule out that OCD is under the control of genes, but it shows the relationship is complex and not driven by a few bits of wonky inherited DNA that can easily be identified.

Mental disorders that run in families do not need a genetic cause. There is the impact of the environment too. Some genes lie dormant until something in the environment triggers them. Other inherited traits are down to the behaviour and influence of our parents. I play golf and so does my brother. That's because my parents both play golf and they encouraged us, not because golf is in the shared DNA of our family. It's especially not in the shared DNA of my dad. You only have to watch him try to chip his ball over a bunker to see that.*

The usual way to tease apart genetic and environmental factors, to separate nature from nurture, is to study twins. Identical twins share all their genes, non-identical twins don't. Twins raised together share aspects of their environment, those raised apart don't. Throw enough of these different twins at a hereditary illness and scientists can start to work out whether their nature or nurture has the most influence. OCD has been studied in twins for decades but the results are hard to interpret. The best guess of scientists

---

* Just kidding dad.

when it comes to OCD is that genes and environment are about as important as each other. So, just as someone with OCD cannot blame the nature they received from their parents, they can't blame the nurture they received from them either. Or, if they wish, they could blame both. (What matters most is that the parents do not blame themselves.)

One way that our environment – parents, pre-school years and cultural background – could seed obsessions is because these early experiences frequently leave us with dysfunctional beliefs, some of which, as we saw in Chapter Seven, are implicated in OCD. Inflated responsibility could come, for example, when parents give older children too much power over their younger siblings at an early age, or conversely as compensation for giving them no power at all. In problem-solving tests, mothers of those with OCD have been seen to demand more of their children, to expect them to take the lead.

The famous OCD of aviation pioneer-turned-bearded-recluse Howard Hughes may have emerged from his child-hood experiences. Hughes died in 1976 and was a fierce defender of his privacy, but details of his bizarre behaviour in later years were pieced together by psychologist Raymond Fowler, a former president of the American Psychological Association who was asked to conduct a 'psychological autopsy' by the law firm that handled the billionaire's estate.

Hughes showed clear symptoms of OCD, which, according to Fowler, may have related to his mother's fear of polio and the extreme measures she took to protect her young son from the disease. By the time he was in his sixties, Hughes had developed severe compulsive behaviour to ward off germs. His staff had to wear white gloves, pass him cutlery wrapped in paper, and he would burn the clothes he was wearing if someone he met became ill. He gave detailed instructions on how others should feed him tinned peaches – remove the label, scrub the can and pour the contents into a bowl without touching it. He wore tissue boxes on his feet.

It is hard to pin down how parenting style contributes to OCD because to draw definitive conclusions, adults with OCD must be asked to recall how their parents behaved some twenty or thirty years or more before. A handful of studies have looked at the impact of parenting style on the mental health of children in real time, but only for the broader problem of anxiety. (High parental control and overprotection did seem to make children more anxious, but it is impossible to tease out the impact on OCD from this research.) The only known study to compare the behaviour of parents of children with OCD, and parents of children with other anxiety disorders, suggested the mothers and fathers of the OCD kids showed less confidence in their children and were less likely to reward independence. The study, however, was small (just eighteen children with OCD) and it does not prove that the parenting style was to blame.

As a parent concerned I will pass OCD on to my children, none of that is very helpful, but that's the way it is. Most parents make it up as they go along anyway. It's hard to stick to a script, even if we knew what it should say.

There is clearer evidence on the damaging impact of what's called family accommodation of someone's OCD – parents and siblings drawn into the obsessive web of a loved one and forced to help perform their ridiculous compulsions. Mrs D, for instance, was obsessed with contamination from other people and would sit only on a single chair that she would disinfect each morning and which nobody else was allowed to touch. Mrs D's compulsions demanded that her three children stay two or three feet away from her. The children had no choice but to comply – their mother made the rules.

In their 1980 book *Obsessions and Compulsions*, Stanley Rachman and Ray Hodgson described an extreme case of accommodation of the contamination rituals of a 19-year-old man called George by his elderly father Harry. Each morning, Harry said, he would help his son dress while taking care not to touch the outside of his clothes. A trip to the toilet was next and, Harry said, it was a palaver. It was easier if George wanted only to urinate, Harry said, because his role then was then only to get down on his hands and knees with a torch to check his son's trousers and boots for splashes, or the floor for pubic hairs. As soon as George did up his trousers, Harry would have to wipe the zip with a pad soaked in antiseptic.

Life was better outside the house, if they could get there. If George saw a speck of brown in the car he said it was dog dirt and Harry had to scrub the seats. About to go out one day, George felt suddenly compelled to have a bath and delayed their departure by three hours. If George felt

Harry had not cleaned properly he would get angry and smash crockery and furniture; he once threw a bar of soap through a window pane and then started to worry about the broken glass, which he insisted that Harry clear away.

Harry was in an impossible situation. And it's one faced time and again by the families of people with OCD. Surveys show that three-quarters of the relatives of people under the age of 17 with OCD become involved in the rituals. More than half the relatives of adult sufferers do too. Some do it because it pains them to see the person they love in such distress; distress which seems easy to lift, at least temporarily. Others indulge the compulsions for the sake of an easier life. It is much simpler, for example, for a family member to agree to leave the house last, than it is to wait for a compulsive checker to do so only after they thoroughly check all doors and windows are closed. And, like Harry, some relatives agree to participate in the rituals because it seems to make the situation worse if they don't. People with OCD can get angry and accuse others of not caring for them if their families do not obey their rules or offer the requested reassurance.

Sometimes the anger is well directed. Children and siblings of people with OCD have been known to exploit the disorder's fear and anxiety as bargaining chips – 'If you don't let me use the car/borrow your jumper/go to the party then I'll walk in my dirty shoes all over your bed.' Together with the insults and mockery that some families hand out to relatives with OCD, psychologists describe such responses as hostile non-compliance. Not surprisingly, hostile non-compliance doesn't help. In fact, criticism can make sufferers more likely to carry out their rituals.

However, compliance – hostile or otherwise – does not help either. Family accommodation of OCD is linked to more severe symptoms and worse functional impairment. And it interferes with some types of treatment, especially behavioural techniques. Families who want to help someone with OCD must aim for the middle ground: non-hostile non-compliance, or non-critical support with no accommodation of rituals. That's easier said than done.

Just as someone with OCD does not respond to reason or appeals to their rational side – 'look, there is no HIV on the towel, just use it' – so it's not as simple as telling a distressed and loving dad such as Harry merely not to wipe his adult son's zip with antiseptic each time he uses the toilet. It seems vital that, when people with OCD seek and receive treatment, those who live with them are made to know and understand what's involved and what's at stake.

When it comes to the possible causes of OCD, the legacy of biology and history – DNA, early experiences and evolution – is only half the story. Biologists talk about short-range and long-range causes of behaviour. (They call them proximate and ultimate.) It's a distinction neatly demonstrated by the tale of the monkey, the snake and the flower, which sounds as if it should be a children's parable or a puzzle about how to get them across a river, but actually describes a series of famous experiments carried out in Wisconsin in the late 1980s. In the studies, psychologists found that hand-reared rhesus monkeys had no instinctive fear of snakes. Why should they have – the animals had never seen one. Pictures of snakes and toy snakes placed next to them had no effect.

That changed after the animals were shown video of the way wild monkeys react to a snake: with lip-smacking fear and restless anxiety. After they saw these images, the lab-reared monkeys quickly developed the same response. Shown the same pictures and toys as before, from then on they would react just as the wild monkeys did. They had learned fear.

When the psychologists tried to use the same mechanism to make the lab monkeys afraid of flowers, they failed. No matter how many times the lab animals watched footage edited to show wild monkeys react with panic to a flower, just as they had to the snakes, the hand-reared animals wouldn't buy it. The difference was down to evolution, the ultimate cause of the monkeys' behaviour. Millions of ancestors who ran away from millions of snakes over millions of years have left their mark on the biology of today's rhesus monkeys in a way that non-threatening flowers simply haven't.

The ultimate causes of OCD could indeed be genetic, or evolutionary, or found in the circumstances of our family home, but this cannot fully explain why some people develop OCD and some don't. And it cannot explain why people who develop OCD do so just when they do. What are the proximate causes of obsessive and compulsive behaviour? What events in our individual lives trigger the dormant OCD threat? One thing is clear. That someone has not developed OCD so far does not mean they will not succumb to it in future.

An American man called Mr Rossi developed an obsessional need to remember people's names. He would write them constantly – those of friends, family, famous baseball players and colleagues from work. It was they who convinced Mr Rossi to seek help, because they were sick of him calling up day and night to check he had them right. He was 87. His obsessions and compulsions did not begin until he was 75. He waited for them almost his whole life.

Obsessive-compulsive disorder strikes most people by early adulthood; fewer than 15 per cent of cases develop in people over 35. So Mr Rossi was unusual, but far from unique. Where did his OCD come from? Did it lie undisturbed for more than seven decades before something brought it to the surface? Or did something change in later life that unsettled him? As we've seen, scientists seem to have solid cognitive explanations of how people develop OCD, but what about why and when they do? Are obsessions a ticking time bomb? You probably have intrusive thoughts, so will you go on to develop OCD? If so, are there danger signs that can be spotted and acted upon? There might be, and a likely one is trauma.

Howard shows the impact of trauma vividly. Howard was 5 years old when he developed OCD. A naturally shy and anxious child, he was intelligent and started to crawl and walk earlier than many of his peers. His OCD started a few days after he witnessed a horrific road traffic accident; a pedestrian was hit by a car and left unconscious and covered in blood. Howard was convinced the pedestrian was dead, and it took him until the next day to stop shaking.

After the accident, Howard started to wash his hands until they cracked and bled. Sometimes he would spend most of the night at the sink. He was not afraid of germs. That was not why he washed. He did it, he said, because it was the only way he could find to make the funny feeling go away. Even that was not enough. He still had to pester his parents and his teachers about whether his hands were really clean. Howard said he wanted to stop his mind making him wash his hands. That *is* pretty bright for a 5-year-old.

Just like Howard, more than half the people with clinical obsessions and compulsions can point to an earlier stressful incident they identify as the trigger for their condition. This trauma does not have to come from horrific and blood-stained events like Howard's. More subtle psychological shocks can lead to OCD as well. Betrayal is one – to be hurt and let down by those you trusted. The mental shock of betrayal can cause mental contamination and it can bring compulsive washing. Treat someone like dirt and they feel dirty.

Bullying has been shown to bring on OCD. Max, a 14-year-old boy from Florida, was victimized at school over his physical appearance and sexual orientation. Max started to shower after he was picked on, to cleanse himself of the insults, then he would avoid wearing clothes he had worn when previously bullied, because he considered them contaminated. He went further; whenever he thought of the bullies, Max would have to clear his throat and restart whatever he was doing. Because he had the thoughts all through the day, this compulsion seriously affected Max's life. He started to associate other places and activities with the bullying, and by the time he was seen by a psychiatrist, he had gone more than a month without a shower, a change of clothes or a night in his own bed.

Direct physical trauma has been linked to the onset of OCD. Mr A recovered from a month-long coma after he fractured his skull in a motorbike crash. Six months later he was back in hospital in Massachusetts, with severe intrusive thoughts of Aids and cancer and obsessions with negative news stories that began the moment he regained consciousness. And two unfortunate people in Istanbul woke from surgery to cure their epilepsy only to find the treatment left them with OCD. They showed some mild obsessive traits before, but afterwards they had to memorize numbers and count objects, or check and clean compulsively. The surgeons who performed the operations were forced to conclude that the patients' quality of life had been better before they tried to help them.

The anxiety of a botched surgical procedure can trigger obsessions as well – at least according to the British legal system. In September 2009, the Dudley Group of Hospitals NHS Foundation Trust agreed to pay £25,000 compensation to a teenager who said his OCD was down to traumatic delays in treatment for appendicitis when he was 8 years old.

If about half the people with OCD can pinpoint a specific trigger event, a trauma that led to obsessions and compulsions, then that still leaves lots of sufferers who cannot. Their OCD appears to come out of the blue. When it does, often it disturbs the innocence of childhood.

Rituals are normal for children. By the time they reach 30 months old most toddlers show some ritualistic and repetitive behaviour; they might line up their toy trains in the same way or pretend to prepare an identical daily meal. Baths and bedtime become a string of familiar routines and any deviation from the expected patterns leads to anxiety and tantrums. The rigid nature of these domestic routines tends to fade by age 4 to 6, but a new set of rituals emerge, commonly seen in play dictated by complex rules. Hopscotch, to someone who has never played it, probably looks like compulsive behaviour. A set number of moves that a child must perform in a specific fashion – four steps forward, touch, turn around twice – and all without a foot on the lines.

Rules of play become more elaborate as a child grows to the age of 10 or 11, and fears of contamination and routines to avoid contagion start to appear, for example in games of tag, or in the way that gangs of girls or boys chase each other to deliver kisses, while the other group reacts by shouting and running away. There are parallels to hoarding behaviour too. Most 7-year-olds collect objects, from action figures to sports cards. Indeed, the children's toy industry exploits this with multiple collectibles connected by a popular theme. Can you collect them all?

Childhood and adolescence are a haven for ritual, but most young people leave them behind and do not progress to obsessions and compulsions. Yet some take them too far and do develop OCD, often while they are still children. So at what point does this normal behaviour become a problem? Some child psychologists think the transition at age 4 to 6 is particularly important. It's a time when the frontal lobes of the brain mature, and mental ability increases.

In 2007, psychologists in the US published the results of a study that tried to test the impact of this cognitive transition point on childhood rituals. They gave 42 children (with their own and their parents' consent) neuropsychological tests to assess two different mental abilities. The first was to get the children to learn and respond to a rule – to sort coloured cards into piles, for instance. The rule was then changed and the children had to adapt to the new regime. The second test measured how well they could stop doing something on demand. They would be asked to match shapes in a certain way, say, and then to resist doing it.

The psychologists gave the children a toy or a five-dollar gift voucher for the local ice cream shop as a thank you, and asked the parents to fill in a series of questionnaires about their child's routines, habits, fears and perfectionism.

When the scientists looked at the results they found a difference between the performances of the younger and older children. For the kids aged 5 and under, the poorer their performance in the tests, the more likely their parents said they were to carry out rituals. For those older than 6 years, a new factor emerged: the older children most likely to show compulsive behaviour were those who, according to the parents' questionnaires again, showed the most fear.

The psychologists interpreted the results like this: rituals and compulsive behaviour in children help them to regulate emotion. Young children, with immature and incomplete mental ability, must rely more on the comfort of familiar ritual to ease the fear and anxiety they feel because they do not yet have full control over their behaviour. Older children can regulate their behaviour better, but they have more complex fears than younger children – of animals and strangers, as well as social fear such as self-consciousness and a need to fit in. As they grow, some older children continue to respond to these new fears as they did when they were younger: with ritual, as a way to ease the anxiety they cause.

We must file the results of this study as unproven. It's pertinent, but the sample is small and the conclusion is pretty speculative. The psychologists themselves point out one of the study's biggest flaws – their analysis of brain development and activity is based on the indirect evidence of test scores.

Still, if we take the findings at face value, there are some eerie parallels to OCD. The younger children could not turn off inappropriate behavioural responses, and tried to quell the anxiety this caused them with ritual. The older children responded to (rational) external fear with an irrational response (rituals such as counting and touching that decreased anxiety only in the short term). The kids in this study were all normal; none had been diagnosed with OCD. But the underlying features of their rituals and their mental condition seem the same.

It's worth noting also that the children who scored the highest on the perfectionism scale showed the most social fear, and so were more likely to carry out ritual. This suggests that increased self-awareness and hypersensitivity are important. We have already seen how sensory hypersensitivity is linked to OCD through excessive disgust, which can be viewed as overreaction to taste, smell and touch.

In 2012, a study in Israel linked the rituals of 4- to 6-year-olds to oversensitivity to everyday tactile and oral stimuli. The children who (according to their parents, again) were more likely to avoid messy play with sand and glue, complain when they had their hair and nails cut, or try to avoid having to brush their teeth were also the most likely to show repetitive behaviour. A further Internet survey of more than three hundred adults showed the most obsessive-compulsive symptoms were reported by those who, for example, didn't like to go barefoot on sand or grass, or who did not like to be touched – and who recalled they felt the same when they were children.

Again, let's not read too much into a single study, but here's what the Israeli team thought might be responsible: The brain takes the different inputs from the senses and combines them to form a picture of the outside world, a cognitive process known as sensory integration. This is a complicated procedure and some brains do it better than

others. Those brains that do it worst can produce development and behavioural problems, especially in young children.
Kids with these sensory dysfunction problems usually show
exaggerated or inappropriate responses to normal sensations
– they might refuse to wear certain clothes or to eat some
textures of food. Sensory dysfunction causes a child distress
and upset. So these children look for ways to calm themselves
down, to create order and predictability. In doing so, they
turn to excessive rituals. As kids with sensory dysfunction
develop, their rituals do too; some become OCD.

If you're a parent and your 5-year-old won't eat baked
beans or wear socks, then please don't panic. To reiterate,
these are preliminary findings and it's still far from clear
what separates the rituals and patterns of happy and
normal development from the foreshadowings of OCD.
Unfortunately, it's just difficult for anyone, parents included,
to spot the difference. Officially, an adapted version of the
Yale-Brown diagnostic test is used to find OCD in children.
Unofficially, there are checklists of danger signs out there,
but the highlighted behaviours are broad and most parents
will recognize at least one – a child who spends more time
than usual in their bedroom for instance, or one who insists
their food is presented to them in the correct way. The core
symptom to watch for is probably distress. Not the instan-
taneous tantrum that flares up when you interfere with one
of their rituals, but premeditated and lingering unhappi-
ness. And most parents can spot that in their kids, even if
we do try to hide it from them.

*

When I turned up for my first assessment at the hospital's mental health unit and walked across the car park, I could see the windows of the maternity ward. The door of the psychiatry unit had no handle on the inside. The staff there declared my OCD severe enough – just – for their assistance. They told me to report back for group therapy the next month. There were no guarantees, they said, but they thought they could help.

TEN

The runaway brain

A popular way to visualize the brain is to clench your fist and stick your thumb out and point it at the ground, as if you are a Roman emperor passing judgement on a defeated gladiator.* Your thumb is now the brain stem and the thumbnail the end of the spinal cord. Your fingers and hand represent the cortex, with the little finger the pre-frontal cortex. Now, do the same, but first squeeze a grape in the grip of your index finger. The grape contains the seat of our obsessions.

The relationship between the mind and the brain is one of the most mysterious in modern science. At their most basic, the thoughts that cause such mayhem in OCD are just electrical and chemical signals. But to say those physical elements alone define and confine the mind would be to say that the Mona Lisa is just some paint. There is a point at

---

* Despite the common image of death signalled by the thumbs down, historians think the opposite is true. Thumb down could have indicated mercy.

which this material pragmatism seems to give way to something greater, a frontier beyond which the sum is greater than the parts. In the brain, that is the moment at which the chemistry and electricity, the nuts and bolts, combine to form the mind, to give humans the sensation of consciousness.

Take the separation of brain and mind too far, and you hit the scientifically awkward idea of a soul – that the mind can and perhaps does exist in isolation of its physical basis. But, refuse to accept the notion of a mind–brain duality at all, and we struggle to explain the human experience. It's a problem as much of philosophy and metaphysics as one of biology.

Biology has one clear advantage over philosophy and metaphysics: it can be measured. But it's natural for scientists to measure either the mind or the brain. Even as modern science scoffs at the false premise of dualism, it inadvertently reinforces it. Neurologists work with brain tissue. Psychologists grapple with functions of the mind. Psychiatrists have a foot in both camps; they diagnose problems of the mind and treat them as problems of the brain, which is perhaps why psychiatry is sometimes regarded with suspicion by both sides.

Since the days of Esquirol and Freud, OCD has been viewed as a problem of the mind. Except, of course, OCD wasn't viewed, not in the literal sense, it was conceived, modelled, re-imagined. Modern technology, however, now allows the brain to be viewed in the literal sense. And that literal view, some neuroscientists believe, can show us the physical basis of OCD.

172

Only a fool or a liar will tell you how the brain works. Even well into the twentieth century, while scientists in other fields could harness technology to split the atom and unravel the molecular structure of DNA, neuroscientists were largely restricted to two types of experiment. They could remove and look at a dead brain, or they could watch for the effects of brutal accidents and dreadful disease on a live brain. The nineteenth-century scientist Paul Broca famously unravelled how the brain processes language with the help of stroke victims who lost the ability to speak. By the 1960s, Canadian neurosurgeon Wilder Penfield made maps of cognitive function with electrical stimulation of the exposed brains of wide-awake epileptic patients he was poised to operate on, to see which part of their bodies activated – the patients might twitch their shoulder or report a memory.

Neuroscience became more high-tech in the 1970s with devices to analyse live brains – an alphabet soup of acronyms. First was the CAT scan, computed axial tomography – which combines X-ray images taken from various directions – and the PET scan, positron emission tomography, which maps radioactively labelled chemicals injected into the bloodstream. Most influential was MRI, magnetic resonance imaging, based on a tool that research chemists had long used to probe molecular structure. The chemists called the technique nuclear magnetic resonance, and one of the first things that doctors did when they started to point the machines at their patients was to drop the word nuclear from the name. The patients preferred it that way.

MRI uses magnets and radio waves to detect blood. Particularly useful to neuroscientists is functional MRI, which takes lots of scans, one immediately after the other, and so shows how the blood moves. Blood flow in the brain means activity. If one part of the brain shows a greater demand for blood, or in the parlance of MRI studies, 'lights up', then neuroscientists believe it shows the 'lit up' part of the brain is more active. If the person whose brain is scanned is engaged in a task at the time, then neuroscientists can claim an association between the task and the region of the brain that lights up. In this way, functional MRI has been used to probe the brain regions associated with love, hate, racism, voting intention, response to adverts and chocolate, and why someone would prefer to drink Coke or Pepsi.

It's a lot easier to look for these regions than to find them. Despite the way these studies are sometimes presented, most don't prove that a certain part of the brain is responsible for a specific activity, thought or intention. The most they can say is that the scan images showed increased activity in that part of the brain at the time, but the pictures say little about cause and effect – whether the area that lit up drives the mental activity under investigation, or if it activates as a consequence of the activity.

There are other weaknesses with this kind of research. Most parts of the brain do different things at different times – the amygdala, for example, plays a role in both sexual arousal and terror – but an MRI scan cannot differentiate between passion and panic. It only tells us when a region is active, or more accurately, more active than normal. So what should we think when the amygdala lights up on an MRI scan when we are shown a picture of Cameron Diaz or Brad Pitt – that we are afraid of them? And then there is the dead fish problem.

In 2005, neuroscientists in California put an Atlantic salmon bought from a local fishmonger into their MRI machine. They showed the dead fish a series of photographs and scanned for its response. 'The salmon', the scientists later reported, 'was asked to determine what emotion the individual in the photo must have been experiencing.' It sounds silly, but it's a common and necessary step to calibrate MRI machines and check all is good before human volunteers are introduced. The California scientists tried it with a pumpkin too, because one is about the same size and weight as a human head.

The test samples – animal or vegetable – of course are not supposed to yield results. Yet, when the neuroscientists looked at the output of the scans of the salmon, they found a curious thing. The results appeared to show the salmon thinking. Shown the photographs, parts of its fishy brain had lit up. The rogue signal was down to a technical and statistical glitch, random noise in the way the scanner's computer software processed the signals. The scientists knew this, but rather than throw the scans away, they decided to publish them to alert others to the problem. MRI studies performed without certain statistical precautions, they said, could give out false positive results.

All of this is not meant to undermine the power and

usefulness of MRI scans in research, just to show that the results are often not as clear-cut as they might appear. Neuroscientists get cross when journalists ignore the caveats and exaggerate the potential of brain scans to determine how we think and behave, but neuroscientists do it themselves. Some sell MRI scans they claim can help companies market their products, or detect liars.

It's pretty grim inside an MRI machine. In 2003, as science correspondent for the *Guardian* newspaper, I had my brain scanned by MRI as part of a research study at University College London into the way we process information. The scientists were interested in how people can find themselves unable to pronounce certain words. It was nothing to do with my OCD. I wanted to write for the newspaper about how it felt to have a scan, and to take part was the only way they would let me through the doors. Time on those machines is too precious to waste on a tourist.

I remember most the sense of entombment; the metal cage to hold my head still and the magnet itself seemed to brush the end of my nose. And the noise – like I was trapped next to someone who typed a chapter of this book on an old-fashioned clickety-clack typewriter and blew an air horn each time they finished a sentence. Given that experience, I have great admiration for the people with OCD who have agreed to venture into these machines in the name of science, and then allowed scientists to poke their obsessions with a sharp stick.

Strapped inside MRI tubes, people with obsessive fears

of contamination have had their hands sprayed with (harmless) water they are told contains drugs. Women with a compulsive need for symmetry have had nail varnish unevenly removed from their fingers. In other experiments, people with OCD have been asked to identify the words that set them off the most – 'scissors' say, for a mother who feared she would stab her child – and then been forced to listen as the scientists repeat the words back to them over and over again through the loudspeakers of the MRI scanner. All the time, the machines record their torment in pixels.

Hundreds of OCD patients have been MRI scanned over the last decade or so, and had their brains compared to those of normal people, schizophrenics and hoarders. They have been scanned before and after treatment, and while they rest or wrestle with deliberately planted intrusive thoughts. Again and again a consistent picture of OCD emerges – unusual activity in and around a brain region called the basal ganglia.

The basal ganglia is the grape held in your crooked index finger. It is a tightly packed and knotty cluster of tissue at the base of the forebrain. Like most of the brain, exactly what the basal ganglia does, and how, remains largely unknown. But the basal ganglia does seem to play a role in ritual, compulsion and in OCD. This was first shown almost a century ago with the work of an Austrian medic called Constantin von Economo, the original flying doctor.

*

Von Economo married a princess but he had two passions: psychiatric medicine and aviation. He piloted one of the first fighter aircraft above the Italian front of the First World War in 1916, before he moved to a hospital in Vienna to care for soldiers with head injuries. It was there he saw his first cases of a bizarre disease that would go on to make him famous. Between 1915 and 1926, nearly a million people across the world died in a largely forgotten epidemic. Millions more were left as living statues in a catatonic state, unable to move or speak. Whatever infectious agent caused the disease (and it has yet to be pinned down with any certainty) seemed to attack and inflame the brain, and specifically, post-mortems of victims revealed, the region around the basal ganglia.

Von Economo reported how some patients with the condition – now known formally as encephalitis lethargica and less formally as von Economo's disease or sleepy sick-ness – reported a strange sensation. They felt compelled to carry out odd movements. In his write-up of 1920, he said: 'These patients do not say I have a twitch in my hand, but rather as a rule, I *have got to* move my hand that way.'* He saw a range of tic-like behaviours too. His patients would cluck, hiss and yell. These disturbances, he said 'were remi-niscent of compulsive movements and compulsive actions, with frequently ensuing utterances of speech and trends of thought of a compulsive character'.

---

* Emphasis mine.

Our brains evolved from the inside out. The clever stuff at the edge, the cortex with its ability to reason, is new in evolutionary terms. The deepest bits of the brain are the oldest. They evolved in some ancestor long before we did and we share these brain units with all the subsequent species that developed later. The basal ganglia is among the deepest and oldest bits of the brain. Birds have a basal ganglia, and so do ugly eels called lampreys, which have been around for more than half a billion years.

Half a billion years is a long time to get something right, and the basal ganglia has its act perfect. It holds set programmes for repetitive, automatic and ritualistic behaviours, any of which a creature can press into service at a moment's notice. A quick response – run! – is usually critical to such situations, so the higher parts of our brain – the middle management, which tend to mull on the pros and cons and just slow everything down – are side-lined. That makes the behaviour directed by the basal ganglia easy to activate and difficult to turn off. When people say that a pattern of behaviour is hardwired into the brain, it's often something that is stored in the basal ganglia.

In that context, it makes sense that OCD could be a problem with the basal ganglia. OCD could be what happens when these programmes go haywire; when they can't be turned off or when they activate at an inappropriate time. That would explain the quasi-instinctive drive in OCD to perform compulsive behaviour. Time and again, scientists see how damage to the basal ganglia can cause OCD-like symptoms. Injuries and diseases such as rheumatic fever,

Huntingdon's and Parkinson's can bring on obsessions and compulsions, and so can something as benign as a wasp sting.

Mr V was French. He was 41 in 1968, when he was stung and suffered an extreme reaction. He had immediate convulsions and fell into a coma for twenty-four hours. He recovered, but scans showed he had suffered damage to the basal ganglia. Two years after he was stung, life began to get strange for Mr V. He started to feel an urge to count inside his head, usually to twelve or a multiple of twelve, though he performed more difficult calculations. Sometimes he wagged his finger as he did so; other times he was compelled to switch a light on and off for an hour or more. His psychiatrist noted: 'When asked about his behaviour he answered that he had to count . . . that he could not stop . . . that it was stronger than him.' Once Mr V was found on his knees as he pushed a stone along the ground with his hands – he simply had to push it, he explained.

Then there was Mr E, a 42-year-old Dutchman who suffered a heart attack in 1992, which choked off the oxygen to the base of his brain around the basal ganglia. He survived but started to compulsively whistle, for up to eight hours a day, always the same tune. He wanted to stop, but when he did he felt annoyed and anxious. After listening to him for almost sixteen years, Mrs E sent her husband for treatment.

Rituals stored in the basal ganglia have been used to explain some of the most puzzling cases of OCD: children who go to bed fine and wake up the next morning with severe obsessions and compulsions. It's a controversial area, but if the scientists and doctors who have investigated these cases are correct then it presents a startling conclusion – OCD can be passed from person to person as easily as a sore throat.

In early 1991, a 10-year-old boy was brought to the US National Institute of Mental Health in Maryland after he seemed to develop OCD overnight. He woke one day with severe obsessive concerns about Aids and other germs, as well as compulsions to clean and hoard. Within two days the boy could not face school, or anything else. He had developed a spitting tic alongside the obsessive thoughts, and jerky, abrupt movements. But the night before his symptoms arrived, his mother said, he had been completely healthy. Well, almost.

She was a medical technologist and she pointed out to the NIMH doctors that, just a couple of weeks before, the boy had been diagnosed with a throat infection; specifically, he had pharyngitis caused by streptococcal bacteria. What's more, the boy's older brother suffered from a tic disorder that waxed and waned, and his most recent bad days, the woman realized, had come after he had been ill with the same throat infection as his younger brother. 'There had to be a connection,' she said.

When the scientists tested the younger boy's blood, they found that levels of antibodies – a sign of the severity of the strep infection – tracked his OCD symptoms. As the antibodies dropped, so his obsessions and compulsions weakened. When his antibodies spiked to indicate renewed strep infection, his OCD symptoms became worse.

The psychiatrists started to track down other similar cases. They advertised nationally and at big medical conferences. Reports of cases started to trickle in, slowly at first, just one or two each month, but as word spread the team would investigate four or five a week. They kept the idea of a possible link to streptococcus to themselves, until they had fifty children who showed a similar pattern: a strep throat infection closely followed by a surge in obsessive-compulsive symptoms or tics. By 1998, the psychiatrists had enough to go public. They published a report in the *American Journal of Psychiatry* that described the fifty cases, and coined a term for what was wrong with them: Paediatric Autoimmune Neuropsychiatric Disorders Associated with Streptococcal Infections; Pandas for short.

The important word in that long title is autoimmune. Scientists think Pandas is down to the strep infection because it makes the body release antibodies against the foreign bacteria that in some people go on to mistakenly attack their own brain cells, probably in the basal ganglia. The exact mechanism, and its contribution to the OCD symptoms in the children, remains unclear and somewhat controversial, given that the idea suggests that common bacteria could provoke infectious outbreaks of OCD and perhaps other psychiatric disorders too.

The 1998 academic paper on Pandas caused a sensation. Patients and anxious parents of children with mysterious obsessions were handed an easy-to-understand explanation, and a possible cure: the scientists successfully treated some of the children by sucking out and replacing the plasma from their blood, so ridding them of the anti-brain antibodies. But the Pandas hypothesis left too many doctors and medical experts sceptical. Disagreement was bitter and polarized the field of child psychiatry for years. It still does. Some said the NIMH team was plain wrong and insisted they scrap the whole idea. A flurry of academic papers attacked and offered support to both camps. The biggest losers were acutely ill children and their parents, who did not know which experts to believe. The research and the controversy continue.

It is not just studies of humans that link damage to the basal ganglia to ritualized and compulsive actions. Experiments with green anoles, a lizard sometimes called the American chameleon, have highlighted the crucial role of the basal ganglia in ritual in reptiles. Male anoles square off with each other for territory with a series of displays and repetitive actions; chiefly they strut and push themselves up and down on their front legs. We do this when we fight over territory too; look how a boxer behaves in the ring when he paces around a downed opponent.

In 2003, brain scientists at the University of Florida showed that anole territorial display routines associate with increased activity in distinct parts of their basal ganglia. The basal ganglia of the reptiles, they observed, seemed to activate to release the behaviour in the appropriate context.

And while one part of the basal ganglia seemed to control dominant behaviour – the squats and struts – a separate part appeared to associate with a separate routine of submissive behaviour shown by the weaker anoles, which squeeze flat to the floor. The results of the Florida experiments supported other research on anoles in the 1970s, which showed that damage to their basal ganglia appeared to switch off control of these territorial rituals, but leave other behaviours intact.

We should be careful not to draw too many comparisons between lizard and human brains, but the anole study does raise an important question. We saw earlier how a capacity, or instinct, for ritual seems hard-wired into the human brain, and how the contents of common human rituals are similar to the themes of OCD. We know from the work of van Economo – on sleepy sickness – and others that damage to the basal ganglia can force some people to perform involuntary and repetitive – ritualistic – movements. And now we see that the basal ganglia relates to ritualistic behaviour, fixed action patterns, in other species too. Is OCD what happens when a fault in the brain leads the basal ganglia to deploy ritual at the wrong time, in an inappropriate context?

Some neuroscientists think that it is. Those who study the basal ganglia, and the brain tissue that surrounds and interacts with it, have developed a model of how the OCD-brain might go wrong. Like all models of the brain, it's massively simplistic to a neuroscientist and maddeningly complex to almost everybody else. It goes something like this.

The basal ganglia works closely with the brain's orbito-frontal cortex (OFC), which sits just behind the eyebrows. The OFC processes sensory information from the eyes and elsewhere and passes signals to a region of the basal ganglia called the striatum. From there, the message goes to a separate brain structure called the thalamus, which controls motor systems. In response, the thalamus passes signals back to the OFC.

This happens in a non-stop loop, and it might help us respond to external threats. Told about events in the world by the OFC, the striatum and thalamus select the appropriate motor response, the right programme, and tell the OFC to make it happen. I see a lion. Yikes. Run away. When the circumstances change, the danger passes, the OFC signals the all-clear and the thalamus stands down.

What's important for the model of OCD is that the OFC can pass these signals to the thalamus in two different ways. The signal to switch on passes through the striatum, and is called direct. The stand-down is indirect; it is sent to the thalamus through the striatum and then via other parts of the basal ganglia.

In this model of obsessive behaviour, OCD occurs when the thalamus runs out of control and sends inappropriate instructions back to the OFC. The instructions and the behaviour no longer suit the circumstance, and this puts the OFC in a bind. Information from the senses, updates from the outside world, indicates everything is fine. Yet signals from the thalamus suggest not. The consequent motor behaviour, the ritual, continues even while the senses tell the OFC that there is no danger, and no need for the behaviour. That's the paradox of OCD right there. The water shrew jumps the removed stone. The clean hands are washed. I check the fresh paper towel for blood.

That's a stripped-down version of the, itself simplified, model of the OCD brain. But here's an even more simplified one: The direct route that excites the thalamus is an accelerator pedal. The indirect route is a brake. In normal function, the accelerator and brake work together to control speed. In OCD, the brake fails.

From this model of the way an obsessive brain works it's clear why a common response from others – that someone with OCD just should not be so ridiculous – does not and will never work. Don't you think we might have tried that? You merely tell us what we can see with our own eyes, that our hands are clean, that the towel is free of blood. We see and yet we can't stop. A driver who points out that a speeding car is going too fast does not slow it down. We need to fix the brake.

One way to try to fix the brake is to use drugs. The Leeds psychiatrist who gave me the rubber band had also convinced me to take Prozac. It was still a wonder drug back then, and Elizabeth Wurtzel's best-selling account of her depression, *Prozac Nation*, had made those little green and cream pills almost a fashion accessory. Prozac didn't help me much. I wasn't depressed, just unhappy. I told the psychiatrist that I didn't feel any better. He offered me an alternative drug. I don't remember what it was called, just that he said it would turn me into a happy zombie. I wasn't sure whether that was an endorsement or a warning. I still don't know. I turned it down.

Some fifteen years later, the first thing that the psychiatrists I went to see at the specialist OCD unit did was to put me back on drugs. Not Prozac, but something similar. This time, the chance they would turn me into a happy zombie wasn't discussed.

ELEVEN

Daddy's little helper

Sertraline hydrochloride is what chemists call a psychotropic medication. I call it a lifeline, a route back to the light from the darkest regions inside my head. I take 200mg every morning. The two white tablets taste bitter, so it's best to swallow them with plenty of water. Here goes. Gulp.

Seconds after I swallow the pills, acidic juice in my stomach starts to eat away at the thin layer of polymer film that covers them; within minutes the film is weak enough to release the crystal powder inside. Some of this powder dissolves quickly in the water and drops into the small intestine, the inch-wide and several-feet-long hosepipe coiled somewhere under my belly button, where it will work gently for hours along my intestinal tract.

As these freed drug molecules rub up against the wall of the gut, they leak through its porous lining and into the blood held by the tributaries of thin vessels on the other side, which trickle and pool into my giant hepatic portal vein. Inside the vein and buffeted by blood cells, most of the dissolved drug binds to giant serum proteins. It must hold tight, because its next stop is the liver.

The armies of PhD chemists who design drugs like sertraline hate the liver, because the liver hates chemicals like sertraline. It's the liver's job to strip foreign bodies from the blood, and sure enough it tears into the sertraline with its most powerful weapons – enzymes to break it down and convert the drug to something else.

Enzymes to the right of them, enzymes to the left of them, enzymes in front of them,* boldly the sertraline charges my liver's metabolic guns. Much of the drug is hit, and changed by the biological defences into clumps of derivative molecules called N-desmethylsertraline – still useful, but weaker. Together with traces of the original drug that manage to slip through, these start to pour with the blood that carries them into the central circulatory system.

It takes about six hours after I swallow the sertraline for the drug to peak in my circulatory blood. After the liver it visits the heart, from where it is flung to all corners of the body – some sertraline uselessly bounces around my toes and floods through my eyes. Some, by chance, takes the route that passes the mouth, where its journey began, and reaches the top of my head. There, the drug molecules face a formidable challenge, to breach perhaps the best-defended wall in all of nature, the blood-brain barrier.

Some four times longer than the former Berlin Wall,

---

* With apologies to Alfred Tennyson.

the blood-brain barrier is a thin layer of tightly knit cells painted onto the outside of the blood vessels that deliver nourishment to the brain. Unlike the cells that line the small intestine, which make it as easy as possible for stuff to move from the gut into the blood, the brain barrier does the opposite. The job of this coating layer is to resist and to make it difficult for the same stuff to shift through it, out of the blood vessels and into the surrounding cells and tissue of the brain. (Picture the barrier as the lagging that surrounds and insulates hot water pipes. The pipe is the blood vessel, the space around it the brain.) There's a good reason for that resistance. Brain cells are fragile and sensitive. They must live a sheltered life, protected from possible poisons or the volatile spikes and dips in blood chemicals that follow food or exercise.

The chemistry of the barrier dictates what goes from the blood into the brain and what does not. Heroin, for instance, is much more addictive than morphine because a quirk of its structure makes heroin a hundred times more soluble in fat, and so more able to cross the fatty blood-brain barrier. Even expert drug designers who can safely guide their best medicines through the liver come up short when they try to access the brain. They discover to their great frustration that the blood-brain barrier blocks even useful molecules like antibiotics and anti-cancer drugs.

Drugs that do penetrate the barrier must either dissolve in its fatty centre, like the heroin, or Trojan horse-style must smuggle themselves in. Sertraline seems able to do the latter and sticks to gateway proteins on the barrier's surface, which confuse the drug with something they were expecting, and so let it pass.

The battle of the liver is tough for the sertraline, but the blood-brain barrier is tougher – most of the sertraline molecules are rebuffed by its defences. But, as each beat of my heart delivers fresh blood and renewed reinforcements, and the sertraline keeps up its assault, it edges into the barrier and eventually through to the other side. It enters my brain.

Just a tiny fraction of the original 200mg, the two bitter tablets, will ever get near a brain neuron. But it is enough. When I swallow the pills, the sertraline hydrochloride renews its daily battle against my OCD. My brain starts to change and my mind changes with it.

Sertraline, sold also as Zoloft and Lustral, is one of a class of widely prescribed anti-depressant medicines known as the SSRIs – selective serotonin reuptake inhibitors. Prozac is another. The SSRI drugs are controversial, partly because of the huge quantity of them routinely dished out, and also because of a claimed association with increased suicide risk in teenagers. There are doubts about if and how they really do work for depression. But they are a popular frontline treatment for OCD.

Psychiatrists have thrown dozens of different drugs at OCD over the years, from LSD, lithium and amphetamines to nicotine patches and the horse tranquilizer ketamine. The only chemicals that seem to consistently help are those that work – like the SSRIs do – on serotonin, a hormone found mostly in the gut but usually recognized for its role in the brain.

Dozens of trials of OCD treatment with SSRIs – sertraline, Prozac and a handful of others – have now been carried out with hundreds of people, and a consistent picture has emerged. Patients with obsessions and compulsions who take the drugs are more likely to improve – measured as a significant decrease in their Yale-Brown scores of obsessive and compulsive symptoms over time – than those who do not. The drugs don't help everybody, but then nothing does.

Before SSRI drugs became available in the 1980s and 1990s, OCD was treated with clomipramine, a brute of an anti-depressant drug with nasty side effects that carried the risk of a fatal overdose. The risks were considered worth it because clomipramine gave hope to people with OCD. Hope that was discovered only thanks to random chance and a little cross-border narcotics smuggling.

Clomipramine is a little different from the SSRI drugs, but it's similar to an antidepressant called imipramine, which was launched by the Swiss drug company Ciba in the 1950s. Both are tricyclic compounds – they have three joined carbon rings at their heart. On a trip to Switzerland in the 1960s, where imipramine was widely available, a French psychoanalyst called Jean Guyotat stuffed some into his pockets and took the pills back to his private practice in

Lyon, where he started to give them to his obsessional patients. 'This was somewhat illegal maybe now but it was possible at the time,' he later recalled.

Guyotat wanted to try the new drug because he believed that some obsessions were masked forms of depression. He treated fifteen obsessional or phobic patients, either with the Swiss imipramine or stocks of clomipramine that his clinic already gave as liquid infusions for severe depression. One patient was a male teacher who turned anger at a colleague who played Wagner records a little too loud into rituals to cope with obsessional thoughts of noise. Another was a woman who for the previous seven years had felt compelled to speak her thoughts out loud. The excitement of extra-marital affairs eased the compulsion but, as Guyotat explained, this method of self-treatment had to stop when her husband found out. The drugs transformed some of his patients, Guyotat said, sometimes within a few days. In 1967 he published his results and announced to the world imipramine and clomipramine as the first chemical treatments for OCD.

Some six hundred miles to the southwest, psychiatrists at a hospital in Madrid learned of the work in France. They had plenty of intravenous clomipramine so they decided to try it on their own severely obsessional patients. Just like the French, the Spanish team reported rapid improvements. Juan Lopez-Ibor, a psychiatrist who worked at the hospital with his father, saw this change in the way one OCD patient on the ward played table tennis. The first sign of recovery came when the man, whose fear of germs had previously left him unable to touch things, was able to hold a communal bat, as long as he went to wash his hands immediately he finished. When Lopez-Ibor saw the man complete his own game and then, without washing, choose to stay and watch other patients play, he knew they had stumbled onto something special.

In northwest England, George Beaumont noted keenly the success with OCD the Spanish doctors reported for clomipramine. Beaumont had worked as a GP in Stockport, near Manchester, but then took a job as medical adviser on psychiatrics with Geigy, a pharmaceutical company. Geigy owned clomipramine and Beaumont saw OCD as a potential new market for it – a big one.

Beaumont suggested to UK psychiatrists that they treat OCD with clomipramine. He arranged for them to visit Lopez-Ibor in Madrid and set up some basic clinical trials of the drug. Beaumont worked closely with staff at the Warrington mental hospital that had treated the claustrophobic American woman we met earlier, who compulsively checked to avoid being buried alive. Just like in France and Spain, some British patients seemed to show rapid improvement.

Encouraged by colleagues in Geigy's marketing department, Beaumont applied for an official licence that would allow doctors to prescribe the drug for obsessions and compulsions. He wrote the 2,000-page application himself – it took three months – and in 1975 clomipramine was approved to treat OCD in the UK, and later other places too. 'Everyone at that time thought that OCD was an unusual, bizarre and rare condition,' Beaumont said later. 'But as soon as you have a treatment for a condition you discover that it is more common than everybody supposed it to be.' *

For years, OCD sufferers in the United States were denied the drug. The licensing body there, the Food and Drug Administration, was wary of what it saw as a copycat antidepressant that offered no benefit beyond those drugs already available. In response, a frustrated Judith Rapoport described in *The Boy Who Couldn't Stop Washing* how – just like Guyotat twenty years earlier – she had helped to bring the unlicensed drug into the country. The FDA relented and approved clomipramine – known in the US as Anafranil – for OCD in 1990.

Sertraline is a powerful drug, especially at the high daily doses given for OCD, but I only notice its impact when I don't take it. Just a day or so without it and, in apparent withdrawal symptoms, my dreams lift from monochrome Kansas to Technicolor Oz. They become so vivid and intense that the emotions they carry linger for most of the day; I can wake myself shouting, once with my eyes wet

---

* Several OCD patients on clomipramine reported delayed or absent orgasms and Beaumont conducted a successful trial of the drug for premature ejaculation. The work was halted in April 1973 when it appeared in the *Sunday Mirror* newspaper as a wonder drug for people's sex lives. His boss was furious: 'We're not having anything to do with this. Stop it.' (Tansey E *et al., Wellcome Witnesses to Twentieth Century Medicine,* vol. 2, Wellcome Trust, 1998, p. 178).

with tears. And the smells – forget to take my pills and I have smelly dreams. I can wake to the aroma of pungent wood smoke or sweet caramel.

On the drugs, it's harder to describe the effect. It's not like the mood lift reported by people given them for depression. It doesn't feel like anything is fixed or restored, though the medication does take the edge off the anxiety that weird thoughts cause. The thoughts still come – no surprise there, as we've seen, they are common and normal – but they seem less sticky. How long will I take the sertraline for? I'm afraid to stop; rapid relapse among those who do is common apparently. I don't see a downside. What gets you well keeps you well, my psychiatrist says.

The impact on OCD of the SSRI and some tricyclic drugs has led scientists who work on the causes and nature of obsession to focus on the chemical that the medicines work on: serotonin.

The brain needs serotonin because, as complex and marvellous as it is, most of its neurons can't communicate directly with each other. At the business end of these neurons there lies a tiny gap that separates them from their neighbours. For neuron A to pass a signal to neuron B it needs serotonin. Specifically, the electrical signal, when activated, releases serotonin molecules into the gap between A and B, some of which bump into B. When that happens, B electrically activates and releases its own chemical messages to pass the signal to C, and so on right through the alphabet.

Spare serotonin sloshing around in the gaps is reclaimed (taken up) by the neurons for when they will need it again.

That is about all we know for sure about how serotonin works in the OCD brain. Much of the rest of the so-called serotonin hypothesis for OCD is based on some reverse engineering. The logic goes like this: the SSRI drugs keep levels of serotonin in the free space between the cells higher than it would be otherwise. They inhibit the uptake. This seems to relieve OCD symptoms, at least in some people. Therefore, the reverse engineering says, OCD must be caused by abnormally low serotonin levels.

It's notoriously difficult to track and measure neurotransmitter activity, so there's no direct evidence to support this hypothesis. It's certainly possible that the extra serotonin might help to ease OCD because it frees the jammed brake in the basal ganglia, and so allows the thalamus to recognize the stand-down signals sent by the orbitofrontal cortex. But it's equally possible that the change is down to something else.

It could be down to dopamine, another neurotransmitter, which tends to cancel out the effects of serotonin. Drugs that boost dopamine levels in the basal ganglia seem to trigger the sudden onsets of compulsive gambling and theft sometimes seen in Parkinson's patients. A failure to produce enough serotonin might allow dopamine levels to rise to the point where they have a stronger influence on the striatum, which plays a key role in the model of the OCD brain. PET brain scans of people with OCD show reduced serotonin transmission and increased dopamine release in the right areas.

Very recently, neuroscientists have fingered a third neurotransmitter, glutamate, for possible conspiracy to cause OCD. Or there could be a role for oxytocin, labelled as the hug-hormone by some because of its role in pair-bonding and maternal behaviour. Oxytocin action is linked to serotonin and can bring on repetitive grooming behaviour in rats. In the mid-1990s scientists at Yale University tried to test its effect on humans. Sadly, regular squirts of oxytocin up the noses of seven OCD patients failed to lift their obsessions with contamination and cleaning.

Although the majority of people with OCD are helped by the SSRIs, a significant number – perhaps up to 40 per cent – see no benefit, even after they have tried four or five different drugs. This has led some scientists to look for obsession elsewhere in the brain, beyond the neurotransmitter systems of the basal ganglia. In 2008, neuroscientists in Turkey reported how they used MRI scans to measure the size of the amygdala and hippocampus in the brains of fourteen OCD patients who had not responded to drug treatment, and compared them to the brains of fourteen normal people. They found both structures were smaller in the OCD group, and the smallest were found in those who had suffered from the condition the longest.

Other studies have found structural differences in the OCD brain, but not consistently enough to build up a clear picture of what they might mean. Bits of the orbitofrontal cortex and basal ganglia have been measured as smaller in

OCD and bits of the thalamus larger (more so in patients with more severe forms of the disease). Some scans find differences in the ratio of grey (functional) to white (supporting) brain tissue. Some of these differences go away when the OCD is treated. But scientists are a long way from making sense of these often contradictory findings.

The conceptual division of the mind and the brain is like the academic separation of neurology, psychology and psychiatry – it seems to make sense until they have a disagreement, at which point it starts to look like a very bad idea indeed.

Can the mind truly develop faults independent of the brain? Or must every shift of mood and change in perception anchor to a chemical and electrical pulse? If so, then can that physical change in the brain be detected? Could it be measured? Could it be treated, as any other physical ailment can be? If it can, should that reassure someone with OCD, or indeed someone with any mental illness? Should it come as a relief that cognitive anguish has a physical root? Or does that just make it more permanent, more of a feature?

Some people with mental illness like to blame the brain, not the mind, as it implies that their problem lies beyond their consciousness and so beyond their control. It's not their fault. I prefer the opposite explanation. That my brain is normal, thanks. The drugs help to keep its complicated and volatile chemistry on track, but it's my mind, the brain's lodger, which has the OCD. My brain is mine to keep and

I would like it to be of sound structure. My mind is transient anyway. My mind today is different from what it was yesterday; I have learned new things and forgotten others. The ephemeral mind is flexible in a way that the material brain is not. And, surely, that makes a broken mind easier to fix than a broken brain? I was on my way to the hospital to find out.

TWELVE

The helicopter view

When I reported to the hospital for my group therapy sessions in the late summer of 2010, if you were to have peered through the window you would not have spotted anything unusual. You would not have seen people wash their hands, or try not to wash their hands. You would have noticed only a group of half a dozen middle-aged people who sat in a circle of chairs and clutched photo-copied handouts, while a much younger, much better dressed man with dreadlocks and a ready smile moved between them. We could have been learning to speak Spanish.

My fellow OCD patients signed up for therapy, as I did, in the full and fair expectation that their involvement would remain confidential. So, I'll be vague. There were two other men and three women. I was the youngest by a good ten years. We were all classed as serious cases (in fact the clinic only treated serious cases). Between us, we ticked most of the big OCD boxes – contamination and checking fears, long-standing symptoms, distress and reduced quality of life. Two of the others had obsessions and compulsions linked to Aids.

We swapped stories and we tried not to swap irrational fears. We agreed to support each other, but, being British, when somebody else told of their darkest moments we mostly shuffled in our seats and looked awkward. And we laughed. We laughed a lot. We laughed at each other and we laughed at ourselves. We had all long passed the time when we feared our OCD, which had announced itself as a mysterious curse on our lives. It was now a hand on our shoulder, a monkey on our back, an irritating shadow. We were fed up with it. We wanted rid of it. But we would probably miss it too. It was simply a part of us.

There was no psychiatrist's couch and no psycho-analysis. We did not talk about our childhoods. The various causes of our obsessions were irrelevant to the treatment, because they would all anyway have been different. The symptoms were what mattered, and to find a way to reduce them. That was what we had in common.

We saw, through wobbly and badly drawn schematic diagrams, how an OCD mind is thought to work. We learned how the compulsions are a short-cut that helps relieve anxiety, but only for a short while. We started to identify dysfunctional beliefs and cognitive errors in ourselves. We started to diagnose them in each other. And we smiled nervously as we did so. This was cognitive behav-ioural therapy (CBT) but it didn't feel like the type of treatment we expected. It was mild. We suspected worse was to come. We were right. I was told to smear my daughter in my own blood.

The psychologist Richard Solomon worked for the US military through the Second World War. Among other things, he used his expertise on perception and hand-eye coordination to improve the defences of the B-29 Superfortress, the aircraft that would go on to drop atomic bombs on the Japanese cities of Hiroshima and Nagasaki. But it was in the early 1950s, with experiments on a pack of mongrel dogs at Harvard University, that Solomon would make his name.

At Harvard, Solomon put individual dogs in a small room he had divided into two with a low hurdle that the dog could easily jump. On each side of the divide, the floor was a metal grid. With the dog on one side, Solomon would flash the lights, and ten seconds later, send an electric current through that side's grid. Shocked, the dog would leap to the other side. When it settled, Solomon would repeat the pattern of lights and electrocution, hundreds or even thousands of times until the dogs grew conditioned to jump to the other side of the room as soon as the lights flashed.

One day, Solomon increased the height of the hurdle, so the dog in the room could not cross. The lights flashed and the terrified dog, unable to escape what it thought would follow, went berserk. It ran around in circles, jumped at the walls, yelped and emptied its bladder and bowel. But this time Solomon did not turn on the electricity.

Gradually, as no shock followed, the dog calmed down. After this version of the test was repeated several times, the dog lost its fear of the lights. Even when the hurdle was lowered again, it would not attempt to jump when they flashed. This reaction is called extinction decay. It's the basis for a treatment for OCD called exposure and response prevention.

Exposure and response prevention works like this: get the person anxious by stimulating them with the object of their obsession, but don't let them take the easy way out – stop the compulsive behaviour. The anxiety has to peak and plateau. In time, it has nowhere to go but down. Once the patient feels their anxiety go away by itself, without the need for compulsions, then, the theory says, like Solomon's dogs they will lose their fear and start to recover. Early attempts, for example, persuaded people with contamination fears to handle rubbish, but told them they could not wash their hands.

My exposure therapy started by accident. In the fifth session we talked about how almost everybody has intrusive thoughts. We read through the list of normal and abnormal obsessions that Stanley Rachman and Padmal de Silva had compiled back in 1977. It had been a rough night, the baby had not slept well, and as I sat there I yawned and rubbed my eyes. The intrusive thought came as I rested my hands back on my knees. What if there was blood on my fingers? I was in a hospital. I had handled the doors and chairs. Who had sat here before me? What were they in here for? Was it Aids? Had they left traces of blood?

Twenty years before I would have reacted with panic. Now it was a weary sense of resignation. Here we go again. I knew that if I checked my fingers for blood, as I wanted to, the anxiety would fade. I would probably have to check again a few more times, but that would be enough. The thoughts would stay in the room. The thoughts would stay, but I knew the OCD would come with me. I had to resist. This was what I was here for. This was what I would have to do to change. This is what it would take to get better. I sat quietly; I thought and then I spoke to the room.

'I'm having a thought right now. What should I do? I rubbed my eyes and now I want to check my fingers for blood. I'm in a hospital and there might be blood on the chair.'

'Stand up,' the therapist said. 'Don't look at your hands.'

I stood.

'Put your arms out to your sides.'

I did.

'Now rub your eyes again.'

No way.

People talk about the power of the mind as if it is a force only for good. Mind over matter represents the triumph of will over physical hindrance. Our thoughts are our weapon against the world. *Cogito ergo sum*, as the man said. I think therefore I am. Thought makes us human. Thoughts shape and define us. Our ancestors benefited from thought so much that their enlarged brains had to fold over themselves just to fit inside their skulls. Thought decides our actions and determines our behaviour. We value the thoughtful; who, after all, wants to be thought of as thoughtless?

I was told as a child that I thought too much. But I liked to think. I liked to roll ideas around my head, to test some to destruction and to rehearse my lines. OCD robbed me of that pleasure. My thoughts became the enemy within; a mocking Lord Haw Haw, a poisonous Tokyo Rose. *Dubito ergo cogito ergo sum*, as he said more fully. I doubt therefore I think; therefore I am. My doubts, my thoughts, now blocked all movement in my hands as I stood with my arms outstretched.

'Now rub your eyes again.'

'I can't. I don't want to.'

We reached a compromise. I did not have to rub my eyes again, but equally I was not allowed to look at my hands. It took three days for the anxiety to subside. Three days during which I went to work, cooked meals, bathed my baby girl, showered, washed dishes and drove a car. I did it all without a single deliberate glance at my hands. Rationally, I knew that any blood there would anyway be long gone. But I still had the urge to check, to make sure. And as I resisted the urge, the fear and the obsession once again came to dominate my life. The three days felt like three years. Three days is a long time on mental high alert. But three days is pretty quick for an extinction event.

That was progress. And that was when I was sent home to cover my daughter in my own blood. Because I feared, probably more than anything else at this point, to touch her with blood on my hands, I was told that the next time

I scratched myself or cut myself shaving or drove a nail through my finger I was to seek her out and daub her face, her head, her exposed arms and legs. The anxiety would peak of course and then, in time, it would come down.

Because so many of the obsessions in OCD are bizarre, so the exposure therapies used to treat them can appear almost comedic. A 37-year-old engineer whose obsessive disgust at semen allowed him only to have sex in a sterile room he kept for that single purpose was told by his therapists to touch clothes soiled with semen stains and to rub objects with a semen-soaked handkerchief that he was to carry in his pocket. A middle-aged woman with an obsessive fear of animals had to watch as a hamster rummaged through her bedclothes and handbag. We have already met Andy, the betrayed civil servant who was dressed by his therapist from head to toe in brown envelopes.

The exposure, remember, only provokes the anxieties. It is the response-prevention that delivers the sting. As the extinction decay kicks in, so someone with OCD – even someone who has had OCD for decades – learns a crucial and life-changing lesson. The events they so fear, the circumstances they spend their lives trying to prevent, do not and will not occur.

Someone with compulsions to tap out numbers or touch blue objects as a way to stop some dreadful thought coming true – that they might hurt their own child, say – find that, if they don't carry out their ritual, then they don't hurt their child. Previously when they had not hurt their child

– they have never done so and never would – they assumed it was because they had touched and tapped. The ritual blocked the necessary reverse conditioning. They could not learn that their fear was misplaced. With the right conditioning, humans learn quickly. Obsessions that have run wild through a mind for thirty years or more can be tamed by just ten hours of exposure and response prevention therapy.

This form of behavioural therapy has proved so effective that few exposure therapists now feel the need to throw their OCD patients in at the deep end, at least not straight away. More commonly they together draw up a list of feared situations and arrange them in a hierarchy. It's our own stepped programme. It's called the subjective units of distress and discomfort scale.

Simon, a 51-year-old middle manager in the US finance industry, received this kind of stepped therapy. Simon was heterosexual and married with two children, but he had intrusive thoughts that he might be gay. Simon did not find himself attracted to men, but he would still keep his distance. If another man walked into his office, Simon would place his hands behind his head, to make sure that he did not touch him. He started to avoid one-on-one meetings with male colleagues and could not bear to watch television programmes or films with masculine characters. He avoided sex with his wife, in case he had thoughts of men.

Simon said his fears were based on what he thought would happen if he was gay: he would have to leave his wife and children and would face hostility from family and friends. Simon had become depressed and started to take SSRI drugs. When they made him less interested in sex (a common side effect) he took that as a further sign that he was gay. By the time Simon was treated at the University of Pennsylvania he was on three separate drugs for obsessions and anxiety, including the anti-psychotic risperidone.

The units of distress scale asks patients to rate the difficulty of a particular activity out of 100. Simon's first exposure was to something he rated as 20: a conversation with another man about gay marriage legislation. As the weeks progressed, Simon would take on tasks that made him feel more and more uncomfortable – sometimes in the formal sessions and sometimes as homework. He would have to strike up conversations with men he met in a sports bar, and then with those men he considered attractive and masculine. He had to stand too close to them. He read gay magazines and then stared at gay pornography. He watched the films *Milk* and *Brokeback Mountain*. He had sex with his wife.

By the end of the treatment, Simon went with his therapist to a gay bar – an activity he originally rated with an expected difficulty of 100 out of 100. After twelve weeks, Simon scored just 3 on the Yale-Brown test of OCD severity, down from 24 before he started.

Unlike the pain and electric shocks of aversion therapy, which we looked at in Chapter Six, the technique of exposure and response prevention harnesses only the patient's own fears. It does not try to plant new ones. Even so, the deliberate stirring of intense anxiety saw many exposure therapists in the early days sail close to the ethical wind. Like Odysseus as he faced the Sirens, some OCD patients were physically restrained so they could not carry out their compulsions. Some doctors certainly went too far, especially those protected from scrutiny within the walls of state institutions.

Victor Meyer, the London psychologist who developed exposure therapy, saw the trouble coming. In 1971 he wrote that exposure therapy would be stressful for all involved because it needed psychologists and psychiatrists to adopt authoritarian attitudes that were alien to the way they usually treated their patients. He said:

> We urge this should only be done where the staff concerned can have the closest supervision and fullest support . . . The line between firm but sympathetic control and unpleasant and inhumane bullying is a thin one indeed and all too easy to cross when one has devoted a lot of time and energy to a patient who relentlessly and monotonously pursues an unchanging course.

Someone with OCD can be pushed too far. There is no evidence that they have higher rates of suicide, but they do sometimes self-harm. Pain seems to offer these people something, and in 2012 psychologists at Harvard University reported that people with OCD are especially tolerant of it.

The scientists studied the reaction of people with and without OCD to a gentle torture device called a portable pressure algometer. It uses a foot-long hinge and weights to exert constant pressure on the back of the index finger, and feels a bit like a butter-knife pressed against the skin. The psychologists asked the two groups to say when the device started to cause them pain, and then when they could bear the pain no longer. The difference between the two signalled their pain tolerance.

The OCD group could bear the pain for an extra 90 seconds. One OCD patient said the pain felt good. Another said he liked it because 'in all the craziness of my OCD, pain is a constant. It's the one thing you can count on.' Just as the Christian flagellant movement of medieval Italy would beat themselves to replace the mental anguish of guilt with physical agony, the Harvard psychologists suggest so people with OCD could use pain to distract themselves from their emotional distress. At the very least, it can make them feel in control of something. It is something they can turn off.

Exposure and response prevention does not work for everyone. Some patients can't or won't try it. Others drop out. And for some obsessions, it's just not plausible to recreate the experience that triggers the anxiety. Mine is one of those – it's pretty hard to expose someone to HIV-infected blood under controlled conditions, or indeed to any kind of blood. That's why I was asked to find and smear my daughter only if and when I cut myself in regular activity such as DIY. Our next example had the same obsessions as me, so let's call him David.

David was a 45-year-old orthopaedic surgeon who sought help in Chicago for obsessive fear of Aids in the early 1990s. He would keep his theatre colleagues waiting while he washed and rewashed his hands between operations. David's therapists drew up a list of exposures, but were hindered by strict guidelines from the US Centers for Disease Control and Prevention on steps that health-care workers had to follow to reduce their risks of HIV infection. Specifically, they had to use appropriate barrier precautions to stop their skin and mucous membranes touching blood or bodily fluids, and if some did splash onto their hands, they had to wash immediately and thoroughly.

These rules removed the most powerful weapon available to the therapists: direct exposure to blood and body fluids. Yet, David would face this every day in work. This put him in an unusual position. He would confront more intense exposures at work than the therapists could conjure up in the treatment sessions. In work he splashed blood onto his hands. In therapy he had to imagine doing so. The CDC requirement to wash after every minor contact with blood was also the last thing the therapists would have recommended, as it could only fuel his fear. And it was hardly reassuring for David to see the psychologists who treated him check with infectious disease experts about whether this or that exposure scenario they wanted to put him through carried any risk of HIV transmission. David didn't get better. In the cold language of the clinical case study, his therapists classed him as a treatment failure.

The therapy sessions helped me. They were a crutch to lean on; a little too much of a crutch, as it turned out. One of the ways that people with OCD centred on irrational and unlikely ways to contract diseases carry out their compulsive checks is to seek reassurance. Usually this is the simple 'can I catch it like this' question. That was clearly banned by the strictures of exposure and response prevention. But OCD is clever, and mine found a way to break the rules.

Under the guise of chat at the group sessions, I would detail some of the obsessive thoughts that had come into my head during the past few days. I had worried, I would say, about how I picked at a spot on my leg and drew blood. What if I had any contaminated blood on my finger? Superficially, this was a way to air our inner thoughts, to open the windows and blow away the obsessive dust that had accumulated since the last session. But I was acting. When I described the thoughts I watched for a reaction, any reaction, in those who listened. I waited for what poker players call a 'tell', for the others to smile with recognition or to laugh and roll their eyes to indicate that, yes, they thought those thoughts were ridiculous. To reassure me that they believed I couldn't catch HIV that way. That caused as much damage as explicit requests for reassurance. It short-circuited the extinction. I may as well have called the National Aids Helpline and asked them.

*

You won't find this description in the textbooks, but behaviour therapy – the BT of CBT – combines two torture devices dreamed up in popular fiction. Like the Room 101 in George Orwell's *1984*, it puts you face to face with your greatest fear. It traps you next to it until you can feel its warm breath on your face. And then there is the Total Perspective Vortex. The vortex, according to Douglas Adams' *Hitchhiker's Guide to the Galaxy* series, is a small room that shows the occupant their true place in the great, universal scheme of things. As the celestial sweep of the cosmos unfolds across trillions of light years and through millennia of time, a small dot appears with a sign that reads 'you are here'.

We saw earlier how much OCD can come down to responsibility. What helped me the most was when somebody else offered to take responsibility for my actions. That's pretty cowardly and I'm not proud to say that it worked, but it did. 'I have a good job and I get paid a lot of money,' the therapist boasted to us one day. 'If I tell you to do something and something bad happens as a result, then you can blame me. I will get sacked. Do you think I would ask you to do something that will get me sacked?'

If I had blood on my fingers and touched my daughter and gave her Aids then it wasn't my fault. He told me to do it. If I rubbed my eyes in a restaurant, did not check them for blood and then rubbed my eyes again, as he told me to, it was his responsibility if I caught HIV. The end result would be the same. I would still have the disease. My daughter would still have the virus. But that didn't seem to matter as much if it was his job to stop it and not mine. It didn't seem as likely to happen.

Boom.

The total perspective vortex fired up. My consciousness soared above my fears, as a camera draws out from a single house on a map to show the street, the town and then the surrounds and countryside. Previously, my OCD interfered with this process. No matter how much I tried to make the camera pan out, the irrational fear stayed in view, like a dirty smudge on the lens. Now the risk of HIV from all those unlikely routes shrank as I rose above to see them in their proper context. Psychologists call this moment of clarity the helicopter view. We see the landscape and all it contains in its proper scale. We regain, in all senses of the word, perspective. From 10,000 feet up, the gap between very low risk and zero risk – so visible and so important to my OCD – is hard to distinguish.

The six months or so of cognitive-behavioural sessions helped everybody in the group. When we met a few months later, the improvement was still there. I haven't seen the others since, but I hope it still is. Such success is not unusual. The therapy, in the words of those adverts that try to sell isotonic sports drinks or spot cream, is clinically proven. In 2012 scientists in Tennessee and Texas published a comprehensive meta-analysis – the top standard for medical investigations – of cognitive behavioural therapy for OCD.

They pooled the results of sixteen randomized-controlled trials that featured 756 people and proved that the therapy was more effective than to do nothing. More people improved with the treatment, in other words, than chance alone would predict.

Cognitive behavioural therapy, as the name suggests, is not just about direct challenge to abnormal behaviour. The cognitive bit is important too. As psychological theories of obsessions and compulsions improved, cognitive therapy was added to exposure treatment. It aims to reveal to patients the dysfunctional beliefs they hold – inflated responsibility, for example – and teaches them how to recognize, to challenge and ultimately to restructure these destructive patterns of thought. It stresses how the interpretation and appraisal of thoughts drive OCD, not the intrusive thoughts themselves.

Some OCD patients refuse cognitive behavioural therapy because it sounds too soft. How can talking and thinking, and talking about thinking, dig out deep-rooted obsessions, overgrown with years and sometimes decades of neglect? Others find it too harsh and quit. Some people find a combination of SSRI drugs and CBT helpful; there is some evidence that OCD patients given so-called 'smart drugs' – supposed to give a short-term boost to mental ability, and popular with college students – can improve the outcome of CBT.

It's common for people who have been through CBT to become evangelists and urge everybody to try it. I'll say only that scientists know it works. They see how the impact can be dramatic and sudden. What's more, they know it can alter the structure and function of the brain. Successful therapy shows up on brain scans – which reveal changes in the kind of activities and brain regions we discussed earlier, those that are implicated in the causes and maintenance of OCD. The mind and the brain are not so separate after all. Change the mind and you can change the brain. It worked for me. It can be hard to access good CBT and I will always be profoundly grateful that I did. And no, I never did smear blood onto my daughter.

THIRTEEN

Long live lobotomy

In the grip of OCD, there were times when I wanted to tear my skull to reach inside and rip the thoughts from my brain. I was desperate to find the cells that held the intrusive thoughts and to squeeze them between my fingers until they burst. I'm not the only one who has felt that way. For some people with severe OCD, the drugs – any of the drugs – and the therapy don't work. The elastic bands don't work. The psychotherapy and the psychodynamics don't work. Desperate and out of options, OCD makes some of these people open their own skulls and burn away the bits of their brains they blame for their obsession. Or at least, they get a surgeon to do it for them.

Mr V, a 62-year-old engineer from Karnataka, an Indian town about four hours' drive from Bangalore, had OCD and had tried everything. Mr V developed depression and obsessions after his father died in 1990. He felt compelled to repeatedly verify documents and count money. He spent three to four hours in the toilet every day, where he would wash his hands again and again. He could not bring himself to sign his pension, so he could not collect it. He did not leave his house for two years. He scored a shocking 38 out of 40 on the Yale-Brown test. Mr V had tried cognitive behavioural therapy more than twenty times. He had taken the highest possible doses of sertraline, Prozac and clomipramine, and a handful of other drugs. After twenty years, Mr V had had enough. And then he met Paresh Doshi, a brain surgeon at the Jaslok Hospital and Research Centre in Mumbai. Doshi drilled two holes in the top of his head, inserted a long electrical pin through each, heated them and held them in place until they melted away Mr V's brain cells. Mr V went home with two holes in his head, each about the size of one of the printed words on this page.*

Lobotomy has a dreadful reputation and one that it fully deserves. In the middle decades of the twentieth century, tens of thousands of people with OCD and other mental illnesses had their brains irreversibly damaged by cavalier surgeons armed with nothing more precise than knitting needles. Hammered up through the tops of the eye sockets, the solid metal was then waggled – there is no other term – around in a clumsy attempt to sever bits of the frontal cortex. Some improved. Plenty didn't.

This form of surgery is now generally referred to as

---

* There are pre- and post-operation interviews with Mr V in videos on the website of the Jaslok centre: www.neurologicalsurgery.in/psychiatry-disorders-surgery/#prettyPhoto.

ice-pick lobotomy, which to those of us in Europe sounds even more horrific. In Europe, ice pick is the common name for an ice axe, the mountaineering tool used to murder the communist leader Leon Trotsky in Mexico City. In the USA an ice pick is a long, sharp needle with a handle on one end that is used to separate blocks of ice. Nobody was lobotomized with an ice axe. At least, not as far as we know.

Those who carry out brain surgery for OCD today recoil from the word lobotomy. They prefer terms like anterior cingulotomy and anterior capsulotomy, which sound reassuringly complex and technical, unless you know that the anterior cingulate cortex and anterior capsule are the names of parts of the brain and that the suffix –tomy is from the Greek for slice. The procedures are certainly more precise than full-scale lobotomy. They target and destroy much smaller amounts of brain. But the principle of psychosurgery has remained the same for more than a century: let's cut here and hope for the best. The doctors responsible don't like the term psychosurgery either. They call it functional neurosurgery for psychiatric disease.

I have some experience of functional neurosurgery for psychiatric disease. In 2004 the *Guardian* photographer Don McPhee and I witnessed its use in Shanghai to treat heroin addiction. Don, who took pictures of the surgery, died in 2007, but his photographs are a fitting legacy; most famous is probably his shot of a miner who wears a toy policeman's helmet and faces up to a young policeman who tries to hold the line during the 1984 coal strike, both poised to break into smiles.

As Don and I stood awkwardly outside the Shanghai operating theatre, both in full surgical scrubs, him with a bulky camera and me with a feeble notebook and chewed biro, I caught his eye. The smiles were about to come, when the surgeon beckoned us inside to where his medical team was struggling to hold down a tall and bald and wide-awake drug addict. The cold turkey withdrawal symptoms had kicked in. This was bad news as it meant his surgery would now be done under a general anaesthetic. The surgeon preferred to use local anaesthetic – there are no pain receptors in the brain once past the skull – so he could converse with patients while he worked on their brains.

The surgeon drilled through the man's shaved skull, inked with two crude crosses, and inserted long needles deep into the brain. Flicking a switch, the needle tips became hot enough to burn away the surrounding tissue. It took just a few minutes. The target was the nucleus accumbens, part of the basal ganglia. It's thought to play a role in motivation, desire and reward. It's been loosely connected to addictive behaviour. So the Chinese surgeons thought the man was better off without it.

When the *Guardian* published my report of his operation – complete with Don's photographs and quotes from western neuroscientists appalled at the risk taken by their Chinese colleagues – the Chinese government stepped in and banned it. But similar procedures are still carried out across the world. Not to cure heroin addiction perhaps, but to treat obsessions and anorexia and anxiety and even obesity. It's done in Dundee and Cardiff, Stockholm and Pittsburgh. Lobotomy is dead. Long live lobotomy.

It takes about five and a half hours to travel by train from Penn Station in New York City to Rutland, Vermont, and on a beautiful day with the autumn leaves in their full glory, you may wish that it took slightly longer. That it does not is down to the backbreaking labour of the men who prepared the New England landscape for the railroad in the mid-nineteenth century, who battered the countryside's lumps and bumps into submission and pinned it down with section after section of fresh track.

One of those men was Phineas Gage, a 25-year-old construction foreman. Born and raised in New Hampshire, Gage was unlikely to have paid too much attention to the colourful leaves that started to dot the trees that provided the backdrop for the work of him and his crew in September 1848. He had seen it all before. But one afternoon, we know that something did distract him. It was a fateful mistake, and one that means his skull is now on permanent display at Harvard University, placed in a glass case next to a metre-long iron bar.

Gage was in charge of blasting away large rocks that littered the intended path of the new railway. He and his men would drill holes into the stones, fill them with explosive powder and detonate them with a fuse. Before the fuse was lit Gage would first prod the sandy mixture into the hole with a 3cm-wide bar called a tamping iron. In the late afternoon of 13 September, Gage pushed the tamping iron directly onto the gunpowder. There was a spark and a flash and a vicious explosion. Stunned, Gage fell to the floor. His men gathered around and were relieved to see him open his eyes and talk. They helped him to his feet. They found his tamping iron some distance away, smeared with blood and what looked like bits of sticky thick mucous. Then they found something else.

There was a hole in Gage's head. A 3cm-wide tunnel opened in what had been Gage's left cheek, passed through his skull and brain, the skull again, and exited through the top of his head. You could have threaded something directly through his head, which, of course, is what had happened. The iron bar, turned into a missile by the premature explosion, had struck Gage in the face, penetrated and passed through his bones and brains, and barely slowed by the experience, hurled itself high into the sky. It was not mucous that covered the bar, lying on the ground some twenty-five metres away. It was bits of Gage's brain.

More extraordinarily still, Gage did not seem unduly troubled. There was lots of blood, and his face and arms were burnt, but he was conscious and helpfully told the doctor, who he was taken to see at a nearby inn, what had happened. No need to send my friends in to see me, he said. I shall be back at work in a few days. Infection nearly killed Gage – the doctor who treated him snipped away fungus that sprouted from his head – but he recovered and lived for another decade. He lived, but he seemed a different man, cruder and more impatient. Gage, his friends said, was no longer Gage.

He is remembered partly because his tamping iron landed in the middle of an argument among nineteenth-century scientists over the role of the brain. Some insisted that the whole brain was involved, and so needed, in every mental process. Others said it had distinct regions, each with their own purpose – this part for language, this part for memory and so on. Many of the scientists who favoured this latter approach believed that the size of each of the bits determined personality – so a large brain region responsible for memory would make someone better able to remember things. As it turns out, they were probably on the right lines, but history scorns them because they also believed that brain regions enlarged in this way would show up as bumps on the surface of the skull. (Working backwards, they reasoned that to measure the lumps and bumps of a person's head could reveal their talents and tastes.)

That Gage lost a large portion of his brain, yet was still able to function, indicated that an entirely intact brain was not essential for well-being. Together with studies of animals and Broca's work with people who had survived strokes, it helped to show that certain regions of the brain controlled specific behaviours. This pushed doctors and scientists who worked with severe mental patients at the time towards a startling idea. Could they manipulate these areas to fix people?

The Swiss psychiatrist Gottlieb Burckhardt thought so.

In late December 1888, at a grand asylum on the banks of Lake Neuchâtel, Burckhardt drilled holes in the heads of six mental patients, five of whom would probably today be diagnosed with severe schizophrenia, and gouged out portions of their cerebral cortex. Burckhardt claimed that the surgery improved the condition of three of the patients, but when he presented his results at a scientific meeting in Berlin the following year, shocked colleagues pressured him not to perform the operation again. Perhaps anticipating their hostile response, Burckhardt had concluded his report on the controversial procedure with a defiant line about the direction he thought medicine should take.

Doctors should challenge the classic medical mantra *primum non nocere* (first do no harm), he said, with an opposing motive: *melius anceps remedium quam nullum* (better an unknown cure than nothing at all). Every path to new victories, he said, must be lined by crosses of the dead, which may be true but it's probably not the motto you would choose for your brain surgeon. Lobotomy had started badly, and would go downhill from there.

July 1935 was warm and sunny in London, so Egas Moniz would have felt very much at home. The Portuguese neurosurgeon, a former ambassador to Spain and minister of foreign affairs in his country's government, had spent the previous fifteen years at the University of Lisbon, where the weather was friendlier than England.

Moniz had come to London to join fellow brain scientists from around the world for a week-long conference at

University College. The event was to prove pivotal for Moniz, who would go on to win a Nobel Prize. Ivan Pavlov was there too, one of his last appearances before his death the following year. So were two scientists from Yale University in the US, John Fulton and Carlyle Jacobsen, who were eager to talk about their work with chimpanzees. In research that wouldn't be allowed in most places these days, Fulton, a physiologist, would sever pathways in the chimps' brains as a way to explore the links between different neural systems. Fulton and Jacobsen told the London meeting how cuts to the frontal lobe areas seemed to make the chimps less anxious. Moniz, in the audience, believed the same could be done to help people with mental illness.

Moniz wanted to use surgery to separate thoughts from emotions, to draw the sting from mental tension. Back in Lisbon, he persuaded a young neurosurgeon called Almedia Lima to operate on twenty psychiatric patients. Lima severed the white matter bundles that connect the frontal lobe regions with the rest of the brain, a procedure called a frontal leucotomy.

The duo went on to perform more than a hundred of these operations – first with injections of ethanol to poison and deactivate the brain tissue, and later with a retractable wire loop on the end of a metal rod to physically destroy it – and though Moniz claimed and celebrated them as successful, he kept few records of what happened to the patients afterwards. Several were quietly returned to asylums. This was the work for which Moniz – still an effective politician – received the 1949 Nobel Prize in Medicine or Physiology. He could not travel to accept the prize, as by then one of his patients had shot and paralysed him.

Moniz wrote positive reports of the surgery, which Walter Freeman, another US scientist, read and was transfixed by. Freeman had also been at the London meeting and he wrote to Moniz in 1936 with a plan to import the procedure to the United States. Freeman's name is mud in medicine now, but at the start he did recognize the risks he was taking, admitting that the scientific basis for the procedure was naïve. He knew that most brain scientists in the US were unimpressed with Moniz's work. One dismissed the whole idea of psychosurgery as burning down a house to roast a pig. But Freeman liked to think of himself as a pragmatist. He had no time for psychodynamics, and he saw how shock cures for mental illness introduced in the 1930s often did more harm than good.

Among these, electroconvulsive therapy (ECT), performed without anaesthetic, led patients to spasm and break bones. Deliberate insulin overdoses put others into terrifying comas for weeks. Meanwhile, the asylums of the United States had long overflowed. In 1937, over 400,000 patients were stuck in some 477 psychiatric institutions across the country. Conditions were dreadful and once a person had been in one for two years, they were unlikely to leave.

Together with the neurosurgeon James Watts, who had the license to operate that Freeman did not, Freeman introduced the Moniz procedure to the USA. Yet when the duo shared the results of their work with colleagues the following year they faced a hostile reaction, just as Burckhardt had done before them. John Fulton – the scientist who had set the ball rolling in London with his research on chimps – defended them (Watts had been one of his students). The work should continue, he said, but as careful clinical trials in the nation's top universities. The work continued, but the trials were never done. It was a pattern that would be repeated.

Fuelled by hype and uncritical reports of patients transformed, lobotomy spread across the country. Neurosurgeons in Florida, Pennsylvania and Massachusetts started to offer the operation. Its profile soared, helped when Freeman and Watts published dramatic accounts in a 1942 book *Psychosurgery* (a tome described by contemporary neurosurgeons as pulp nonfiction). The *New York Times*, *Life* magazine and *Newsweek* all hyped what some surgeons routinely called a miracle cure for America's ills. Joseph Kennedy, the father of John and Robert, took their sister Rosemary to Freeman. An editorial in the *Lancet* medical journal on 5 July 1941, while cautious, predicted that the prefrontal lobotomy would prove most useful to relieve acute anxiety and obsessions.

At the centre of the firestorm was Freeman, who became high on the fumes. Fed up with Watts denying lobotomies to patients he considered not severe enough, Freeman took matters into his own hands. He picked up an ice pick and started to perform a cruder version of the operation himself. The prefrontal lobotomy became the transorbital lobotomy – the ghastly hammer of the spike through the top of the eye socket followed by the destructive waggle.

Watts, disgusted, walked away. Freeman, disgusting, hit the road. He toured the states in a Winnebago camper van and offered lobotomies to all who wanted them, and many who didn't. When Freeman's lobotomobile rolled into town, mental hospitals saw a way to get long-term patients out of the door. The scientist-turned-surgeon would knock the patient out with ECT, and perform the operation there and then. No sterile conditions. No medical back-up. No over-sight.

In their decade together, Freeman and Watts recorded 625 operations. In the decade that followed, Freeman alone lobotomized 2,400 people. He managed 225 in less than a fortnight. One in Iowa died when the ice pick slipped as Freeman stopped to take a photograph. He lobotomized children. He lobotomized a 4-year old. Fulton was aghast. 'What are these terrible things I hear about you doing lobotomies in your office with an ice pick,' he wrote. 'Why not use a shotgun?' Lobotomy was much less traumatic than a shotgun, Freeman replied, and almost as quick.

Lobotomy was now divorced from neuroscience. No theory or hypothesis underpinned Freeman's actions. The operations were uncontrolled and the results largely unknown. Some did try to curtail this clinical drift. Surgeons in other countries had also started to perform versions of Moniz's prefrontal leucotomy (there is good evidence that Eva Perón was lobotomized in Argentina towards the end of her life) and in 1945 the UK hospitals board of control started an enquiry. Two years later it published the results of 1,000 cases where the surgery had been performed in England and Wales. Two-thirds of the cases were women. Significant numbers had OCD.

More than two-thirds of the lobotomized obsessional patients, the report claimed, had their problem removed or relieved. One of these was a 33-year-old man who was admitted to the Bristol Mental Hospital in June 1940 as Britain reeled from the fall of Paris to the Nazis and steeled itself for invasion. The man had a compulsive need to get his hair cut. He refused to eat and became severely emaciated. The Bristol psychiatrists diagnosed obsessional neurosis and performed a prefrontal leucotomy. The day after the operation, the man began to eat ravenously and he put on almost four stone in three months. All traces of his obsessions vanished, the doctors claimed. He left hospital, became engaged, obese and found a job as a railway station clerk.

The brain mutilations of what *Time* magazine called the age of mass lobotomies ended not because of protests and outcry, or due to a crisis of confidence or conscience from Freeman, but with a common allergy medicine. In 1952, a surgeon in Paris, Henri Laborit, noticed the sedative effect of antihistamine drugs and started to use them to calm people anxious before operations. It produced what he called 'euphoric quietude'. Word reached a psychiatrist called Pierre Deniker, who tried an antihistamine called chlorpromazine on his most agitated mental patients. He saw disturbed people who previously had to be restrained transformed and able to mix with others with no supervision. US authorities approved use of chlorpromazine in 1954. Even if there had been widespread demand for lobotomy, there was now no need. The chemical cosh had arrived.

Freeman never accepted that his miracle was redundant. He tracked down former patients and showed off what he claimed were boxes of letters of support from them. He need not have worried. His legacy was secure. Chlorpromazine and subsequent medications such as the SSRI drugs did not work for everyone with OCD and other conditions. Desperate cases remained. And so lobotomy, or a version of it, refused to die.

Mr V in India, the engineer with OCD who could not sign his pension, received an anterior capsulotomy, one of four neurosurgical procedures with their roots in lobotomy that are still performed on people with OCD. The others – cingulotomy, subcaudate tractotomy and limbic leucotomy – take a similar approach but hit slightly different targets. All are designed to disrupt signals in the brain circuits identified as important in the maintenance of obsessions and compulsions.

This kind of more limited psychosurgery first took place in 1947, inspired by the popularity of lobotomy, and it has continued ever since, largely under the public's radar. Collectively, it's called stereotactic surgery. Mr V's operation was stereotactic. So was the rogue attempt to cure the

heroin addict in Shanghai. And so was the disastrous operation performed in 1998 on a 58-year-old Kansas woman
with OCD called Mary Lou Zimmerman.

A former book-keeper, Zimmerman had suffered from
contamination OCD for thirty years. She wasted several
hours a day showering and washing her hands. Drugs and
counselling had not helped. When she saw surgery for
OCD advertised on the website of the Cleveland Clinic in
Ohio, she decided she had little to lose. A surgeon at the
clinic gave Zimmerman a combined capsulotomy and
cingulotomy. She had four pieces of brain tissue destroyed.
But something went horribly wrong. The operation left
Zimmerman crippled with brain damage. She developed
dementia, became mute and needed full-time care. Her
family sued and in June 2002, an Ohio jury awarded
Zimmerman and her husband Sherman $7.5m in damages.

Advocates of stereotactic surgery highlight two differences between it and lobotomy. The volume of brain
destroyed is smaller. And the lesion, the damage, is more
precisely targeted. The waggle has gone. That's because the
surgeons first draw up a three-dimensional map of the
brain, which they use to guide the placement of the electrodes. As technology has improved, so has this targeting.
In early stereotactic procedures surgeons clamped their
patients into crude metal frames and often fatally pierced
blood vessels by mistake. Mr V's operation was guided by
CAT and MRI scans of his brain's precise anatomy.

Still, just like early lobotomy, stereotactic surgery for
OCD has fierce critics. The procedure has certainly had its

shameful moments, just like lobotomy. In the late 1960s and early 1970s, scientists in Germany performed ethically dubious stereotactic psychosurgery on sex offenders and homosexuals. The Russian government was forced to ban stereotactic brain surgery for drug addiction in its hospitals in 2002; the Chinese, as we saw, followed in 2004. Scientists in Copenhagen have tried it to cure obesity.

Three months after his surgery, Mr V seemed to be doing well – that was all the follow-up that his surgeon reported. But there are concerns about the long-term impact on patients given these kinds of procedures. In a 2003 editorial in the scientific journal *Acta Psychiatrica Scandinavia*, titled 'Psychosurgery for obsessive-compulsive disorder – concerns remain', the clinical neuroscientist Susanne Bejerot warned that not enough is known about possible side effects. 'There is no doubt that neurosurgery can dramatically reduce obsessions and compulsions,' she wrote. 'The question is to what price.' Neurosurgery for mental disorders, she concluded, should only be allowed in controlled research settings – exactly what Fulton had urged in vain for lobotomy.

In 2008, a group of psychiatrists and neurosurgeons published a rare analysis of the long-term effects of stereotactic surgery for OCD. They tracked down all 25 patients (14 women and 11 men) who had a capsulotomy at the world-class Karolinska University Hospital in Stockholm between 1988 and 2000. (That is an important difference from lobotomy: the numbers of people involved are much smaller). Nine patients were classed as in remission, but only three of these showed no adverse effects. Ten patients were considered to have significant problems with mental ability or function. The more brain material they had lost in surgery, the worse they were. The team concluded that capsulotomy is an effective way to treat OCD, but carries 'a substantial risk' – and one larger than previously assumed.

Against these risks and warnings, neurosurgeons have to balance the impact on quality of life of OCD left unchecked. Life with a Yale-Brown score in the high 30s is no life at all. OCD may not provoke suicide, but plenty consider it. And some people with OCD who have improved after surgery are keen for others to try it too.

Gerry Radano was a cheerleader for psychosurgery. A former flight attendant, Radano developed severe contamination OCD when pregnant with her second child. Drugs and therapy did not work. Numerous psychiatrists told her she could not be helped. A decade on, she had lost the career she had wanted since she was a little girl and her husband walked out. Radano was selected by scientists at Brown University in Rhode Island for a new and experimental type of capsulotomy. Rather than physically drill into the skull, the surgeons used technology called gamma knife surgery. These machines – invented in the 1950s and common in the treatment of cancer – use radioactive cobalt to generate 200 beams of gamma radiation.

Alone, the streams of radiation are harmless, but focused to combine at a specific site in a tumour, or in the brain, they sizzle where they cross and fry surrounding cells. It's called non-invasive brain surgery, if a technique that burns holes in the brain can ever be non-invasive. In November 1999, Radano was treated for OCD with a gamma knife. She was the first to persuade her medical insurers to meet the $30,000 cost of the surgery. And she was the first to write a book, in which she described what she calls a miraculous recovery. Radano no longer talks publicly about the gamma knife procedure. The Brown University team put its work on hold in 2011 to investigate why several patients developed brain cysts, though it hopes to restart. The procedure is still done elsewhere.

Just as accidental damage to the brain can trigger OCD, so, in very rare cases, accidental damage can remove it. A 44-year-old woman in Iran was freed of severe obsessions and compulsions she had suffered since a teenager when she banged her head in a car crash. And a Canadian student called George inadvertently cured himself of his OCD when he tried and failed to commit suicide. Driven to desperation by his obsessions, George put a rifle in his mouth and pulled the trigger. The bullet did not kill him but it did give him a successful leucotomy. Do not try this at home.

Functional neurosurgery is not the only treatment of last resort for OCD. Other people have metal wires planted into their brains, attached to a battery that sends through them a powerful electrical current, which changes the way the surrounding neuronal circuits communicate. Called deep brain stimulation, the therapy arrived in the late 1980s, when it was found to reduce tremor in patients with

Parkinson's disease. Electrical stimulation seems to reduce the seizures in epileptic patients too. By the early twenty-first century, electrical wires in the brain were considered a form of reversible capsulotomy, and tried for depression and OCD. They have also been used to tackle obesity, alcoholism, drug addiction, anorexia and Tourette's.

Deep brain stimulation has a history as rich and controversial as lobotomy. Electrical modulation of the brain was recommended by Scribonius Largus, court physician to the Roman emperor Claudius, who suggested in AD 46 that a live electric fish be applied to the head of a patient who suffered a headache. It would fall to another former protégé of the lobotomy pioneer John Fulton to show that electricity could do a lot more to the brain than that.

Jose Delgado was born in 1915 in Ronda in the mountains of western Andalusia. He studied medicine at the University of Madrid and worked as a doctor for the Republicans in the Spanish civil war against Franco. In 1946 he won a fellowship to Yale University, and then took a job in the university's physiology department under John Fulton. Interviewed in 2005, Delgado said he had been determined to undermine his mentor's work on lobotomy. 'I thought Fulton and Moniz's idea of destroying the brain was absolutely horrendous,' he said. 'My idea was to avoid lobotomy, with the help of electrodes.'

Delgado is most famous for a publicity stunt at a bullring in Córdoba, back in Spain. He wanted to demonstrate the power of what he called his stimoceiver – radio-controlled electrodes he placed in the brain that delivered a sharp pulse of electricity at the touch of a button. In one stunning trial of the technology he allowed a fighting bull to charge him until, when it was just a few feet away, he remotely activated the stimoceiver placed in the bull's caudate nucleus. The bull skidded to a halt and Delgado, unhurt, made the front page of the next day's *New York Times*.*

Delgado experimented with people too. In the early 1950s he placed electrodes into the exposed brains of twenty-five patients at a Rhode Island mental hospital, mainly people with schizophrenia and epilepsy. He showed how electrical stimulation of the motor cortex could make people react with involuntary movements. One patient clenched his fist, even when he tried to resist. 'I guess doctor, that your electricity is stronger than my will,' he said.

Despite Delgado's intention to offer an alternative to lobotomy, he was dragged into a similar and public controversy. Some of this he courted. He wrote of possible two-way communication between the brain and computers, which would sieve neuronal activity and step in to correct abnormal patterns with electrical pulses. He was talking about detection and treatment of epileptic fits, but his rhetoric frequently strayed into the uncomfortable territory of mind and thought control. In 1969 he published a book called *Physical Control of the Mind: Toward a Psychocivilised Society*.

---

* Footage on YouTube.

In 1972 any distinction between lobotomy and brain stimulation in the public's eye dissolved when two Harvard researchers, Frank Ervin and Vernon Mark – one-time collaborators of Delgado – published their own book, *Violence and the Brain*. The duo provoked a national scandal with their suggestion that both brain stimulation and psychosurgery might help to calm the violent tendencies of rioters in American inner cities. Robert Heath, a neuro-surgeon at Tulane University, fanned the flames further when in 1972 he announced he had tried to reverse homo-sexuality through electrical stimulation of a gay man's brain while he had sex with a female prostitute.

Debate became so heated that the US Supreme Court weighed in with a series of announcements on whether 'government programs of thought control' were unconsti-tutional because they breached the First Amendment's protection of free speech. The court concluded that the state 'cannot constitutionally premise legislation on the desirability of controlling a private person's thoughts'. In a free society, 'one's beliefs should be shaped by his mind and his conscience rather than coerced by the state'.

Judges in Michigan used these grounds to halt a 1973 scientific experiment into anger and sexuality. A criminal sexual psychopath committed to a state mental hospital was to have electrodes placed into his brain to probe the reasons for his behaviour. The research team hoped to identify, stimulate and then destroy the brain regions responsible for the criminal's thoughts of sexual violence. The man consented to the experiment on his brain, which was approved by a scientific review committee and a human rights review committee. The court blocked it because it would contravene the convict's rights to freely generate ideas, even those of brutal rape.

In the same year, a Washington DC psychiatrist, Peter Breggin, published an influential article in the *Congressional Record* that said Delgado and other scientists who researched brain stimulation were as bad as the now-reviled lobotomists. Those whose thoughts deviated from the norm would be 'surgically mutilated', he said. Congress launched an investigation into psychosurgery, and Delgado returned to Spain.

Just like stereotactic surgery, the modern use of deep brain stimulation for OCD has its critics, who argue that experimental treatments for mental illness should be regulated more strictly and that more research is needed to check if they are safe and effective. History, once again, shows that these critics shouldn't hold their breath, or too much hope that stricter regulation will follow.

The National Commission investigation of psychosurgery set up after the badgering of Congress by Peter Breggin reported its findings in 1976. Despite misgivings, the report was favourable. The government, it suggested, should encourage further research. Kenneth Ryan, the chairman of the commission, told *Science* magazine at the time:

> We looked at the data and saw they did not support our prejudices. I, for one, did not expect to come out in favour

of psychosurgery. But we saw that some very sick people had been helped by it and that it did not destroy their intelligence or rob them of feelings. Their marriages were intact. They were able to work. The operation shouldn't be banned.

Ryan did not endorse Walter Freeman's technique of prefrontal lobotomy, but gave a cautious green light to the more selective stereotactic surgery such as cingulotomy. Still, the commission was nervous about possible side effects and potential abuse of psychosurgery. If the research was to continue, it said, the United States must make more effort to ensure it was safe. No patient should have psychosurgery, the commission said, unless details of their presenting symptoms, preoperative diagnosis, past medical and social history and – crucially – the outcome of their operation were recorded and stored in a new national registry. Psychosurgery should become a reportable operation, not something that could be done without public and professional scrutiny.

It never happened. Patients still wait for anyone involved to set up such a registry. The calls for caution have, once again, gone unheeded. The surgery, for OCD and other mental disorders, continues anyway. Long live lobotomy.

FOURTEEN

Politics and prejudice

The UK parliamentary record *Hansard* notes every word spoken in the House of Commons and the House of Lords since 1909. Winston Churchill's battles as First Lord of the Admiralty to convert the Royal Navy from coal to oil in the years before the First World War are in there. So is the famous putdown from Labour politician Denis Healey that to be attacked in a speech by Conservative rival Geoffrey Howe was to be savaged by a dead sheep. The compilers of *Hansard* have seen it all. But if they can still be surprised by a political turn of phrase, then Charles Walker probably managed it. In the summer of 2012, Walker, the Conservative MP for the Hertfordshire town of Broxbourne, told the House of Commons he suffered from OCD and had done so for 31 years. During a debate on mental health, Walker announced to the centre of British democracy that he was a 'practising fruitcake'.

He described his compulsions to count and turn off lights four times, and his fears of contamination – he must leave biscuit wrappers throughout the house because of anxiety around bins. He touched also on the darker side of OCD – the terror of thoughts he cannot control. He said:

> One is constantly striking deals with oneself. Sometimes these are quite ridiculous and on some occasions they can be rather depressing and serious. I have been pretty healthy for five years but just when you let your guard down this aggressive friend comes and smacks you right in the face. I was on holiday recently and I took a beautiful photograph of my son carrying a fishing rod. There was my beautiful son carrying a fishing rod, I was glowing with pride and then the voice started, 'If you don't get rid of that photograph, your child will die.' You fight those voices for a couple or three hours and you know that you really should not give into them because they should not be there and it ain't going to happen, but in the end, you are not going to risk your child, so one gives into the voices and then feels pretty miserable about life.

Following his speech, Walker received deserved plaudits for his honesty and his bravery, including from the prime minister. People wrote to thank him for raising the issue in such a public way. But he is not the first MP to talk about his obsessions and compulsions. Gerald Kaufman, the former Labour government minister, received a different reception.

At the height of a 2009 scandal over abuse of parliamentary expenses, Kaufman was ridiculed when he blamed (self-diagnosed) OCD for his decision to claim back £220 of taxpayers' money for the purchase of two crystal grapefruit bowls for his London home. He had identical bowls at his constituency home in Manchester, Kaufman said, and his OCD demanded that he repeat the same breakfast each morning: half a grapefruit, a bowl of muesli with semi-skimmed milk and a cup of coffee with a Rich Tea biscuit. Given what we've seen of OCD in this book, we shouldn't jump to conclusions. It's possible that Kaufman's thoughts did demand superior crockery. But it's much less clear why he thought the rest of us should pay for it.

Part of the reason that Charles Walker wanted to speak out, he said, was to tackle prejudice. That's a goal that lots of people credited me with, when they found out I was writing this story of OCD. They assumed I wanted to raise awareness. I didn't, not at the beginning at least. I hadn't faced prejudice, because I had kept my OCD to myself. Perhaps I feared prejudice and that's why I kept it a secret, but I don't think it was that either. I just didn't want people to know I was a practising fruitcake. I didn't want to accept it myself.

The reason it is important to raise awareness, I realize now, is more fundamental. The reality of OCD is scary for all involved. But it's not dangerous. Yet it can be, especially for people who believe the condition is nothing more serious than a need to wash hands. That's why it's necessary to show and talk about the reality of what OCD is and what it is not. That's why there's no bar of soap on the cover of this book.

On a rainy day in Wales in November 2012, the charity OCD-UK organized a series of talks and discussions at Cardiff University. On the bill were numerous experts – academic psychologists, psychiatrists and former sufferers turned advocates. And in the audience were people from across the UK with OCD. A room full of two hundred people with OCD sounds like the set up to a joke, the punch line of which would be something like 'and you should have seen the queue for the sink'. But for the people who attended it was a serious matter.

Many had brought along friends and family for support. Teenage girls were there with a best friend. Men in their twenties were accompanied by both parents. I heard one husband tell his wife, in the queue for their lunch, that only now did he understand her. Many of the attendees were probably confronting their OCD for the first time. Certainly some were speaking in public about it for the first time. Lots were in tears, while others sat in silence and shook their heads gently or closed their eyes as they listened.

Yvette sat a few rows behind me, towards the back. A few people craned their necks to look as she indicated she wished to speak and asked for the microphone. By the time she handed it back, all eyes were on her. Yvette wasn't keen to cooperate for this book, so what appears here is what she said at the open meeting, which was broadcast on the Internet, and no more.

Yvette (not her real name) was a secondary school teacher. She suffered from OCD and was visited by a particular type of intrusive thought. When Yvette drove her car, she could not shake the feeling that she had been in an accident. She worried that she might have knocked someone down as she drove through dark country lanes at night.

This is a fairly common obsession. The driver finds their thoughts are not relieved by a quick glance in the rear-view mirror, so sometimes they stop and reverse or circle around to check. They might get out and check their car repeatedly for damage, paint or blood. Some ring hospitals and ask if any victims of road traffic accidents have been brought in. One night, convinced she had hit someone yet equally certain that she hadn't, Yvette called and checked with the local police. No, the confused officer on the phone replied, there had been no such accident. But, why do you ask? Who are you? The police told the headmaster at Yvette's school about her enquiry, who then suspended her for nine weeks, while the school tried to decide if Yvette was a danger to the children. She had worked as a teacher for nine years. The kids she taught, Yvette said, understood her condition better than her colleagues.

Of course, those who work with children must be checked out. And Yvette was later able to return to work. But others are not so fortunate. Mental health advocates regularly deal with cases of people who have been separated from their families because a medical professional became alarmed when they reported harmless obsessions. Even when the facts of OCD are made clear, and the individual reunited with their family, the problems and the injustice can continue. If they go for a job that demands a criminal records check, and many do – in counselling or charities, for example – then the question of their mental health is often raised. In a section of the records check that asks for other relevant information, chief constables have the discretion to write: 'We are aware that this person was detained for a mental health problem at this institution. We are not aware that they are a threat to adults or children.' Would you give them a job?

Charles Walker raised this issue in his speech to Parliament. 'I am afraid that in our ultra risk-averse world, that is a career death sentence for those people.' In September 2012, after pressure from campaigners, the UK government did tweak the emphasis of the records check with respect to mental illness. Police are now asked only to report incidents they believe are relevant. The changes introduced an appeals procedure too. It remains to be seen how effective they will be.

A more fundamental way to sort this out is increased awareness. At first I thought awareness was a worthy sentiment but too vague and nebulous to address directly, but I was wrong. The more that OCD is cemented in the public consciousness as a behavioural tic, the more times that a Hollywood celebrity who likes to keep their house tidy describes themselves as having OCD, the more times companies cash in on the apparent quirks of the condition as a gimmick, then the more times people like Yvette suffer. Some National Health Service trusts in the UK demand their psychiatrists refer any parent who reports intrusive thoughts about harming children to child protection authorities.* One impact of that can only be that more parents with OCD fail to seek help, and so continue to believe they are a danger to their child when they are not.

We're getting there with other mental illnesses. Schizophrenia is no longer acceptable shorthand for a split personality – its use in that way was banned by the style guide at the *Guardian*, which told writers how to use language. People with autism are not expected to memorize and recall the order of three combined packets of cards. Some who suffer from depression may still be told to pull themselves together, but hopefully fewer than a decade or so ago. OCD is perhaps a more serious challenge because fewer people regard it as a serious illness.

The US television show *Monk* features a policeman with OCD – the defective detective – whose obsessive attention to detail gives him superior ability to solve crimes, even though he regularly has to interrupt interviews or stop pursuits of villains to touch and arrange objects. Jack Nicholson won an Oscar for his quirky and humorous portrayal of a misanthropic obsessive-compulsive in the film *As Good as it Gets*, who skipped down the street with a grin on his face to avoid cracks in the pavement.

Fed up with having to watch Nicholson play OCD for laughs, the Welsh actor and writer Ian Puleston-Davies co-wrote what he hoped would be a more realistic portrayal. Called *Dirty Filthy Love*, and with Michael Sheen in the lead

---

* The Department of Health says it does not instruct NHS trusts to do this.

role as an architect with both OCD and Tourette's, the 2004 ITV film won a Royal Television Society award the following year. In the two hours after it was screened, OCD-UK received 2,000 phone calls.

Puleston-Davies, who as I write this stars in the long-running British soap opera *Coronation Street*, has severe OCD and has described how intrusive thoughts can join him on stage – forcing him to think about when he last went to the toilet rather than his lines in a play. He based the script of *Dirty Filthy Love* on his own experiences. But even he admits that some scenes are unrealistic, particularly those when the lead character goes to a self-help group. Puleston-Davies had originally written the group as they appear – like a class sat around to learn how to speak Spanish. This was too dull for the producers. The final screened version, to his despair, looked more like something from *One Flew over the Cuckoo's Nest* – all white clinical walls and intense oddballs who rock in their chairs.

OCD gets a raw deal in the media, especially film and television. It's pretty clear why: obsessive thoughts are internal and hard to film, so the focus tends to fall on the compulsions. The distress is invisible, but the checks, the hand washing and the lining up of shirts in a wardrobe can appear sinister and funny, sometimes both at the same time.

In 2009, Paul Cefalu, an English professor at Lafayette College in Pennsylvania, investigated this media misrepresentation further. He published an article in *PMLA*, the house journal of the Modern Language Association of

252

America, called: 'What's so funny about Obsessive-Compulsive Disorder?' 'What distinguishes representations of OCD from depictions of other mental disorders', he wrote, 'is the frequency with which OCD is treated with humour and levity.'

Earlier incarnations of obsession were portrayed – by Edgar Allen Poe and others – in melodrama, tragedies and Gothic literature, Cefalu said. Yet more recent books and films suggest that sufferers of OCD 'can always be counted on to make us laugh'. The reason, and the answer to the question in the title of his essay, he decided, is irony. 'Not only is there something fundamentally ironic about the extent to which obsessives with OCD concentrate on tasks that they believe ridiculous, but compulsions, usually orchestrated to relieve underlying obsessions, tend to worsen the motivating obsession.'

OCD is funny, he says, because it is based on incongruity, and incongruity is funny. The action makes no sense, but even after it acknowledges its own senselessness, it carries on regardless. That makes OCD postmodern irony; slapstick misery.

Funny or not, some psychologists have suggested that peer pressure and societal expectations are crucial to the perception of obsession. People with OCD, they suggest, might experience less distress if they live in cultures where commonplace superstition makes their mental and behavioural rituals more acceptable. (If everyone around you touches wood for luck, you might feel less bothered about having to touch it compulsively to see off intrusive thoughts.)

Such acceptable and unacceptable cultural context for obsessions has been highlighted by the US academic Lennard Davis to explain the rise in the visibility and apparent prevalence of clinical OCD in the last few decades. In his 2008 book *Obsession: A History*, Davis writes:

> In the requirement that the behaviours produce marked distress in the person, how one arrives at distress is crucial. The same behaviour in different cultures might produce different results. In other words, it takes a community, a culture, a family to make an obsessive. If your behaviour, say the meticulous lining up of objects, is seen as an oddity, you will be distressed that you do it. If it is seen as the useful quality of a master bricklayer, then you will not be distressed.

Davis, a professor in the Departments of English, Disability and Human Development and Medical Education at the University of Chicago, argues that obsession – and OCD – is better framed as a disease entity, a temporary and fluid definition that shifts with culture and history; sometimes useful and valued, but sometimes malevolent and feared. Dickens' huge output, he says, shows he was an obsessive writer. We demand that lovers are infatuated with each other in films. We respond to driven athletes and single-minded musicians.

Plenty of psychologists and psychiatrists have taken issue with his argument already. It misleads to bundle all these different types of obsessive behaviour together, they say. It conflates the general definition of obsession and the clinical term, and in doing so it dilutes the significance of the latter. Here's my objection: when Davis writes that the distress caused by repetitive behaviour, to line up objects say, is subjective, he misses a crucial point. In my experience, and that of most people with OCD I've met, the compulsive behaviour does not cause distress, it lessens it. That is why we do it. As the character Mark Renton in Irvine Welsh's 1994 novel *Trainspotting*, puts it, to explain why he and his friends take heroin. It feels good. 'Otherwise we wouldn't do it. After all, we're not fucking stupid. At least, we're not that fucking stupid.'

My paternal great-grandmother's temper was legendary. It was said she could start a fight in an empty room. My OCD can cause me distress in an empty room. It doesn't need a community or a culture or a family to disapprove. I'm not that fucking stupid.

Davis is not alone in the quest for possible benefits to OCD. Plenty of writers on the subject, including some who should know better, are keen to point out the up-side of a personality that repetitively focuses on detail. Armed with little more than some vague references in his diaries to how his mind would fix on an object and would sometimes be taken by insane feelings of anger, some websites dedicated to mental illness claim that Charles Darwin had OCD. Others, in an apparent effort to challenge the view of OCD as a handicap, have credited Winston Churchill's obsessional nature for giving him the strength of character to see through the dark days of the Second World War. OCD helps defeat global fascism! Way to go Winston.

I can't think of a single positive thing about OCD. And I've thought about OCD a lot. In 1785, after a particularly rough Atlantic crossing to Southampton, the US inventor Benjamin Franklin designed a sea anchor – a submerged sail a ship could tow behind itself in the water to slow and stabilize itself in heavy seas.

People who live with OCD drag a mental sea anchor around. Obsession is a brake, a source of drag, not a badge of creativity, a mark of genius or an inconvenient side effect of some greater function. That's not to say that some people with OCD don't achieve great things. But – given what we have seen of how OCD might develop – that's only what you would expect, just as some people with OCD are criminals, teachers, politicians and writers. Some have it worse than others and some perform better than others. Certainly, some people with severe OCD are quite brilliant.

At Christmas 2009, a plaque was unveiled on the door of room 3327 on the 33rd floor of the New Yorker Hotel in Manhattan. It commemorates the life of electricity pioneer Nikola Tesla, who lived in the room for the last ten years of his life, and the confluence of numbers is no coincidence. Tesla was obsessed by the number three, one of a series of intrusive thoughts and compulsive behaviours that affected him his whole life.

Tesla wasn't diagnosed with OCD, but his experiences fit the model. Aged 5, he suffered a terrible trauma when his older brother Daniel was killed. Tesla always maintained Daniel died of injuries inflicted by a horse, but another account says Daniel fell down the cellar stairs and banged his head. Drifting in and out of consciousness before he died, he accused his younger brother of pushing him. In her 1981 biography of Tesla, US writer Margaret Cheney says:

> We can only speculate about the degree to which Daniel's death may have been responsible for the fantastic array of phobias and obsessions that Nikola subsequently developed. All we can say for certain is that some manifestations of his extreme eccentricity seem to have appeared at an early age.

As a teenager in what is now Croatia in the 1870s, Tesla indulged in what sounds like maladaptive daydreaming (see page 92). He would invent complex and detailed places and live there in his head, where he would meet people and make friends. As a student he opened a book by Voltaire and then felt compelled to read his entire works, close, he discovered with dismay, to one hundred volumes. As an adult he counted steps when he walked and had to calculate the cubic volume of his food and drink to enjoy it. He tended to dine alone. He had issues with touch and tactility and said he could not bear to feel other people's hair, 'except perhaps at the point of a revolver'.

Tesla's greatest invention was the alternating-current (the AC in AC/DC) motor. It revolutionized the supply and distribution of electricity and remains the basis for power in the modern world. Like many of his creations, he designed the motor in his head. 'Ideas came in an uninterrupted stream,' he said. 'The only difficulty I had was to hold them fast.'

As his fame and wealth grew, so did the impact of his obsessions and compulsions. He would dine each evening at exactly eight o'clock and needed a stack of eighteen clean linen napkins to wipe his cutlery. Walking the Manhattan streets to his laboratory, if he took a certain route he felt forced to circle the block three times before he could continue on his way.

By the Second World War, just as Walter Freeman was descending to his lobotomizing pomp and the hoarding Collyer brothers were at the height of their unwanted fame, Tesla's obsessions and compulsions ruled his life. His fear of germs meant even close friends could not approach him; he preferred the company of pigeons. He died alone in his hotel room in January 1943.

FIFTEEN

A new dimension

When I started to write this book I had an anxiety disorder. As you read it, I don't. That change is not as positive as it might seem – I still have OCD. But OCD is no longer *considered* an anxiety disorder. In May 2013, the American Psychiatric Association (APA) officially reclassified OCD as a different type of mental illness. It's now one of the obsessive-compulsive and related disorders, a new group that includes a handful of the OCD spectrum conditions we discussed in Chapter Five: body dysmorphic disorder, hair pulling, skin picking and hoarding disorder. It sounds a trivial change, but the implications are great – not just for OCD, but for the way we think about mental illness.

The APA reclassification, as well as the shift towards the concepts of the OCD spectrum and the autism spectrum, starts the important process of building connections between mental disorders, which traditionally have been viewed as separate. There is a strong link, for example, between OCD and post-traumatic stress disorder, PTSD. As we have seen, some people who suffer trauma develop

OCD. Yet others convert precisely the same kind of experience into PTSD, a particularly vicious mental syndrome linked to intrusive thoughts. The thoughts of PTSD usually show as harrowing memories, and when they strike, the sufferer seems to lose touch with reality. They re-experience the trauma as vividly as they did the first time, with all the accordant terror, fear and shock. They re-live the incident, time and time again.

PTSD and OCD can be triggered by the same event, and co-exist in the same person. Soldiers with post-traumatic stress disorder are ten times more likely to develop obsessions and compulsions. Studies of Israeli combat veterans from the 1982 Lebanon war show an elevated risk for OCD.

A US soldier called B.A. had both OCD and PTSD. By the time he received the help of Roger Pitman, a psychiatrist at Harvard University, B.A. was about 40 years old. Bored with high school, B.A. had looked for adventure in the army. He was a good soldier and a brave one. When, on a military exercise, an armoured personnel carrier fell onto its side and pinned its commander to the ground, B.A. ignored the risk of an explosion and crawled underneath to dig him out.

B.A. went to the war in Vietnam, where he served on helicopter gunships. He flew more than four hundred combat missions and won medals: two Purple Hearts and the Bronze Star. He was an all-American hero. He frequently volunteered for extremely risky missions to rescue soldiers in desperate situations and once jumped from his helicopter into an enemy boat armed only with a machete.

While he fought in Vietnam, B.A.* developed the symptoms of OCD. After he loaded his rifle, intrusive thoughts made him doubt that he had done so, which forced him to unload and load it again. He went through hundreds of bullets in this way. Further worried that a kink in the ammunition belt would jam his machine gun, while his buddies drank beer in the evenings B.A. would return to the helicopter and pass the ammunition through his hands to make sure it ran smoothly. Finished and walking back to his tent, the intrusive thoughts and the doubts would return, and so would B.A. to the helicopter to make sure. 'He's counting bullets again,' the other soldiers would shout. He was compelled to order and touch the sockets in his wrench kit and hoarded so many spare parts that he earned the nickname Requisition.

B.A.'s intrusive thoughts and OCD gripped his mind even during the mortal danger of warfare. Shot at from the ground during missions, he would compulsively count the tracer rounds headed his way. And when he shot back, he would count the rounds in sets of threes. During what the helicopter crews called a meat-run – the evacuation of the dead – as the landing helicopter's downdraft would blow away the ponchos that covered the waiting corpses, often those of fresh-faced and frightened teenage recruits they

---

* *A-Team* fans – B.A. really is the name used in the case report.

had carried into the area earlier that day, B.A. could not resist thoughts to count their feet, two by two. Some bodies had only one foot, and then B.A. would become distressed that his count had been thrown off and have to start again.

B.A. served two tours of duty in Vietnam and when he returned to the US, he was a psychological wreck. But nobody noticed – or cared. On discharge from the army, a military psychiatrist said B.A. had signs of anxiety but otherwise 'nothing unusual'. Ten years after Vietnam he went for help at a specialist mental health clinic for veterans. He was told: 'this too shall pass'.

B.A. beat his dog, destroyed furniture and mentally played out how he would shoot, stab and strangle people he met. He worked in a helicopter repair workshop, until the day he saw a shot-up aircraft from Vietnam and his reaction – a war hero who had flown four hundred missions – forced him to hide in the toilet.

B.A. would wash and rewash his hands – to get the 'dead stuff' off them –and repeatedly checked the stove and locks on the doors, sometimes driving eight miles home just to do so. He kept a machete under the bed, took a gun to the bathroom at night and would compulsively check he had a knife in his pocket a hundred times a day. Despite thinking to himself: 'This is stupid. What kind of an asshole am I?' he could not resist the thoughts.

By the time Pitman treated him several years later, B.A. had a baby son, who he was compelled to check on ten or twenty times each night. At the same time, he had to fight intrusive thoughts to strangle him. He could not close his eyes in the shower, because of the dread that someone would grab him. When his wife zipped up her dress, B.A. heard the sound and felt the chill of a body bag.*

B.A. is an extreme case but he is far from alone. A grim parade of people with OCD and PTSD and a mixture of the two, kicked into life by all sorts of terrible events, have trooped through psychologists' offices in recent times. Mrs Y, who was tied up and raped by a man who videoed the attack and forced her to watch it, afterwards felt compelled to arrange objects in her house into specific positions. That might seem an irrational response, but recall how the children would respond with ritual to their complex fears of situations beyond their control.

Aged 20, Miss B was enjoying a picnic with her family when an aircraft in distress looking to make an emergency landing approached. Seeing the family at the last minute, the pilot swerved, crashed and died. Miss B felt upset and guilty but her OCD only struck a few years later when, driving in heavy traffic, she inadvertently blocked an ambulance. In response, she developed obsessions about harming people, particularly by bumping into them, and found it difficult to walk through swing doors, in case she let them go and hit someone. When a friend of hers was murdered, Miss B then started to compulsively check her food to make sure it was not human flesh, and that crumbly dishes did not hide human ashes. When she menstruated, she could

---

* Pitman last saw him in 2000. 'He gets by,' he says.

not shake the idea that the blood belonged to someone she might have killed. As with all cases of OCD, Miss B knew her thoughts were absurd, but she could not stop them.

In 2012, scientists discovered a possible explanation for why some people who experience trauma can develop OCD or PTSD, or both. The scientists of the University of Arkansas worked with forty-nine women who had suffered physical or sexual abuse. Many had gone on to develop psychological problems. Gently asking them to recall how they felt during the assault and immediately afterwards, the researchers found those who experienced pure fear, and a sense of disgust they directed at their attacker, showed the symptoms of PTSD. But many of the women said they felt disgusted at themselves, even while the assault was ongoing. They were the ones who developed signs of OCD.

If this finding is correct then OCD and PTSD could overlap, with the degree to which someone leans more towards one or the other determined by their emotional response to the original trauma. Already, some psychiatrists think a similar mechanism could help explain the origins of other mental syndromes too. OCD, for example, might relate to schizophrenia.

As we know, the same strange thoughts strike everybody from time to time, and it is how someone responds to them – the different settings on our thought factories – that can help dictate if someone will develop OCD. Perhaps this response could play a role in selecting who will develop schizophrenia too. Take, for instance, an intrusive thought of stabbing an old lady in the street. If someone brushes it off as a weird idea that deserves no attention then it is unlikely to lead to mental illness. If they were to fight the thought, to try to make it go away, then as we have seen, they could develop OCD. And if they were to attribute the thought to another person, or the devil, or the CIA, then they could turn that same thought into schizophrenia.

There is some evidence for this. Those patients with OCD who also show symptoms of schizophrenia are usually those who show less insight. They are less aware than others with OCD that the strange thoughts and urges originate in their own head. Up to 40 per cent of people with schizophrenia also have OCD, while some OCD patients show signs of schizophrenia. Already, psychiatrists say some people suffer from schizo-obsessive disorder.

It makes sense. The problem is that such overlap in the causes and presentation of mental illnesses – OCD with schizophrenia and PTSD, for instance – threatens to undermine the current way that doctors and psychiatrists diagnose and treat psychiatric conditions. And not just those linked to OCD, but all of the rest too.

The American Psychiatric Association declared that OCD was no longer an anxiety disorder when it published the fifth version of what's commonly referred to as the bible of psychiatrists, the *Diagnostic and Statistical Manual of Mental Disorders* (DSM). The DSM is a list of officially recognized mental conditions and a reference tool for hard-pressed and busy doctors and psychiatrists across the world to diagnose their patients. More, it is a powerful focus for powerful forces. It is a ticket to the asylum for some and a ticket to riches for others. The inclusion of a condition in the DSM is an official stamp of approval and one that opens doors, especially so in the USA, where health insurance policies typically insist that a mental illness is DSM-listed before they pay out on a claim. A condition included in the DSM is one that psychiatrists can be paid handsomely to treat, and one for which pharmaceutical companies can supply expensive drugs.

The first DSM grew in the 1950s from the need for the postwar US military to gather information on how many of its veterans were affected by psychiatric problems. It was 130 pages long and listed 106 mental disorders, which it called reactions. OCD was listed as obsessive-compulsive reaction. The DSM has since been updated and revised several times. In the 1970s it dropped its controversial listing of homosexuality. By the time DSM-III emerged in 1980 it had swollen to almost 500 pages, which presented mental illnesses as products of the human condition in the way that the menu of a Chinese restaurant displays the products of its kitchen, with endless sub-categories added to try to account for sometimes very small differences.

DSM-III had 265 diagnosable disorders. DSM-IV followed in 1994, with 297 conditions across 886 pages. The new DSM-5 (the scrapping of Roman numerals was one of its less controversial changes) has about the same. In the DSM-5 obsessive-compulsive and related disorders have their own chapter, which gives the new grouping the same status as depression and schizophrenia. The DSM change implies that OCD and its related disorders have something in common. So, therefore, must the people who suffer from them. I have a new family.

On one level, it is irrelevant whether I suffer from an anxiety disorder or an obsessive-compulsive and related disorder. Labels to some extent are just that, labels. They can be peeled off and swapped around as fashion dictates. Some psychiatrists talk of 'treatment nihilism': the diagnosis – the official label – is irrelevant. They have drugs and treatments and they can try each of them in different doses and combinations until something works. That's a direct progression from the end-justifies-the-means approach of the behaviourists, and it's as far as you can get from the probing, causal analysis of Freudian psychodynamics. In some patients it works. But to work, it needs drugs and treatments to be available. And to work with more people, it requires new and better treatments and drugs to emerge. And here's the problem: the drugs aren't coming.

Just as public and political awareness of psychiatric illness is rising and more people are being encouraged to acknowledge their own mental problems and seek help, the drug industry we rely on to offer some of that help is in full retreat. Mental illness is too difficult. Drugs against it are too expensive to develop, because so many fail. Just as the APA has extended the OCD family, the industry has given up on us. Since 2011, the major drug firms GlaxoSmithKline, AstraZeneca, Pfizer, Merck and Sanofi have all ended or scaled back their research to develop new drugs to treat brain disorders. It now takes more than

13 years and more than a billion dollars to deliver a new psychiatric drug to market. Even nihilists have to pay the bills.

At present, it simply makes more financial sense for these firms to invest in areas of medicine where the chances of success and profit are higher. One reason for this retreat from mental illness is that drug companies and scientists are starting to realize that modern psychiatry is a castle built on sand.

The first two DSM books were based on Freudian psychodynamics, which dominated the field when they were written. Psychiatrists today often airbrush them away when they talk about the history of their discipline. The modern age of psychiatry, they say, began with the DSM-III in 1980.

That was when psychiatry got in touch with its scientific side and started to use evidence and empirical observations of patients to decide who was sick and what illness they had, rather than guesswork over childhood toilet habits. The DSM-III and the two versions that followed looked not to Freud but a different role model, one as far away from Freud as it is possible to imagine.

Emil Kraeplin was born the same year as Freud. They worked in the same field and they both spoke German, but the two men never met and never corresponded. They didn't agree on anything. Kraeplin had some unpleasant views on racial purity, but he was a true psychiatric scientist in the way that Freud was not. Kraeplin looked to biology for the causes of mental disorder, and he looked for evidence of how biology showed itself as common symptoms in his patients. He found plenty of both, and is most famous in psychiatric circles for using the results to identify and describe the syndromes we now call schizophrenia and bi-polar disorder. Crucially, Kraeplin said these were separate conditions, with different causes and unique outcomes.

Kraeplin's work was overshadowed by Freud's and lay largely unnoticed in academic journals for decades, until it was rediscovered and given fresh momentum by scientists in the United States in the 1960s. This re-emergence of the need for empirical evidence to identify and group patients set the tone for the DSM-III – and all of modern psychiatry since.

It's called the category approach and it places firm boundaries between different mental disorders, each of which are viewed as discrete conditions to be diagnosed and treated separately. It uses fixed criteria and checklists that psychiatrists compare to the symptoms of a patient. Those criteria and checklists are modified as more or fewer patients seen in the real world seem to correspond to them. A big part of the DSM revision process is to gather the data on how well the various categories seem to fit those who report mental illness – how efficiently sick people can be placed in the categorical boxes.

Unfortunately for Kraeplin – and for the countless millions of patients around the world who still rely on his ideas for help with their mental illness – it now looks like he, just like his great rival Freud, was wrong. Unlike in

Kraeplin's day, modern scientists have the tools to probe how accurately the various categories map onto genuine biological differences in patients. And as science has started to peek behind the curtain of psychiatry in this way, it has revealed the category approach to be a giant conjuring trick.

The most fundamental problem with the category approach is that people with a mixture of symptoms are believed to suffer from several different mental disorders at the same time. Psychiatrists call this co-morbidity. Patients call it confusing and demoralizing. At the most extreme, it's possible for a single person – who by definition can only have a single personality – to be diagnosed with three or four separate personality disorders simultaneously.

This problem arises because the underlying biology and pathology of most mental illnesses remain a complete mystery. No other branch of medicine relies so heavily on self-reported symptoms to make a diagnosis. No blood test can detect OCD. No X-ray can find depression. No biopsy can label someone as anxious or bi-polar. In this important respect, the science of psychiatry has hardly moved on since its earliest days. It is still based around the simple question: so how do you feel today? Depression, for instance, can be diagnosed with a check-list. Tick five items and you are depressed, tick four and you are not. It really is as arbitrary as that.

To improve the situation, neuroscientists have long searched for biological differences in patients they can use to distinguish the diagnostic categories of the DSM. They look for gene mutations implicated in depression, or a part of the brain that is smaller or larger in OCD, or more and less active in schizophrenia. These so-called biomarkers would be the first step to reliable tests. But they remain elusive.

This could be because there are no such biological differences. Studies show that various mental illnesses, such as schizophrenia and bi-polar disorder, have similar genetic signatures. They show that what the DSM describes as separate conditions seem, in fact, to have plenty in common. This has pushed psychiatrists to confront an awkward truth. The categories of the DSM probably don't reflect the situation on the ground. They may not exist at all. They do not, in a phrase they are fond of, carve nature at the joints.

This would be one reason why current treatments for mental illness fail so often. It's because people classified with depression, or OCD, or mania or whatever, and so grouped together by the listings of the DSM, are in fact different from each other, perhaps very different. And those differences mean that the same treatment won't help them in the same way.

That's something biologists are becoming more aware of as they learn about physical illness, where patients with the same disease also respond in radically different ways to identical treatment. A diagnosis of cancer on its own says nothing about a patient's condition, their day-to-day health and their survival chances. It's not even enough to stratify cancer by type – lung or breast for example – or even by the nature of the tumour. There are important differences between and within common types of tumours, and these differences can dictate whether a patient will, in many cases, live or die.

It sounds obvious. Of course two people with breast cancer or depression are different from each other. But without knowing why and how they are different, it's impossible to separate them, and equally impossible to link them to other people with a shared specific form of the illness. This separating and linking are essential to probe the underlying biology and so develop new drugs to target and treat them. It has taken decades of painstaking study of the way tumour cells live, die and interact, and a revolution in genetics, for oncologists to start to stratify their cancer patients. Psychiatrists can't do it as long as their solitary tool remains to ask people how they feel.

That's why the drive to establish links between mental illnesses and the reclassification of OCD as a disorder with something in common with other mental syndromes is important. Even though most psychiatrists acknowledge that the category approach is flawed, nobody is about to tear up the DSM; it's a product of politics as well as science. And existing categories do serve some useful purposes, such as helping to allocate treatment. They are likely to continue to exist for some time. A flawed but familiar system is better than nothing at all, right?

Not for research scientists, the people who patients and psychiatrists and drug companies all rely on to make the discoveries that will lead to better treatments. The category approach ties one hand behind their back. Here's why: To get a drug approved, it has to make sick people better. In psychiatric medicine, those sick people are those who have a DSM-listed disorder. That means clinical trials must be done with those same DSM groups – this drug for schizophrenia, this one for bi-polar. And so, for basic research to stand any chance of being converted to useful medicines, it must analyse the problems of those groups as well. Research with brain scans and DNA scans recruits patients with 'depression' or 'obsessive-compulsive disorder' as if they are two separate species. It's not just the DSM that is tied to the flawed category approach to mental illness, it's the entire scientific and medical system. Panels that award research grants and promotions to scientists, and journal editors who decide which research to publish, all tacitly support and follow it. They endorse it, even though many of them know it doesn't work and isn't based on science.

Given these shortcomings of the existing system, and the unwillingness to change, it does at least make sense to group together those DSM categories that seem to have the most in common. The conceptual shift in recent years to view autism as a spectrum of related conditions rather than an isolated problem has significantly changed the way it is considered by scientists, patients and the public alike. It may not have brought a revolution in treatment, but at least we understand those affected better now, and can help them to understand themselves. The creation of the OCD spectrum could do something similar.

In practical terms, the DSM shift to obsessive-compulsive

and related disorders means that research scientists now have official permission to ask for money to work on those conditions as if they are connected. In their studies they can group together people with OCD and compulsive hair pulling, for example, and look for things they have in common. It's a small step, but it does go some way towards breaking Kraeplin's stranglehold on psychiatry, just as Freud's was broken before.

Some neuroscientists argue we will never understand the brain and the mind and how they relate in mental illness until we unravel how the 90-odd billion neurons in the brain connect to each other, and how those connections form, break and re-arrange over time.

There are plans to draw up such a brain map – called the functional connectome. The connectome project assumes that it is not the performance of individual portions and regional segments of the brain that drives behaviour and motivation, but the careful choreography of many. That could explain why so many MRI studies of OCD brains give results that are all over the place. The brain is an orchestra, and to focus at any one time on the violins or the percussion section alone misses the point. The connectome conducts and the interplay of different regions of the brain, acting at the same time, delivers the symphony.

We see hints of this in the apparent importance of the circuit between the orbitofrontal cortex and the thalamus thought to play a role in OCD. That loop probably does not operate in isolation. More likely it draws input and variance from surrounding brain cells, and whatever affects them.

All this complexity means that, in the long term, the only way to develop better treatments for mental illness could be to scrap the category approach and go back to the drawing board. A different strategy would be to assume that the causes of mental illness are not divided according to the categories of the DSM, but are spread much more evenly through the population. The symptoms that emerge do so only when the causative agents – genes, environment, misfiring brain circuitry, whatever – reach a certain threshold. Diagnosis then becomes a matter of tuning in to the correct signal, rather than blindly punching clunky buttons until a crude approximation of a picture emerges.

This way of thinking about mental illness is called dimensionality. Blood pressure is dimensional, and so is weight. Both operate on a continuum and are best represented by a number. At some point, doctors class those numbers as too high, and they treat the patient for obesity or hypertension. Could something similar be done with mental health? The US National Institute of Mental Health thinks it could. It has launched a new project that aims to find biological traits in mental illness that, just like blood pressure, can be measured in everybody, and which can be classed as too high and then treated.

Anhedonia, for example, is a trait found in many mental illnesses, depression and schizophrenia among them. It's the inability to take pleasure from activities that should be fun

– exercise, hobbies, sex or just hanging out with friends. It's a good way to describe the sense in OCD that life is lived on autopilot. Anhedonia has been linked to malfunctions in the normal reward circuits and systems of the brain. In theory, as neuroscientists develop more powerful brain scans and better genetic tests, these malfunctions could be identified, measured and quantified. Anhedonia could be tested for, and it could be treated. People could get to feel better, and all without a diagnosis of depression or schizophrenia or both.

This idea of a continuum between mental illness and normality, and that our position on the scale is determined by how a circuit in our brain functions or malfunctions, feeds back directly to what we know about sub-clinical OCD. Some people with OCD get annoyed when others use the phrase 'a little bit OCD'. They think it trivializes their distress. They don't believe that someone can experience their own omnipresent misery in microcosm. I don't agree. As we saw with the results of the Dunedin longitudinal study in New Zealand that revealed the high number of non-clinical cases of obsessions and compulsions, plenty of people do experience life as a little bit OCD. Our reaction when people use the phrase should not be 'no you don't'. It should be: 'imagine that you can never turn it off'.

When I was a young kid and I first saw someone with a guide dog, I couldn't get my head round the idea that some people simply could not see. What about colours? Did they still find other people attractive? I used to try to find out what it was like by closing my eyes and then trying to do day-to-day stuff – walk downstairs or see if I could tell who was approaching from the sounds they made. The longest I ever lasted with my eyes closed was about twenty minutes.

I still have no real idea what it must be like to be blind. But I know how hard those twenty minutes were. People who say they are a little bit OCD probably have no real idea what it's like to have a full-blown mental disorder. But they do know how hard, or annoying or time-consuming or unusual, their little bit is. Now, imagine you can never turn it off.

The beauty of the dimensional approach to mental illness is that nobody need be 'a little bit' OCD at all. Why be so vague? We can put an exact number on it. Everybody can take the Yale-Brown test. Everybody can have their own OCD score. That's the dimensional approach to mental illness right there. OCD is not present or absent, it's a Yale-Brown score of 6, 11 or 26.*

A dimensional approach – the scoring of certain symptoms on a sliding scale – is especially useful to psychiatrists because OCD is not the only mental illness that lurks at sub-clinical levels in the general population. Signs of sub-clinical psychoses – the most severe conditions – are everywhere. Surveys show that about a quarter of normal people say they have some experience of hearing voices in

---

* You can take the Yale-Brown test online at http://psychology-tools. com/yale-brown-obsessive-compulsive-scale.

their heads, or of their own thoughts being spoken aloud. In 1999, psychologists in London measured what they called delusional ideation in 272 normal people and found that most of them endorsed what could be considered symptoms of psychosis. Almost half said they believed in the power of witchcraft, voodoo or the occult, and six in ten believed in telepathy. More than four in ten felt they were very special or unusual people and more than a third thought there was a special purpose or mission to their life. When the scientists compared the scores from the normal population and the results from similar tests performed with patients at an acute psychiatric unit, they found that one in ten of the people considered normal scored above the average rating of these medicated and 'floridly psychotic' patients. Now, imagine you can never turn it off.

SIXTEEN

Final thoughts

This should probably be the point in the book where it all comes together. Having discussed the possible causes of OCD – the genetic, evolutionary, family, social, Freudian, environmental, infectious, psychological, medical, traumatic and just plain unfortunate pressures that might contribute – I should reach a triumphant and emotional conclusion. I should explain my own OCD. It was my parents what did it or my childhood fear of dogs, or the shock when I wrapped myself and my brand new ten-speed bicycle around a barbed wire fence at high speed. The sore throat I had when I was 6, or 8, or 13. The betrayal by the boy I thought was my friend who called me into a deserted school toilet so four of his mates could hit and kick at me in the dark. That my mother had a stroke and couldn't hold me as a baby, and that my dad – an arch rationalist – can't bear to look out of high windows. The trauma of Stoke City's relegation in 1985 and 1990 (by 1998 it was too late). The psychological conflict I suffered and buried when I was cruelly separated from my faeces and potty trained.

The death of Sebastian my pet rabbit. That fucking Aids advert.

It's not there. I don't know. A teenager in the United States said his OCD, centred like mine on an obsessive fear of Aids, started when he almost slipped and fell to his death from a high cliff. I've had near misses and I've fallen off my share of things and into things, but I seem to have bounced.

What I do know is that my OCD probably didn't start when I was 19. That was when I went full-blown, but the signs were there before. I was sub-clinical. On a caravan holiday in the late 1970s, I remember that I checked the gas fire was switched off dozens of times before I could sleep. We didn't have a gas fire at home and my dad had told me it was important that we didn't leave it on. He and mum slept in a different room. My little brother didn't know about the danger. It was my responsibility.

As a 10-year-old I would write the names of people who had wronged me in a special book. It became a nightly ritual that seemed to help dissipate anger and hurt. If I had an argument and then bad thoughts about my parents, I would have to punish myself and undo the damage by trying to sleep without the duvet. When I was 13, having watched the black and white film the previous Sunday, one day at school I felt like I had to hum the Dambusters March to myself during a maths lesson. I did it for months, but only in maths.

One of my earliest memories is a feeling I had to tap out numbers from one to ten when I heard someone say them out loud. I was probably 5 or 6 years old and sat cross-legged in assembly hall at my primary school. As I tapped the floor I remember a teacher watched me. She gave an awkward smile. The previous day I had learned two things that were important: that it hurt when someone hit you in the face. And that it hurt more when someone let you down.

This is probably the closest we will get to the genesis of my condition. It could of course be a creation myth: it was summer and we were playing on the field behind the school. The grass had been mown that morning and smelled sweet. I heard cries and saw a friend pinned to the ground by an older boy. Just like in the cartoons, I threw myself at the assailant and we kicked up the cut grass as we rolled. The older boy finished on top, and, startled and annoyed, started to punch me. My friend stood and watched. Worse, as I spat the grass from my mouth and wiped tears on my blue Miami Dolphins T-shirt as we walked back together when the bell rang, I heard my friend say there was no space in our gang for boys who cried. I saw the older boy at assembly the next morning and he ignored me. When I saw my friend sitting a couple of rows away, I wanted to cry again. Instead I started to count.

This is not intended as a self-help book. But if it does help, if it connects to someone directly affected by the issues it raises, or helps someone close to them to understand, or if it can merely prise open the eyes of others, then I am glad. Something good will have come from what was a frightening and miserable experience. My strange thoughts will finally have meant something.

If you are distressed by intrusive thoughts, if you think you might have OCD, then the bad news is that it probably won't go away by itself. The good news is that scientists are constantly finding out more about the condition and the best way to diagnose and treat people with it. The idea of mental contamination, for example, is really starting to take off. It just takes a while for these ideas to soak through to clinical practice, for even experienced and overburdened mental health workers to catch up.

Not everyone who wants professional help can get it. Tell someone about your thoughts, a friend or a relative. If you're worried about their reaction then show them this book first. Most likely, they will have those kinds of thoughts too. The only difference is that their thought factory works differently from yours. Try the Internet. There are web forums and blogs that allow people to anonymously share their stories with others who will understand. OCD charities help people like you – confused, frightened, convinced your thoughts are different – every single day. Tell someone. If you want to defeat a vampire then you can chase it with a wooden stake or holy water, or mess about with crucifixes and garlic, or throw seeds at it to count, but it's more effective to throw open the curtains and let in the light.

If you find it hard to talk about your thoughts then you are not alone. When I signed the deal to publish this book, I told the publishers they could not announce it. I needed to tell my parents and brother and my friends about my OCD first. If it helps, the charity OCD-UK has produced a simple introduction to the condition that you can print off its website and give to people. It's intended to help break the ice with health professionals, but will work just as well on friends and family. There is also a specific ice-breaker for those who have intrusive thoughts about hurting children. Both are published as an appendix to this book.

It's not often possible to cure OCD in the conventional sense. Even on the drugs and after CBT, if they work, then for most people it's a bit like being a recovering alcoholic. You are always a certain number of days past your most recent obsessive-compulsive episode. You are always one drink from disaster. Most people with OCD can't be cured, but they can be helped to manage their condition and they can be helped to feel better. In many cases, they can feel much better. I feel much better. But I will probably always have OCD. The psychiatrists who helped me have warned that it will be a lifelong struggle. My case is still open and I am still on their books. I am still their patient. I have an open invitation to go back and see them again, if I think it's necessary.

I don't think it will be. My OCD rarely causes me distress now. It's still a constant companion and the intrusive thoughts on HIV continue to come – the snowflakes still tumble from the summer sky. But I have learned how to watch them come and go. They don't settle in my mind, not always. But every now and then, one catches me unawares.

*

In the spring of 2012, life was pretty good. It had been a year since I last saw the psychiatrists at the mental health unit, and almost eighteen months since they had told me to rub my eyes again. A baby boy had joined our family and my daughter was flourishing. I had spoken to a literary agent about writing a book on OCD and had started to sketch out some ideas.

I went for a skiing holiday to the French Alps with some friends. I'm no Markus Wasmeier but I love to ski. It's the activity that comes closest to recreating the impact of a Stoke City goal. When I throw myself down a mountain on skis, the intrusive thoughts can't touch me. And I don't need to count backwards from 999 to keep them away, the combination of exhilaration, physical effort and the concentration required to keep me upright does that for me.

About halfway through the week, on an early run before the morning warmth had melted the crispy ice layer that coated the snow, one member of our group had a nasty fall. He wasn't wearing a helmet and his face took the full force. He was briefly unconscious and his mouth and nose were bleeding badly. I tend to tense up when there is blood around and I was happy when the others agreed to my suggestion that I would head down to find help. As I clicked my boots into my skis, I saw one of my friends pass our fallen comrade her blue water bottle.

Later that morning, the temperature had soared as the sun flew high in the thin mountain sky. There were two of us now, and we laughed and poked fun at each other as we struggled with a bumpy mogul field. The secret, apparently, is to turn the skis on the top of the bump, just as the secret to beat OCD is not to perform the compulsions. It's almost as hard. It's even harder for someone on a snowboard, as my friend was, so she took a shortcut out and was waiting for me at the bottom. Drenched in sweat, I pulled off my hat and scarf. She removed the lid and offered me her water bottle. Her blue water bottle.

I looked at the bottle and at her. As I hesitated, she put it to her lips and took a long slurp. Then she passed it back to me. She didn't know about my OCD. She didn't know that I had spent more than twenty years trying, largely successfully, to avoid moments like this. She couldn't hear the screams in my head that urged me not to take the bottle. She didn't see the panic flash across my mind. I took the bottle, and I took a drink from it. I passed it back with a mumbled thank you. She put the lid back on and she moved on with the rest of her life.

In therapy, the subject of what is an irrational thought and what is therefore a compulsive response to an obsession was one of the things we discussed. Most people would be anxious about HIV if they jabbed themselves with a bloody needle they found on the floor, but most people, I was surprised to learn, would not be anxious about touching a door handle if they had a bleeding finger. Most people, it turns out, though you probably know this already, are more concerned about them dripping blood onto the handle than they are that anything on the handle will pass into their blood. Most people are weird.

What would most people do? That has become my

response to an intrusive thought. If most people would do something, then, to keep away the nonsense of OCD, so must I. That was another part of my treatment.

So when my friend took a drink from the blue bottle that I feared was contaminated with my other friend's red blood, I knew what I had to do. It wasn't easy, but she wouldn't have noticed anything amiss. In the time it took me to raise the bottle to my lips and take a drink, two decades of intrusive thoughts and my responses to them flooded my mind. HIV is a fragile virus. It can't live long outside the body. Lots of infected blood would have to enter my mouth. It would have to get into my bloodstream. I have no open cuts in my mouth. The virus would perish in the acid of my stomach. My injured friend is married, he has a child and his wife is pregnant. They test for HIV in pregnancy. The water would dilute it. Did he actually bleed into the water? Maybe it's a different bottle. He doesn't have Aids. How can you be sure? How can you be sure it's safe to drink? We can't be sure of course. That's the point.

I might have escaped from the thoughts, but a couple of hours later the bottle came out again. 'Ha! I hope he's right when he told me he doesn't have any blood-borne diseases,' she said as she took another gulp.

I didn't ski the next day, I surfed the Internet. I read how HIV was a fragile virus. How it can't live long out-side the body. How lots of infected blood would have to have entered my mouth. How it would have to get into my bloodstream. How the virus would perish in the acid of my stomach. I turned the computer off and then turned it back on and read it all again. I found and tried to decode scientific papers on virology. And with every Google search I found page after page of people on Internet forums dedicated to OCD and to HIV who were desperate for the same impossible certainty as I was. I told my friends I was working on the book.

The anxiety came and went and then came back again every time I turned the computer off and on. This is where the therapy helped. I knew what I had to do. I had to ignore the thoughts, resist the compulsion, let the anxiety build, and then let it decay to extinction all over again. That's what I've learned. I've done it many times since. The hardest thing is that the anxiety each time feels just as severe as it has always been. The fear is as acute. The sense of impotence is just as debilitating. It feels like I am thrust right back into the maelstrom again, each and every time. But I trust, and I know, that it will pass.

The journey is almost at an end, but before we finish I must offer sincere apologies to anybody who reads this book and is offended by the way I have throughout used HIV as something to be feared and avoided. I have portrayed life with HIV as something so bad that I have spent my life without it worrying about it. I know that, somewhere deep down, I can make the choice not to worry about HIV. Someone who is HIV-positive cannot.

All I can say is that to me HIV is no longer the reality of the virus and the disease, it has become instead a symbol of a lost life, a destiny denied. It has become something to fear in its own right, not because of the consequences – perceived or otherwise. If I was to prick my finger on an executioner's axe before he lifted it to remove my head, my final thought as he brought the blade down would be if his previous victims had left behind contaminated blood.

The celebrated Danish children's author Hans Christian Andersen probably had OCD. He was plagued by obsessive thoughts, way darker than anything that appeared in his fairy tales. A dreamy child – he spent much of his time with his eyes closed – Andersen the man converted his thoughts to classically compulsive behaviour. He had to rise several times each night to confirm he had extinguished the candle by his bed, ruined many an evening out with doubts about whether he had locked the front door and became anxious when he posted letters that he had mixed up the envelopes or written the wrong names.

Andersen did see his obsessions as the flip side of the creative imagination that made him wealthy and famous.

I possessed a peculiar talent, that of lingering on the gloomy side of life, or extracting the bitter from it, and tasting it; and understood well, when the whole was exhausted, how to torment myself.

He showed all the signs of inflated responsibility. Once given a banknote in his change in a Frankfurt restaurant, he later described in a letter to a friend how he discovered it was not legal tender. After he posted the letter, he became consumed with thoughts that his comment would lead to the waiter being fired. So he returned to the post office and retrieved it. He feared being burned in a house fire, so in his trunk he carried a rope he could use to escape from an upstairs window. He had the obsessive fear that he would be buried alive, and left a note by his bed on which he had written 'Jeg er skindød' or 'I only appear to be dead.'

Andersen said once of his work:

> There is something elevating, but at the same time some-thing terrific in seeing one's thoughts spread so far, and among so many people; it is indeed, almost a fearful thing to belong to so many.

This book is my thoughts spread so far. You cradle them as you turn these final pages. I belong to you now and to so many. I'm not fearful though, it feels wonderful.

There is a point towards the end of a live album recorded by the Los Angeles band Jane's Addiction when their perfor-mance dissolves into audience noise, drums and breathless vocals. It's a glorious mess and from it emerges their version of the song 'Rock & Roll' by the Velvet Underground. That was the music I listened to on that sunny 1991 summer's day, just a few hours before my intrusive thoughts would turn into obsessive-compulsive disorder. The tape was still in the machine the next morning.

In my more melodramatic moments, I used to believe that listening to that subtle shift from song to song was the moment my happiness ended. I found it impossible to listen to that tape for years. Working for the *Guardian* more than a decade later I got to interview the band's singer, the man who offered the soundtrack to my own transition. I wanted to kick him. I wanted to hug him. (I had my photo taken with him.)

My happiness did not end that day, but it was the last time that I felt happy – truly happy – for a long time. It was the last time that my thoughts were free to move and to transform. Even if what my mind produced was banal and uninspiring, it was spontaneous. It was my thought, my idea. It was not pre-ordered by OCD or programmed millions of years ago by evolution or performed by well-drilled electrical and chemical signals in my brain or broadcast as an inevitable sequel of my psychological history. It was new. It was mine.

Lots of people have asked me whether to write this book will help me. They mean, I think, whether it will help me address my OCD, to come to terms with the condition and to challenge my illness. I think it probably will. But, more importantly to me, this book is new and it is mine. To write it has reminded me how I felt on that summer's day and shown me I can feel that way again. This book and the journey it involves have proven to me that OCD no longer holds my thoughts captive. They are free to dissolve to glorious mess. And from that, they can begin again.

ACKNOWLEDGEMENTS

My name is on the front, but a bunch of people helped to make this book. My agent Karolina Sutton turned a series of rambling thoughts into a solid idea. Liz Gough and then Cindy Chan at Pan Macmillan, together with Jon Butler, helped me translate that idea into a manuscript. Iain Lauchlan, Adam Rutherford, Tim Radford and Jack Rachman all commented on drafts. I asked Geoff Brumfiel to be rude about some early pages and he was.

Numerous friends and colleagues have encouraged and improved my writing over the years. I unfairly single out three for particular thanks: Vanessa Bridge, Peter Aldhous and Emily Wilson.

Sincere gratitude to Professor Naomi Fineberg and her team at the QEII Hospital in Welwyn Garden City for their compassion and professional insight; God bless the National Health Service. Thanks to Tim Appenzeller for giving me time off from a new job to attend their sessions.

Apologies to the friends who will say: 'gosh, I had no idea'. I did tell a handful and still appreciate the help offered by Debbie Brunt, Elaine Bond and Joy Edmondson. Thanks also to Andy and Tony Bailey, Giles Millington and my brother Douglas for times on the Boothen End that meant more to me than you knew.

As a father I understand how hard it must have been for my Mum and Dad to now learn what I kept from them. Their positive reaction since only emphasizes my original folly. Love and thanks to my wife Natalie for her patience, understanding and support. I do this for Lara and Dylan, my new obsession.

NOTES AND REFERENCES

A note on sources

Most case studies in this book are drawn from accounts published in scientific and medical reports, written by the doctors who treated them and the scientists who have researched their conditions. These people allowed their lives to be described in this way on the condition they were granted anonymity. As such, I have not tried to contact them or to identify them. I hope I have done their stories justice. Names have been changed and invented throughout, but where a given name was included in the original report, I have used it too.

Suggestions for further reading

A good place to start for more on the science of OCD is *Obsessive-Compulsive Disorder* by Dan Stein and Naomi Fineberg (Oxford University Press, 2007).

The most comprehensive and up-to-date academic review of the science of OCD and related disorders I have found is *The Oxford Handbook of Obsessive Compulsive and Spectrum Disorders,* edited by Gail Steketee (Oxford University Press, 2012).

For more on human stories of OCD it's still hard to beat *The Boy Who Couldn't Stop Washing* by Judith Rapoport (Penguin, 1991).

A recent memoir of life with OCD is *The Woman Who Thought Too Much* by Joanne Limburg (Atlantic Books, 2010).

A good general account of OCD is *Tormenting Thoughts and Secret Rituals* by Ian Osborn (Dell Publishing, 1999).

For an alternative view on OCD see *Obsession: A History* by Lennard Davis (University of Chicago Press, 2008).

For a scientific exploration of the nature and importance of intrusive thoughts see *Intrusive Thoughts in Clinical Disorders,* edited by David A. Clark (Guildford Press, 2005).

Rachel Herz has written a book that describes the emerging science of disgust: *That's Disgusting* (W. W. Norton, 2012).

For more on Freud and Lanzer see *Freud and the Rat Man* by Patrick Mahony (Yale University Press, 1986).

For more on Esquirol and monomania and the politics of the era see *Console and Classify* by Jan Goldstein (University of Chicago Press, 1987).

I glossed over a century or so of important medical and scientific thinking on OCD in the nineteenth century. For a fuller account see German Berrios, 'Obsessive-compulsive disorder: its conceptual history in France during the 19th century', *Comprehensive Psychiatry* Volume 30 (1989) pp. 283–95.

For more on the Collyer brothers see *Ghosty Men* by Franz Lidz (Bloomsbury, 2003).

For a fuller account of the history of lobotomy see *Great and Desperate Cures* by Elliot Valenstein (Basic Books, 1986).

For more on the development of drugs for OCD and other psychiatric conditions see David Healy's *The Psychopharmacologists* series (CRC, 1998–2000).

I wrote a feature article for *Nature* on the problems with the DSM and the category approach to mental illness: 'On the Spectrum', *Nature* (25 April 2013).

For a biography of Nikola Tesla try *Tesla: Man out of Time* by Margaret Cheney (Touchstone, 2001).

References

ONE: Our siege mentality

1 'Bira', Y. Baheretibeb *et al.*, 'The Girl Who Ate Her House – Pica as an Obsessive-Compulsive Disorder: A Case Report', *Clinical Case Studies*, 7 (2008), pp. 3–11.

2 'Four thousand thoughts', D. Clark and S. Rhyno, 'Unwanted Intrusive Thoughts in Nonclinical Individuals' in D. Clark (ed.), *Intrusive Thoughts in Clinical Disorders* (Guildford Press, 2005), p. 1.

8 'Marcus prodded himself blind', A. Torres *et al.*, 'Loss of Vision Secondary to Obsessive-Compulsive Disorder: a Case Report', *General Hospital Psychiatry*, 31 (2009), pp. 292–4.

8 'six hours', A. Ruscio *et al.*, 'The Epidemiology of Obsessive-Compulsive Disorder in the National Comorbidity Survey Replication', *Molecular Psychiatry*, 15 (2010), pp. 53–63.

9 'between 2 per cent and 3 per cent' and 'fourth most common', Karno *et al.*, 'The Epidemiology of Obsessive-Compulsive Disorder in Five US Communities', *Archives of General Psychiatry*, 45 (1988), pp. 1094–9.

9 'World Health Organization', C. Murray and A. D. Lopez, 'Global Burden of Disease: A comprehensive assessment of mortality and disability from diseases, injuries and risk factors in 1990 and projected to 2020', *Global Burden of Disease and Injury Series*, vol. I (Harvard School of Public Health, 1996).

9 'more severe than diabetes', L. Koran *et al.*, 'Quality of Life for Patients with Obsessive-Compulsive Disorder', *American Journal of Psychiatry*, 153 (6) (1996), pp. 783–8.

9 'wait a decade', M. Demet *et al.*, 'Risk Factors for Delaying Treatment Seeking in Obsessive-Compulsive Disorder', *Comprehensive Psychiatry*, 51 (2010), pp. 480–85.

9 'men and women', C. Lochner and D. Stein, 'Gender in Obsessive-Compulsive Disorder and Obsessive Compulsive Spectrum Disorders', *Archives of Women's Mental Health*, 4 (2001), pp. 19–26.

9 'It begins usually', C. Carmin *et al.*, 'OCD and Spectrum Conditions in Older Adults', in G. Steketee, *Oxford Handbook of Obsessive Compulsive and Spectrum Disorders* (Oxford University Press, 2012), p. 455.

10 'unemployed', A. Torres *et al.*, 'Obsessive-Compulsive Disorder: Prevalence, comorbidity, impact and help-seeking in the British National Psychiatric Morbidity Survey of 2000', *American Journal of Psychiatry*, 163 (11) (2006), pp. 1978–85.

10 'unmarried', L. Koran, 'Quality of Life in Obsessive-Compulsive Disorder', *Psychiatric Clinics of North America*, 23 (2000), pp. 509–17.

10 'live with their parents', G. Steketee and N. Pruyn, 'Families of Individuals with Obsessive-Compulsive Disorder', in R. Swinson *et al.*, *Obsessive-Compulsive Disorder: Theory, Research and Treatment* (Guildford Press, 1998), pp. 120–40.

10 'divorce', A. Torres *et al.*, 'Obsessive-Compulsive Disorder: prevalence, comorbidity, impact and help-seeking in the British National Psychiatric Morbidity Survey of 2000', *American Journal of Psychiatry* 163 (11) (2006), pp. 1978–85.

10 'fail to recognize', K. Wahl *et al.*, 'Obsessive-Compulsive Disorder is Still an Unrecognised Disorder: A study on the recognition of OCD in psychiatric outpatients', *European Psychiatry*, 25 (2010), pp. 374–7.

10 'two-thirds of sufferers never see', J. Calamari *et al.*, 'Phenomenology and epidemiology of obsessive-compulsive disorder', in G. Steketee, *The Oxford Handbook of Obsessive Compulsive and Spectrum Disorders* (Oxford University Press, 2012), p. 36.

12 'Kurt Gödel', H. Szechtman and E. Woody, 'Obsessive-compulsive disorder as a disturbance of security motivation', *Psychological Review*, 111 (2004), pp. 111–27.

TWO: Bad thoughts

15 'survey after survey', P. Salkovskis and J. Harrison, 'Abnormal and Normal Obsessions: A Replication', *Behaviour Research and Therapy*, 22 (1984), pp. 549–52.

15 'off the road', C. Purdon and D. Clark, 'Obsessive Intrusive Thoughts in Nonclinical Subjects: Part 1. Content and relation with depressive, anxious and obsessional symptoms', *Behaviour Research and Therapy*, 31 (1993), pp. 713–20.

15 'high-place phenomenon', J. Hames *et al.*, 'An Urge to Jump

Affirms the Urge to Live: An empirical examination of the high place phenomenon', *Journal of Affective Disorders*, 136 (2012), pp. 1114–20.

15 'Stanley Rachman', S. Rachman and P. de Silva, 'Abnormal and Normal Obsessions', *Behaviour Research and Therapy*, 16 (1978), pp. 233–48.

21 'Winston Churchill', I. Osborn, *Tormenting Thoughts and Secret Rituals* (DTP, 1999), pp. 56–7.

22 'idea generator', D. Clark and S. Rhyno, 'Unwanted Intrusive Thoughts in Nonclinical Individuals', in D. Clark, *Intrusive Thoughts in Clinical Disorders* (Guildford Press, 2005), pp. 18–19.

22 'Mozart . . . Beethoven', S. Rachman and R. Hodgson, *Obsessions and Compulsions* (Prentice Hall, 1980), pp. 10–11.

23 'Arnold Schwarzenegger', N. Berman *et al.*, 'The "Arnold Schwarzenegger Effect": is strength of the "victim" related to misinterpretations of harm intrusions?', *Behaviour Research and Therapy*, 50 (2012), pp. 761–6.

24 'under stress', L. Parkinson and S. Rachman, 'Part III – Intrusive Thoughts: The effects of an uncontrived stress', *Advances in Behaviour Research and Therapy*, 3 (3) (1981), pp. 111–18.

24 'Tolstoy', R. Bartlett, *Tolstoy: A Russian Life* (Houghton Mifflin Harcourt, 2011), p. 53.

24 'Playboy', D. Wegner and D. Schneider, 'The White Bear Story', *Psychological Inquiry*, 14 (2003), pp. 326–9.

25 'worst thing', D. Wegner, 'How to Think, Say or Do Precisely the Worst Thing for Any Occasion', *Science*, 325 (3 July 2009), pp. 48–50.

25 'Tolstoy trial', D. Wegner *et al.*, 'Paradoxical Effects of Thought Suppression', *Journal of Personality and Social Psychology*, 53 (1987), pp. 5–13.

26 'quit cigarettes', B. Toll *et al.*, 'The Relationship Between Thought Suppression and Smoking Cessation', *Addictive Behaviors*, 26 (2001), pp. 509–15.

26 'obese', B. Soetens and C. Braet, 'The Weight of a Thought: Food-related thought suppression in obese and normal-weight youngsters', *Appetite*, 46 (2006), pp. 309–17.

26 'resurface in a dream', R. Bryant *et al.*, 'Dream Rebound of

Suppressed Emotional Thoughts: The Influence of Cognitive Load', *Consciousness and Cognition*, 20 (2011), pp. 515–22.

26 'mental processes', D. Wegner, 'Ironic Processes of Mental Control', *Psychological Review*, 101 (1) (1994), pp. 34–52.

27 'Wasmeier', J. Beckmann, interview with author.

29 'odd and meaningless rituals', P. Muris *et al.*, 'Abnormal and Normal Compulsions', *Behavioural Research and Therapy*, 35 (3) (1997), pp. 249–52.

31 'worms', M. Nguyen *et al.*, 'A case of severe adolescent obsessive-compulsive disorder treated with inpatient hospitalisation, risperidone and sertraline', *Journal of Behavioral Addictions*, 1 (2) (2012), pp. 78–82.

32 'Eddie', W. Marshall and C. Langton, 'Unwanted Thoughts and Fantasies Experienced by Sexual Offenders', in D. Clark (ed.), *Intrusive Thoughts in Clinical Disorders* (Guildford Press, 2005), pp. 206–7.

32 'Mike . . . Jennifer', G. Doron *et al.*, 'Flaws and All: Exploring partner-focused obsessive-compulsive symptoms', *Journal of Obsessive-Compulsive and Related Disorders*, 1 (2012), pp. 234–43.

34 'Israel . . . Jack', G. Doron *et al.*, 'Tainted Love: Exploring relationship-centred obsessive compulsive symptoms in two non-clinical cohorts', *Journal of Obsessive-Compulsive and Related Disorders*, 1 (2012), pp. 16–24.

37 'Nanaimo Correctional Centre', M. O'Neill *et al.*, 'Intrusive Thoughts and Psychopathy in a Student and Incarcerated Sample', *Journal of Behavior Therapy and Experimental Psychiatry*, 40 (2009), pp. 147–57.

THREE: The mademoiselle and the Rat Man

40 'Aids-phobia', M. Jenike and C. Pato, 'Disabling Fear of AIDS Responsive to Imipramine', *Psychosomatics*, 27 (1986), pp. 143–4.

40 'Munich', Proceedings published as H. Jäger, *Aids Phobia: Disease Patterns and Possibilities of Treatment* (Ellis Horwood, 1988).

40 'syphilis-phobia', F. Cormia, 'Syphilophobia and Allied Anxiety States', *The Canadian Medical Association Journal* (October, 1938), pp. 361–6.

40 'asbestos', P. De Silva, 'Culture and Obsessive-Compulsive Disorder', *Clinical Conditions* (2006), pp. 402–4.

40 'it was HIV', J. Rapoport, *The Boy Who Couldn't Stop Washing* (Penguin, 1991), pp. 161–4.

41 'climate change', M. Jones *et al.*, 'The Impact of Climate Change on Obsessive Compulsive Checking Concerns', *Australian and New Zealand Journal of Psychiatry*, 46 (3) (2012), pp. 265–70.

42 'Andy Warhol', B. Dillon, *Tormented Hope: Nine Hypochondriac Lives* (Penguin, 2010), pp. 255–261.

42 'Warrington', D. Walton and M. Mather, 'The application of learning principles to the treatment of obsessive-compulsive states in the acute and chronic phases of illness', *Behaviour Research and Therapy*, August (1963), pp. 163–74.

43 'coffins', J. Bondeson, *Buried Alive: The terrifying history of our most primal fear* (W. W. Norton, 2002), p. 118.

43 'Washington . . . Chopin', L. Dossey, 'The Undead: Botched burials, safety coffins and the fear of the grave', *Explorations*, July/August 2007, pp. 347–54.

43 'Nobel', www.nobelprize.org/alfred_nobel/will/will-full.html.

45 'mad disease', S. Freud, *Introductory Lectures on Psychoanalysis* (1920), p. 220.

46 'Lanzer', S. Freud, *Notes Upon a Case of Obsessional Neurosis* (1909).

49 'Ernest Jones', E. Jones, *Sigmund Freud Life and Work, Vol. 2: Years of Maturity 1901–1919* (The Hogarth Press, 1958), p. 42.

49 'Sulloway', F. Sulloway, 'Reassessing Freud's Case Histories', *Isis*, 82 (1991), pp. 245–75.

50 'Mademoiselle F', J. Esquirol, *Mental maladies: a treatise on insanity* (Lea and Blanchard, 1845/1938), pp. 348–51.

52 'To see madhouses', quoted in J. Goldstein, *Console and Classify: The French Psychiatric Profession in the Nineteenth Century* (University of Chicago Press, 1987), p.141.

55 'field of law', J. Goldstein, 'Professional Knowledge and Professional Self-Interest: The Rise and Fall of Monomania in 19th-century France', *International Journal of Law and Psychiatry*, 21 (1998), pp. 385–96.

56 'Harrington Tuke', H. Tuke, 'Monomania and homicide', *Lancet* (12 October 1867), pp. 472–3.

56–7 'Newgate', J. Gibson, 'Bordier's case', *Lancet* (2 November 1867), pp. 567–8.

FOUR: An emerging obsession

62 'UK government', www.dh.gov.uk/health/category/policy-areas/social-care/mental-health.

63 'Tavistock Clinic', J. Sandler and A. Hazari, 'The "Obsessional": On the psychological classification of obsessional character traits and symptoms', *British Journal of Medical Psychology*, 33 (1960), pp. 113–22.

65 'bowel movements', see for example E. Hetherington and Y. Brackbill, 'Etiology and Covariation of Obstinacy, Orderliness and Parsimony in Young Children', *Child Development*, 34 (1963), pp. 919–43.

65 'Selfridges', L. Warren, 'The OCD Chopping Board with Etched Lines for a Perfectionist', *Daily Mail* online (1 September 2011), http://www.dailymail.co.uk/news/article-2032812/The-OCD-chopping-board-etched-lines-perfectionist.html.

66 'OCD for dummies', C. Elliot and L. Smith, *Obsessive-Compulsive Disorder for Dummies* (Wiley, 2008).

66 'Zohar', D. Stein and N. Fineberg, *Obsessive-Compulsive Disorder* (Oxford University Press, 2007), p. 10.

67 'Yale-Brown', W. Goodman *et al.*, 'The Yale-Brown Obsessive Compulsive Scale', *Archives of General Psychiatry*, 46 (1989), pp. 1006–16.

68 'all white here', 'Cricket: West Indies Seeing Red Over "All White" Slogan', *New Zealand Herald* (23 November 2008).

69 'cannabis', L. Arseneault *et al.*, 'Cannabis Use in Adolescence and Risk for Adult Psychosis: Longitudinal Prospective Study', *British Medical Journal*, 325 (2002), pp. 1212–13.

69 'quarter of the cohort', M. Fullana *et al.*, 'Obsessions and Compulsions in the Community: Prevalence, Interference, Help-Seeking, Developmental Stability and Co-Occurring Psychiatric Conditions', *American Journal of Psychiatry*, 166 (3) (2009), pp. 329–36.

69–70 'Belgium', M. Fullana *et al.*, 'Obsessive-Compulsive Symptom Dimensions in the General Population: Results from an epidemiological study in six European countries', *Journal of Affective Disorders*, 124 (2010), pp. 291–9.

70 '**two-week spell**', A. Ruscio *et al.*, 'The Epidemiology of Obsessive-Compulsive Disorder in the National Comorbidity Survey Replication', *Molecular Psychiatry*, 15 (2010), pp. 53–63.

70 '**Murray Stein**', M. Stein, 'Worrying About Obsessions and Compulsions', *American Journal of Psychiatry*, 166 (March 2009), pp. 271–3.

73 '**pure-O**', see www.ocduk.org/pure-o.

74 '**just-not-right**', C. Sica *et al.*, 'Not just right experiences predict obsessive-compulsive symptoms in non-clinical Italian individuals: A one-year longitudinal study', *Journal of Obsessive-Compulsive and Related Disorders*, 1 (2012), pp. 159–67.

74 '**high-place phenomenon**', J. Hames *et al.* 'An Urge to Jump Affirms the Urge to Live: An empirical examination of the high place phenomenon', *Journal of Affective Disorders*, 136 (2012), pp. 1114–20.

76 '**dentist**', L. Altman, 'AIDS and a dentist's secrets', *New York Times*, 6 June 1993, http://www.nytimes.com/1993/06/06/weekinreview/aids-and-a-dentist-s-secrets.html?pagewanted=all&src=pm.

77 '**Concordia**', A. Radomsky *et al.*, 'Repeated Checking Really Does Cause Memory Distrust', *Behaviour Research and Therapy*, 44 (2006), pp. 305–16.

78 '**two checks**', M. Coles *et al.*, 'Exploring the Boundaries of Memory Distrust from Repeated Checking: Increasing external validity and examining thresholds', *Behaviour Research and Therapy*, 44 (2006), pp. 995–1006.

78 '**to stare**', M. Van den Hout *et al.*, 'Uncertainty About Perception and Dissociation After Compulsive-like Staring: Time Course of Effects', *Behaviour Research and Therapy*, 47 (2009), pp. 535–9.

FIVE: **The OCD family**

81 '**Collyers mansion**', A. Newman, '"Collyers Mansion" is Code for Firefighters' Nightmare', *New York Times* (5 July 2006).

81 '**Homer and Langley**', Most details taken from M. Natanson, 'The Rock Cried Out', *Prairie Schooner*, 24 (1950), pp. 7–12 and F. Lidz, *Ghosty Men* (Bloomsbury, 2003).

85 'tried to rename', C. Gray, 'Streetscapes', *New York Times* (23 June 2002).

85 'autism', A. Wakabayashi *et al.*, 'Do the traits of autism spectrum overlap with those of schizophrenia or obsessive-compulsive disorder in the general population?' *Research in Autism Spectrum Disorders*, 6 (2012), pp. 717–25.

85 'a tenth', J. Stern, 'Update on Tic Disorders and Tourette Syndrome', *Paediatrics and Child Health* 20 (9) (2010), pp. 411–15.

86 'teleshopping', A. Bonfanti *et al.*, 'Kleptomania, an Unusual Impulsive Control Disorder in Parkinson's Disease?', *Parkinsonism and Related Disorders*, 16 (2010), pp. 358–9.

86 'gambling', D. Drapier *et al.*, 'Pathological Gambling Secondary to Dopaminergic Therapy in Parkinson's Disease', *Psychiatry Research*, 144 (2006), pp. 241–4.

87 'sexsomniac', Y. Béjot *et al.*, 'Sexsomnia: An Uncommon Variety of Parasomnia', *Clinical Neurology and Neurosurgery*, 112 (2010), pp. 72–5.

88 'nonparaphilic . . . Matt . . . Robert', J. Abramowitz, 'Is Nonparaphilic Compulsive Sexual Behavior a Variant of OCD?', in *Obsessive-Compulsive Disorder* (Elsevier, 2007), pp. 271–86.

89 'Charles Marc', M. Goldman, 'Kleptomania: Making Sense of the Nonsensical', *American Journal of Psychiatry*, 148 (1991), pp. 986–96.

89 'Mathey', R. Fullerton and G. Punj, 'Shoplifting as Moral Insanity: Historical Perspectives on Kleptomania', *Journal of Macromarketing*, 24 (2004), pp. 8–16.

89 'rise in tension', D. Simeon and H. Berlin, 'Impulse-Control Disorders', in *Psychiatry* (John Wiley, 2008).

90 'dashboard', J. Dean *et al.*, 'Pathological Hair-Pulling: A Review of the Literature and Case Reports', *Comprehensive Psychiatry*, 33 (1992), pp. 84–91.

90 'Rapunzel syndrome', I. Kirpinar *et al.*, 'Recurrent Trichobezoar Due to Trichophagia: A Case Report', *General Hospital Psychiatry*, 35 (2013), pp. 439–41.

90 'near-fatal', R. O'Sullivan *et al.*, 'Near fatal skin picking from delusional body dysmorphic disorder responsive to fluvoxamine', *Psychosomatics*, 40 (1999), pp. 79–81.

91 '**BDD by proxy**', M. Kelly and K. Phillips, 'Phenomenology and Epidemiology of Body Dysmorphic Disorder' in G. Steketee, *The Oxford Handbook of Obsessive Compulsive and Spectrum Conditions* (Oxford University Press, 2012), p. 55.

92 '**a quarter**', M. Kelly and K. Phillips, 'Phenomenology and Epidemiology of Body Dysmorphic Disorder' in G. Steketee, *The Oxford Handbook of Obsessive Compulsive and Spectrum Conditions* (Oxford University Press, 2012), p. 57.

92 '**Morselli**', K. Phillips, 'Body Dysmorphic Disorder: Recognising and Treating Imagined Ugliness', *World Psychiatry*, 3 (1) (2004), pp. 12–17.

92 '**Body Integrity**', R. Blom *et al.*, 'Body Integrity Identity Disorder', *PLoS ONE*, 7 (April 2012), e34702.

93 '**hypochondriasis**', S. Taylor *et al.*, 'Hypochondriasis and Health-Related Anxiety', in P. Sturmey and M. Hersen (eds.), *Handbook of Evidence-Based Practice in Clinical Psychology* (Wiley, 2012).

94 '**unrelated to food**', D. Garner *et al.*, 'Cognitive-Behavioural Therapy for Anorexia Nervosa', in D. Garner and P. Garfinkel, *Handbook of Treatment for Eating Disorders*, Guildford (1997), pp. 94–144.

94 '**Rachel**', C. Schupak and J. Rosenthal, 'Excessive Daydreaming: A case history and discussion of mind wandering and high fantasy proneness', *Consciousness and Cognition*, 18 (2009), pp. 290–92.

95 '**academic survey**', J. Bigelsen and C. Schupak, 'Compulsive Fantasy: Proposed evidence for an under-reported syndrome through a systematic study of 90 self-identified non-normative fantasisers', *Consciousness and Cognition*, 20 (2011), pp. 1634–48.

96 '**jealousy**', D. Marazziti *et al.*, 'Normal and Obsessional Jealousy: A Study of a Population of Young Adults', *European Psychiatry*, 18 (2003), pp. 106–11.

97 '**pet rabbit**', S. Taylor *et al.*, 'Cognitive Approaches to Understanding Obsessive Compulsive and Related Disorders' in G. Steketee, *The Oxford Handbook of Obsessive Compulsive and Spectrum Disorders* (Oxford University Press, 2012), p. 234.

98 '**signs of a tail**', C. Volz and I. Heyman, 'Case Series: Transformation obsession in young people with obsessive-compulsive

disorder', *Journal of the American Academy of Child and Adolescent Psychiatry*, 46 (2007), pp. 766–72.

SIX: Cruel to be kind

99 '**pleaded**', A. Solomon, *The Noonday Demon: An Anatomy of Depression* (Vintage, 2002), p. 84.

100 '**zero evidence**', K. Ponniah *et al.*, 'An update on the efficacy of psychological treatments for obsessive-compulsive disorder in adults', *Journal of Obsessive Compulsive and Related Disorders*, 2 (2013), pp. 207–18.

100 '**Holy Ghost**', V. Meyer, 'Modification of Expectations in Cases with Obsessional Rituals', *Behaviour Research and Therapy*, 4 (1966), pp. 273–80.

101 '**compromise**', www.ocdhistory.net/20thcentury/the_term_ocd.html.

101 '**reflex at a distance**', D. Todes, 'From the Machine to the Ghost Within: Pavlov's transition from digestive physiology to conditional reflexes', *American Psychologist*, 52 (1997), pp. 947–55.

102 '**wallpaper**', H. Eysenck, 'Personality and Behaviour Therapy', *Proceedings of the Royal Society of Medicine*, 504 (1960), pp. 18–22.

102 '**gamblers**', J. Barker and M. Miller, 'Aversion Therapy for Compulsive Gambling', *Lancet* (26 February 1966), pp. 491–2. 100 '**alcoholics**', R. Elkins, 'An appraisal of chemical aversion (emetic therapy) approaches to alcoholism treatment', *Behaviour Research and Therapy* 29 (5) (1991), pp. 387–413.

103 '**doughnut**', J. Foreyt and W. Kennedy, 'Treatment of Overweight by Aversion Therapy', *Behaviour Research and Therapy*, 9 (1) (1971), pp. 29–34.

103 '**gay men**', M. MacCulloch *et al.*, 'Anticipatory Avoidance Learning for the Treatment of Homosexuality: Recent developments and an automatic aversion therapy system', *Behavior Therapy*, 2 (1971), pp. 151–69.

103 '**eel**', P. Kellaway, 'The part played by electric fish in the early history of bioelectricity and electrotherapy', *Bulletin of the History of Medicine*, 20 (1946), pp. 112–37.

103 '**chaplain**', P. De Silva, 'Buddhism and Behaviour Modification', *Behaviour Research and Therapy*, 22 (6) (1984), pp. 661–78.

103 '**Birmingham**', A. Le Boeuf, 'An automated aversion device in the

treatment of a compulsive handwashing ritual', *Journal of Behavior Therapy and Experimental Psychiatry*, 5 (3–4) (1974), pp. 267–70.

103–4 **'Kenny'**, F. Kenny et al., 'Faradic disruption of obsessive ideation in the treatment of obsessive neurosis', *Behavior Therapy*, 4 (1973), pp. 448–57.

105 **'brainwash, Rockefeller Nazis** and **McConnell'**, A. Bandura, 'Swimming Against the Mainstream: The early years from chilly tributary to transformative mainstream', *Behaviour Research and Therapy*, 42 (2004), pp. 613–30.

108 **'great line'**, B. Dillon, *Tormented Hope: Nine Hypochondriac Lives* (Penguin, 2009), p. 2.

109 **'seventeen years'**, M. Jenike, 'Obsessive-Compulsive Disorder', *The New England Journal of Medicine*, 350 (2004), pp. 259–65.

110 **'erect penises'**, W. Butler-Bowdon, *The Book of Margery Kempe, A Modern Version* (Jonathan Cape, 1936), pp. 352–3.

110 **'porpoise'**, R. Hunter, *300 Years of Psychiatry 1535–1860* (1963), pp. 338–41.

111 **'some stories'**, P. De Silva, 'Culture and Obsessive-Compulsive Disorder', *Clinical Conditions* (2006), pp. 402–4.

111 **'enlightenment'**, K. Wong, *The Complete Book of Zen* (Tuttle, 2002), p. 293.

111 **'Boswell'**, http://www.ocdhistory.net/philosophical/johnson.html.

111 **'Luther'**, M. Luther, *Luther: Letters of Spiritual Counsel.* (Regent College, 2003), p. 90.

SEVEN: **The God obsession**

115 **'misled'**, C. Sica et al., 'Religiousness and Obsessive-Compulsive Cognitions and Symptoms in an Italian Population', *Behaviour Research and Therapy*, 40 (7) (2002), pp. 813–23.

116 **'Climacus'**, J. Climacus, *The Ladder of Divine Ascent* (Paulist Press, 1982), pp. 211–13.

116 **'Antoninus'**, www.ocdhistory.net/earlypastoral/antoninus.html.

117 **'display this trend'**, H. Van Megen et al., 'Obsessive-Compulsive Disorder and Religion: A Reconnaissance', in P. Verhagen et al., *Religion and Psychiatry: Beyond Boundaries* (Wiley, 2010), p. 274.

119 **'Sermon'**, Matthew 5:27–28.

119 '**Lutheran**', B. Deacon *et al.*, 'Lutheran Clergy Members' Responses to Scrupulosity: The effects of moral thought-action fusion and liberal vs conservative denomination', *Journal of Obsessive-Compulsive and Related Disorders*, 2 (2) (2013), pp. 71–7.

120 '**Protestant**', N. Berman, 'The Relationship Between Religion and Thought-action Fusion: Use of an In Vivo Paradigm', *Behaviour Research and Therapy*, 48 (2010), pp. 670–74.

121 '*waswaas*', M. Awais Tahir, 'Islamic Solution for OCD (Waswaas) – A Comprehensive Guide', *Islam and Psychology blog* (August 2011).

121 '**Islamic text**', 'Forgetfulness in prayer and prostration as compensation for it', *Sahih al-Muslim*.

121 '**Jewish people**', J. Huppert and J. Siev, 'Treating scrupulosity in religious individuals using cognitive behavioural therapy', *Cognitive and Behavioral Practice*, 17 (2010), pp. 382–92.

122 '**Joan**', F. Tallis, 'Obsessions, Responsibility and Guilt: Two case reports suggesting a common and specific aetiology', *Behaviour Research and Therapy*, 32 (1994), pp. 143–5.

123 '**broken glass**', V. Bream Oldfield, 'Hoarding – A New Chapter', Presentation at OCD-UK conference at Cardiff University (10 November 2012).

123 '**cognitive model**', P. Salkovskis, 'Obsessional-Compulsive Problems: A Cognitive Behavioural Analysis', *Behaviour Research and Therapy*, 23 (1985), pp. 571–83.

124 '**turn them into**', Obsessive Compulsive Cognitions Work Group, 'Cognitive Assessment of Obsessive-Compulsive Disorder', *Behaviour Research and Therapy*, 35 (1997), pp. 667–81.

125 '**mixed pills**', R. Ladoucheur *et al.*, 'Excessive Responsibility in Obsessional Concerns: A Fine-Grained Experimental Analysis', *Behaviour Research and Therapy*, 35 (1997), pp. 423–7.

125 '**snakes**', B. Fritzler *et al.*, 'From Intrusive Thoughts to Obsessions: The role of perceptions of responsibility, salience and thought suppression', *Journal of Behavior Therapy and Experimental Psychiatry*, 39 (2008), pp. 610–24.

127 '**soldier**', A. Kalman, 'State Admits Soldier Developed OCD Guarding Military Secrets', *The Times of Israel* (7 April 2013).

127–8 '**Sara**', L. Christian and E. Storch, 'Cognitive behavioural treatment of postpartum onset obsessive-compulsive disorder with aggressive obsessions', *Clinical Case Studies*, 8 (1) (2009), pp. 72–83.

128 '**one in ten**', E. Miller *et al.*, 'Obsessive Compulsive Symptoms During the Postpartum Period: A Prospective Cohort', *Journal of Reproductive Medicine* (8 May 2013).

128 '**worsen**', M. Altemus and K. Brogan, 'Pregnancy and Postpartum', *CNS Spectrums*, 9 (2004), pp. 10–11.

129 '**psychosis**', N. Fairbrother and J. Abramowitz, 'New parenthood as a risk factor for the development of obsessional problems', *Behaviour Research and Therapy*, 45 (2007), pp. 2155–63.

130 '**Rachman**', S. Rachman, personal communication with author.

EIGHT: **Animals and other relatives**

133 '**Lorenz**', K. Lorenz, *King Solomon's Ring* (Methuen, 1957), p. 108.

134 '**sniffy**', J. Abramowitz *et al.*, 'Animal Models of Obsessive-Compulsive Disorder', *Biological Psychiatry*, 69 (2011), pp. 29–30.

134 '**veterinary scientists**', A. Goto *et al.*, 'Risk Factors for Canine Tail-Chasing Behaviour in Japan', *The Veterinary Journal*, 192 (2012), pp. 445–8.

135 '**birds**', For review see N. Fineberg *et al.*, 'Translational Approaches to Obsessive-Compulsive Disorder: From Animal Models to Clinical Treatment', *British Journal of Pharmacology*, 164 (2011), pp. 1044–61.

135–6 '**Vienna**', Quoted in D. Eilam *et al.*, 'Rituals, Stereotypy and Compulsive Behaviour in Animals and Humans', *Neuroscience and Biobehavioral Reviews*, 30 (2006), pp. 456–71.

136 '**rituals**', All of these examples from S. Dulaney and A. Fiske, 'Cultural Rituals and Obsessive-Compulsive Disorder: Is there a common psychological mechanism?' *Ethos*, 22 (3) (1994), pp. 243–83.

139 '**rape**', R. Thornhill and C. Palmer, *A Natural History of Rape* (MIT Press, 2001).

140 '**anxiety**', W. Lee *et al.*, 'The Protective Role of Trait Anxiety: A Longitudinal Cohort Study', *Psychological Medicine*, 36 (2006), pp. 345–51.

140 '**contradiction**', W. Lee, personal communication with the author.

141 '**immune**', R. Abed and K. de Pauw, 'An Evolutionary Hypothesis

for Obsessive-Compulsive Disorder: A Psychological Immune System?', cogprints.org/1147/1/ocd-final.htm (1999).

142-3 'Speculated . . . Congo people . . . Waica', J. Polimeni et al., 'Could obsessive-compulsive disorder have originated as a group-selected adaptive trait in traditional societies?' Medical Hypotheses, 65 (2005), pp. 655-64.

144 'Seligman', R. Littlewood and S. Dein, Cultural Psychiatry and Medical Anthropology (Athlone Press, 2000), p. 10.

145 'Ghana', V. Curtis et al., 'Masters of Marketing: Bringing private sector skills to public health partnerships', American Journal of Public Health, 97 (4) (2007), pp. 634-41.

146 'filthy toilets', S. Moritz et al., 'Larger than Life: Overestimation of object size is moderated by personal relevance in obsessive-compulsive disorder', Journal of Behavior Therapy and Experimental Psychiatry, 42 (2011), pp. 481-7.

146 'Darwin', C. Darwin, The Expression of the Emotions in Man and Animals (Fontana, 3rd edn, 1998), p. 257.

147 'Andy', S. Rachman, personal communication with author.

148 'dirty kiss', C. Elliot and A. Radomsky, 'Mental Contamination: The effects of imagined physical dirt and immoral behaviour', Behaviour Research and Therapy, 50 (2012), pp. 422-7.

149 'Claire', K. Wagner and M. Sullivan, 'Fear of AIDS related to development of obsessive-compulsive disorder in a child', Journal of the American Academy of Adolescent Psychiatry, 30 (5) (1991), pp. 740-42.

NINE: Man hands on misery to man

152 'run in families', J. Samuels et al., 'Genetic Understanding of OCD and Spectrum Disorders' in G. Steketee, The Oxford Handbook of Obsessive Compulsive and Spectrum Disorders (Oxford University Press, 2012), p. 113.

153 'eye colour', R. Sturm and M. Larsson, 'Genetics of Human Iris Colour and Patterns', Pigment Cells and Melanoma Research, 22 (2009), pp. 544-62.

153 'obsessive family', C. Mathews et al., 'Genome-wide linkage analysis of obsessive-compulsive disorder implicates chromosome 1p36', Biological Psychiatry, 72 (2012), pp. 629-36.

154 'parallel study', S. Stewart *et al.*, 'Genome-wide Association Study of Obsessive-Compulsive Disorder', *Molecular Psychiatry* (2012), pp. 1–11.

155 'twins . . . best guess', J. Samuels *et al.*, 'Genetic Understanding of OCD and Spectrum Disorders' in G. Steketee, *The Oxford Handbook of Obsessive Compulsive and Spectrum Disorders* (Oxford University Press, 2012), pp. 112–13.

156 'too much power', K. Renshaw *et al.*, 'The Role of Family and Social Relationships in OCD and Spectrum Conditions' in G. Steketee, *The Oxford Handbook of Obsessive Compulsive and Spectrum Disorders* (Oxford University Press, 2012), pp. 171–3.

156 'tests', L. Farrell *et al.*, 'Do mothers enhance responsibility in children with obsessive-compulsive disorder? A preliminary study of mother-child interactions during a problem solving discussion', *Journal of Obsessive-Compulsive and Related Disorders*, 2 (2) (2013), pp. 76–84.

156 'Raymond Fowler', R. Fowler, 'Howard Hughes: A Psychological Autopsy', *Psychology Today* (May 1986).

157 'overprotection', P. Salkovskis *et al.*, 'Multiple pathways to inflated responsibility beliefs in obsessional problems: Possible origins and implications for therapy and research', *Behaviour Research and Therapy*, 37 (1999), pp. 1055–72.

157 'known study', P. Barrett *et al.*, 'Do parent and child behaviours differentiate families whose children have obsessive-compulsive disorder from other clinic and non-clinic families?' *Journal of Child Psychology and Psychiatry*, 43 (2002), pp. 597–607.

158 'Mrs D.', S. Rachman and R. Hodgson, *Obsessions and Compulsions* (Prentice Hall, 1980), p. 61.

158 'George and Harry', S. Rachman and R. Hodgson, *Obsessions and Compulsions* (Prentice Hall, 1980), pp. 66–8.

159 'become involved', K. Renshaw *et al.*, 'Role of Family and Social Relationships in OCD and Spectrum Conditions' in G. Steketee, *The Oxford Handbook of Obsessive Compulsive and Spectrum Disorders* (Oxford University Press, 2012), p. 178.

159 'can get angry', E. Storch *et al.*, 'Family Accommodation in Paediatric Obsessive-Compulsive Disorder', *Journal of Clinical Child Adolescent Psychiatry*, 36 (2007), pp. 207–16.

159 '**bargaining**', C. Purdon, 'Assessing Comorbidity, Insight, Family and Functioning in OCD' in G. Steketee, *The Oxford Handbook of Obsessive Compulsive and Spectrum Disorders* (Oxford University Press, 2012), p. 283.

160 '**monkey, snake and flower**', M. Cook and S. Mineka, 'Second-order conditioning and overshadowing in the observational conditioning of fear in monkeys', *Behaviour Research and Therapy*, 25 (5) (1987), pp. 349–64.

162 '**Mr Rossi**', J. Calamari *et al.*, 'Obsessive-Compulsive Disorder in Late Life', *Cognitive and Behavioral Practice*, 19 (2012), pp. 136–50.

162 '**fewer than 15 per cent**', S. Rasmussen and J. Eisen, 'The Epidemiology and Clinical Features of Obsessive-Compulsive Disorder', *Child and Adolescent Psychiatric Clinics of North America*, 15 (1992), pp. 743–58.

162 '**Howard**', D. Tolin, 'Case Study: Bibliotherapy and extinction treatment of obsessive-compulsive disorder in a 5-year old boy', *Journal of the American Academy of Child and Adolescent Psychiatry*, 40 (2001), pp. 1111–14.

163 '**more than half**', J. Pollitt, 'Natural History Studies in Mental Illness: A discussion based on a pilot study of obsessional states', *Journal of Mental Science*, 106 (1960), pp. 93–113.

163 '**Max**', E. Storch *et al.*, 'Peer Victimization and the Development of Obsessive-Compulsive Disorder in Adolescence', *Depression and Anxiety*, 21 (2005), pp. 41–4.

164 '**Mr A.**', M. Jenike and A. Brandon, 'Obsessive-Compulsive Disorder and Head Trauma: A Rare Association', *Journal of Anxiety Disorders*, 2 (1988), pp. 353–9.

164 '**Istanbul**', I. Baral Kulaksizoglu *et al.*, 'Obsessive-Compulsive Disorder After Epilepsy Surgery', *Epilepsy & Behavior*, 5 (2004), pp. 113–18.

164 '**Dudley**', N. Lewis *et al.*, 'Delayed Diagnosis of Appendicitis and Peritonitis, Resulting in the Onset of OCD: D *v.* Dudley Group of Hospitals NHS Foundation Trust', *Clinical Risk*, March 2011, p. 73.

165 '**most toddlers**', H. Leonard *et al.*, 'Childhood Rituals: Normal Development or Obsessive-Compulsive Symptoms?', *Journal of the American Academy of Child and Adolescent Psychiatry*, 29 (1) (1990), pp. 17–23.

166 '**test the impact**', A. Pietrefesa and D. Evans, 'Affective and neuropsychological correlates of children's rituals and compulsive-like behaviours: Continuities and discontinuities with obsessive-compulsive disorder', *Brain and Cognition*, 65 (2007), pp. 36–46.

168 '**oversensitivity**', R. Dar *et al.*, 'The relationship between sensory processing, childhood rituals and obsessive-compulsive symptoms', *Journal of Behavior Therapy and Experimental Psychiatry*, 43 (2012), pp. 679–84.

169 '**adapted version**', L. Scahill *et al.*, 'Children's Yale-Brown Obsessive Compulsive Scale: Reliability and Validity', *Journal of the American Academy of Child and Adolescent Psychiatry*, 36 (1997), pp. 844–52.

TEN: The runaway brain

173 '**Penfield**', for example R. Hogan and E. English, 'Epilepsy and Brain Function: Common Ideas of Hughlings-Jackson and Wilder Penfield', *Epilepsy & Behavior*, 24 (2012), pp. 311–13.

173 '**drop the word**', S. Goldberg, 'MRIs and the Perception of Risk', *American Journal of Law and Medicine*, 33 (2007), pp. 229–37.

175 '**Atlantic salmon**', C. Bennett *et al.*, 'Neural correlates of interspecies perspective taking in the post-mortem Atlantic Salmon', *Journal of Serendipitous and Unexpected Results*, 1 (2010), pp. 1–5.

176 '**my brain scanned**', D. Adam, 'I Feel as if I've Been Entombed', *Guardian* (20 November 2003).

176 '**inside MRI tubes**', C. Adler *et al.*, 'fMRI of neuronal activation with symptom provocation in unmedicated patients with obsessive-compulsive disorder', *Journal of Psychiatric Research*, 34 (2000), pp. 317–24.

177 '**normal**', J. Hou *et al.*, 'Localization of cerebral function deficits in patients with obsessive-compulsive disorder: A resting state fMRI study', *Journal of Affective Disorders*, 138 (2012), pp. 313–21.

178 '**fighter aircraft**', J. Sak and A. Grzybowski, 'Brain and Aviation: On the 80th anniversary of Constantin von Economo's (1876–1931) death', *Neurological Sciences*, 34 (3) (2013), pp. 387–91.

178 '**write-up**', C. von Economo, *Encephalitis Lethargica: Its Sequelae and Treatment* (tr. K. Newman, Oxford University Press, 1931), p. 121.

179 'lampreys', M. Stephenson-Jones et al., 'Evolutionary Conservation of the Basal Ganglia as a Common Vertebrate Mechanism for Action Selection', Current Biology, 21 (2011), pp. 1081–91.

180 'Mr V.', D. Laplane et al., 'Pure psychic akinesia with bilateral lesions of basal ganglia', Journal of Neurology, Neurosurgery and Psychiatry, 47 (1984), pp. 377–85.

180 'whistle', Polak et al., 'Compulsive Carnival Song Whistling Following Cardiac Arrest: A Case Study', BMC Psychiatry, 12 (2012).

182 'Pandas', S. Swedo et al., 'Paediatric Autoimmune Neuropsychiatric Disorders Associated With Streptococcal Infections: Clinical Description of the First 50 Cases', American Journal of Psychiatry, 155 (2 February 1998), pp. 264–71.

183 'replacing the plasma', S. Perlmutter et al., 'Therapeutic plasma exchange and intravenous immunoglobulin for obsessive-compulsive disorder and tic disorders in childhood', The Lancet, 354 (1999), pp. 1153–8.

183 'disagreement', S. Swedo et al., 'From Research Subgroup to Clinical Syndrome: Modifying the Pandas Criteria to Describe Pans', Paediatrics and Therapeutics, 2 (2012).

183 'green anoles', L. Baxter, 'Basal Ganglia Systems in Ritualistic Social Displays: Reptiles and Humans; Function and Illness', Physiology & Behavior, 79 (2003), pp. 451–60.

184 'supported other research', N. Greenberg et al., 'Role of the paleostriatum in species-typical display behaviour of the lizard (Anolis carolinensis)', Brain Research, 172 (1979), pp. 229–41.

184–5 'something like this', D. Mataix-Cols and O. van den Heuvel, 'Neuroanatomy of Obsessive Compulsive and Related Disorders', in G. Steketee, The Oxford Handbook of Obsessive Compulsive and Spectrum Disorders (Oxford University Press, 2012), pp. 126–7.

ELEVEN: Daddy's little helper

190 'six hours', 'International Programme on Chemical Safety Poisons Information Monograph', Pharmaceutical, 177 (1997).

191 'heroin', S. Everts, 'Brain Barricade', Chemical and Engineering News (4 June 2007), pp. 33–6.

192 'gateway proteins', for overview see M. Alavijeh et al., 'Drug

metabolism and pharmacokinetics, the blood brain barrier and central nervous system drug discovery', *NeuroRx*, 2 (4) (2005), pp. 554–71.

193 '**consistent picture**', D. Dougherty *et al.*, 'Pharmacological Treatments for Obsessive-Compulsive Disorder' in G. Steketee, *The Oxford Handbook of Obsessive Compulsive and Spectrum Disorders* (Oxford University Press, 2012), pp. 293–5.

193 '**Guyotat**', D. Healy, *The Psychopharmacologists*, vol. 3 (Arnold, 1998), pp. 40–45.

194 '**table tennis**', D. Healy, *The Psychopharmacologists*, vol. 2, (Arnold, 1998), pp. 412–15.

195 '**Beaumont**', D. Healy, *The Psychopharmacologists* (Arnold, 1998), pp. 310–15.

196 '**Rapoport**', J. Rapoport, *The Boy Who Couldn't Stop Washing* (Penguin, 1991), p. 115.

197 '**rapid relapse**', D. Dougherty *et al.*, 'Pharmacological Treatments for Obsessive-Compulsive Disorder' in G. Steketee, *The Oxford Handbook of Obsessive Compulsive and Spectrum Disorders* (Oxford University Press, 2012), pp. 296–7.

198 '**serotonin hypothesis**', for overview see D. Stein and N. Fineberg, *Obsessive-Compulsive Disorder* (Oxford University Press, 2007), pp. 18–19.

198 '**PET**', D. Perani *et al.*, 'In vivo PET study of 5HT(2A) serotonin and D(2) dopamine dysfunction in drug-naïve obsessive-compulsive disorder', *Neuroimage*, 42 (2008), pp. 306–14.

199 '**glutamate**', C. Pittenger *et al.*, 'Glutamate Abnormalities in Obsessive-Compulsive Disorder: Neurobiology, Pathophysiology and Treatment', *Pharmacology and Therapeutics*, 132 (2011), pp. 314–32.

199 '**squirts**', C. Neill Epperson *et al.*, 'Intranasal Oxytocin in Obsessive-Compulsive Disorder', *Biological Psychiatry*, 40 (1996), pp. 547–9.

199–200 '**Turkey . . . measured as smaller**', M. Atmaca *et al.*, 'Hippocampus and amygdala volumes in patients with refractory obsessive-compulsive disorder', *Progress in Neuro-Psychopharmacology and Biological Psychiatry*, 32 (2008), pp. 1283–6.

TWELVE: The helicopter view

205 'Solomon', V. LoLordo, 'Experimental Psychologist Richard L. Solomon (1918–1995)', *APS Observer*, 9 (2) (1996).

205 'dogs', J. Abramowitz *et al.*, 'Exposure-Based Treatment for Obsessive-Compulsive Disorder' in G. Steketee, *Oxford Handbook of Obsessive Compulsive and Spectrum Disorders* (Oxford University Press, 2012), p. 323.

209 'semen', S. Rachman and R. Hodgson, *Obsessions and Compulsions* (Prentice Hall, 1980), p. 304.

209 'hamster', S. Rachman *et al.*, 'The Treatment of Chronic Obsessive-Compulsive Neurosis', *Behaviour Research and Therapy*, 9 (1971), pp. 237–47.

210 'tamed', J. Abramowitz, 'Effectiveness of psychological and pharmacological treatments for obsessive-compulsive disorder: A quantitative review', *Journal of Consulting and Clinical Psychology*, 65 (1997), pp. 44–52.

210 'Simon', M. Williams *et al.*, 'Treatment of sexual-orientation obsessions in obsessive-compulsive disorder using exposure and ritual prevention', *Clinical Case Studies*, 10 (1) (2011), pp. 53–66.

212 'Meyer', R. Levy and V. Meyer, 'Ritual Prevention in Obsessional Patients', *Proceedings of the Royal Society of Medicine*, 64 (1971), pp. 1115–18.

212 'especially tolerant', D. Hezel *et al.*, 'Emotional Distress and Pain Tolerance in Obsessive-Compulsive Disorder', *Journal of Behavior Therapy and Experimental Psychiatry*, 43 (2012), pp. 981–7.

214 'David', B. Bruce and V. Stevens, 'AIDS-related Obsessive-Compulsive Disorder: A Treatment Dilemma', *Journal of Anxiety Disorders*, 6 (1992), pp. 79–88.

217 'meta-analysis', B. Olatunji *et al.*, 'Cognitive-Behavioural Therapy for Obsessive-Compulsive Disorder: A meta-analysis of treatment outcome and moderators', *Journal of Psychiatric Research*, 47 (1) (2013), pp. 33–41.

218 'smart drugs', M. Norberg *et al.*, 'D-Cycloserine for Treatment Nonresponders with Obsessive-Compulsive Disorder: A Case Report', *Cognitive and Behavioral Practice*, 19 (2012), pp. 338–45.

219 'shows up', S. Vázquez Rivera *et al.*, 'Effects on the Brain of Effective Psychological Treatments for Anxiety Disorders: A Systematic Review', *Actas españolas de psiquiatría*, 38 (4) (2010), pp. 239–48.

THIRTEEN: Long live lobotomy

221 'Mr V.', P. Doshi, 'Anterior Capsulotomy for Refractory OCD: First case as per the core group guidelines', *Indian Journal of Psychiatry*, 53 (2011), pp. 270–73.

223 'miner', M. Wainwright, 'Snapshot Revisited: The Miner and the Copper', *Guardian* (23 February 2009).

224 'my report', D. Adam, 'Open Your Mind', *Guardian* (11 November 2004).

224 'banned it', N. Li *et al.*, 'Nucleus Accumbens Surgery for Addiction', *World Neurosurgery*, 80 (3) (2013), pp. S28.e9–S28.e19.

226 'doctor who treated', J. Harlow, 'Recovery from the Passage of an Iron Bar Through the Head', *Publ Mass Med Soc.* (2) (1868), p. 327.

227 'Burckhardt', S. Manjila *et al.*, 'Modern Psychosurgery Before Egas Moniz: A Tribute to Gottlieb Burckhardt', *Neurosurgery Focus*, 25 (2008), pp. 1–4.

229 'Pavlov', E. Reynolds, 'The John Hughlings Jackson 1935 Centenary Congress Medal', *Journal of Neurology, Neurosurgery and Psychiatry*, 76 (2005), pp. 858–9.

229 'sever pathways', G. Mashour *et al.*, 'Psychosurgery: Past, Present and Future', *Brain Research Reviews*, 48 (2005), pp. 409–19.

229 'quietly returned', E. Valenstein, *Great and Desperate Cures: The Rise and Decline of Psychosurgery and Other Radical Treatments for Mental Illness* (Basic Books, 1986), p. 112.

230 'roast a pig', J. Pressman, *Last Resort: Psychosurgery and the Limits of Medicine* (Cambridge University Press, 1998), pp. 83–4.

230 '400,000 patients', G. Mashour *et al.*, 'Psychosurgery: Past, Present and Future', *Brain Research Reviews*, 48 (2005), pp. 409–19.

230 'two years', B. Kopell and A. Rezai, 'Psychiatric Neurosurgery: A Historical Perspective', *Neurosurgery Clinics of North America*, 14 (2003), pp. 181–97.

231 'defended them', J. Pressman, *Last Resort: Psychosurgery and the Limits of Medicine* (Cambridge University Press, 1998), p. 146.

231 'Lancet', 'Prefrontal Leucotomy', *Lancet* (5 July 1941), p. 13.

232 'Freeman alone', B. Kopell and A. Rezai, 'Psychiatric Neurosurgery: A Historical Perspective', *Neurosurgery Clinics of North America*, 14 (2003), pp. 181–97.

232 'Iowa . . . 4-year-old', B. Goodman, *The Lobotomist*, American Experience PBS Documentary (2008).

232 'shotgun', J. Pressman, *Last Resort: Psychosurgery and the Limits of Medicine* (Cambridge University Press, 1998), p. 342.

232 'Perón', D. Nijensohn *et al.*, 'New evidence of prefrontal lobotomy in the last months of the illness of Eva Perón', *World Neurosurgery*, 77 (3/4) (2012), pp. 583–90.

233 'published the results', 'Prefrontal Leucotomy: Report on 1000 Cases', *Lancet* (15 February 1947), p. 265.

233 'Bristol', R. Hemphill, 'Return of virility after prefrontal leucotomy with enlargement of gonads', *Lancet* (9 September 1944), pp. 345–6.

235 'Mary Lou Zimmerman', the court docket is a matter of public record and can be accessed online at http://cpdocket. cp.cuyahogacounty.us/CV_CaseInformation_Docket. aspx?q=Rw1eHnTVIqL0oQenQx7mcg2. Case was Mary Lou and Sherman Zimmerman v. Cleveland Clinic Foundation, Cuyahoga County Common Pleas Case No. CV-00-399411.

236 'in Germany', I. Rieber and V. Sigusch, 'Psychosurgery on Sex Offenders and Sexual "Deviants" in West Germany', *Archives of Sexual Behaviour*, 8 (1979), pp. 523–7.

236 'Russian', N. Walsh, 'Russia Bans Brain Surgery on Drug Addicts', *Guardian* (9 August 2002), p. 12.

236 'obesity', 'Stereotaxy for Obesity', *Lancet* (4 May 1974), p. 867.

236 'editorial', 'Psychosurgery for Obsessive-Compulsive Disorder – Concerns Remain', *Acta Psychiatrica Scandinavica*, 107 (2003), pp. 241–3.

236 'rare analysis', C. Rück *et al.*, 'Capsulotomy for Obsessive-Compulsive Disorder: Long term follow up of 25 patients', *Archives of General Psychiatry*, 65 (8) (2008), pp. 914–22.

237 'Radano', freeofocd.com and http://www.ocfoundation.org/radano. aspx.

238 'hopes to restart', S. Rasmussen, personal communication with the author.

238 'Iran', S. Hosseini *et al.*, 'Suppression of Obsessive-Compulsive Symptoms after Head Trauma', *Case Reports in Medicine* (26 August 2012).

238 'suicide', L. Solyom *et al.*, 'A Case of Self-Inflicted Leucotomy', *British Journal of Psychiatry*, 151 (1987), pp. 855–7.

239 'Claudius', K. Kane and A. Taub, 'A History of Local Electrical Analgesis', *Pain*, 1 (1975), pp. 125–38.

239 'interviewed', J. Horgan, 'The Forgotten Era of Brain Chips', *Scientific American* (October 2005), pp. 67–73.

239 'Córdoba', J. Osmundsen, 'Matador with a Radio Stops Wired Bull', *New York Times* (17 May 1965), p.1.

240 'Rhode Island' and 'I guess doctor', J. Horgan, 'The Forgotten Era of Brain Chips', *Scientific American* (October 2005), pp. 67–73.

240 'two-way communication', J. Delgado, *Physical Control of the Mind* (Irvington, 1971).

241 'Robert Heath', C. Moan and R. Heath, 'Septal Stimulation for the Initiation of Heterosexual Behavior in a Homosexual Male', *Journal of Behavior Therapy and Experimental Psychiatry*, 3 (1972), pp. 23–30.

241 'Supreme Court', S. Beyer, 'Thought Control and the First Amendment', *Behavioral Sciences and the Law*, 1 (1983), pp. 59–76.

241 'Michigan', Kaimowitz *v.* Michigan Department of Mental Health, No. 73-19434-AW (Michigan, Wayne County Circuit Court, 10 July 1973). See S. Beyer, 'Thought Control and the First Amendment', *Behavioral Sciences and the Law*, 1 (1983), pp. 59–76.

242 'Breggin', P. Breggin, *US Congressional Record*, 118 (26) (1972).

242 '*Science* magazine', B. Culliton, 'Psychosurgery: National Commission Issues Surprisingly Favourable Report', *Science* (15 October 1976), pp. 299–301.

243 'never happened', N. McLaughlin and B. Greenberg, 'Other Biological Approaches to OCD', in G. Steketee, *The Oxford Handbook of Obsessive Compulsive and Spectrum Disorders* (Oxford University Press, 2012), p. 309.

FOURTEEN: Politics and prejudice

245 'Walker', 'I'm a fruitcake! (but that doesn't mean I can't work): MP reveals his battle against OCD as he campaigns against stigma of mental illness', *Daily Mail* online (16 June 2012).

246 'Kaufman', 'Veteran labour MP Gerald Kaufman blames claim for Waterford crystal grapefruit bowls on OCD', *Daily Mail* online (6 June 2009).

250 'child protection', P. Salkovskis, personal communication with the author.

251 'Puleston-Davies', Presentation at OCD-UK conference at Cardiff University (10 November 2012).

252 'Cefalu', P. Cefalu, 'What's So Funny about Obsessive-Compulsive Disorder?' *PMLA*, 124 (1) (2009), pp. 351–2.

254 'Lennard Davis', L. Davis, *Obsession: A history* (University of Chicago Press, 2008), p. 18.

256 'Tesla', M. Cheney, *Tesla: Man out of Time* (Touchstone, 2001).

FIFTEEN: A new dimension

259 'officially reclassified', www.dsm5.org.

260 'B.A.', R. Pitman, 'Posttraumatic Obsessive-Compulsive Disorder: A Case Study', *Comprehensive Psychiatry*, 34 (2) (1993), pp. 102–7.

263 'grim parade', P. De Silva and M. Marks, 'The role of traumatic experiences in the genesis of obsessive-compulsive disorder', *Behavior Research and Therapy*, 37 (1999), pp. 941–51.

264 'Arkansas', C. Badour *et al.*, 'Specificity of fear and disgust experienced during traumatic interpersonal victimization in predicting posttraumatic stress and contamination-based obsessive-compulsive symptoms', *Journal of Anxiety Disorders*, 26 (2012), pp. 590–98.

264 'develop schizophrenia', A. Morrison, 'Psychosis and the Phenomenon of Unwanted Intrusive Thoughts' in D. Clark (ed.), *Intrusive Thoughts in Clinical Disorders: Theory, Research, and Treatment* (Guildford Press, 2005), pp. 175–9.

265 'less insight', M. Poyurovsky and L. Koran, 'Obsessive-compulsive disorder with schizotypy vs schizophrenia with OCD: Diagnostic

dilemmas and therapeutic implications', *Journal of Psychiatric Research*, 39 (2005), pp. 399–408.

267 '**full retreat**', for example 'A. Abbott Novartis to Shut Brain Research Facility', *Nature*, 480 (8 December 2011), pp. 161–2.

267–8 '**13 years**', D. Nutt and G. Goodwin, 'Pharma Fears', *Public Service Review: European Science and Technology*, 14 (2012), pp. 129–30.

269 '**rediscovered**', W. Compton and S. Guze, 'The Neo-Kraepelinian Revolution in Psychiatric Diagnosis', *European Archives of Psychiatry and Clinical Neuroscience*, 245 (1995), pp. 196–201.

274 '**functional connectome**', J. Buckholtz and A. Meyer-Lindenberg, 'Psychopathology and the Human Connectome: Toward a Transdiagnostic Model of Risk for Mental Illness', *Neuron*, 74 (2012), pp. 990–1004.

275 '**new project**', T. Insel and B. Cuthbert, 'Research Domain Criteria: Toward a new classification framework of research on mental disorders', *American Journal of Psychiatry*, 167 (7) (2010), pp. 748–9.

277 '**sub-clinical psychoses**', W. Rössler *et al.*, 'Psychotic Experiences in the General Population: A Twenty-year Prospective Community Study', *Schizophrenia Research*, 92 (2007), pp. 1–14.

278 '**delusional ideation**', E. Peters *et al.*, 'Measurement of Delusional Ideation in the Normal Population: Introducing the PDI (Peters et al Delusional Inventory)', *Schizophrenia Bulletin*, 25 (3) (1999), pp. 553–76.

SIXTEEN: Final thoughts

280 '**high cliff**', D. Lafleur *et al.*, 'Traumatic events and obsessive-compulsive disorder in children and adolescents: Is there a link?' *Journal of Anxiety Disorders*, 25 (2011), pp. 513–19.

288 '**Andersen**', F. Toates and O. Coschug-Toates, *Obsessive-Compulsive Disorder* (Class, 2002), pp. 193–9.

APPENDIX 1

Notes for a doctor, prepared by OCD-UK

To a professional who can help:

I think I have obsessive-compulsive disorder:
- It's hard for me to talk about this.
- Other people don't seem to understand.
- I've become secretive about my habits.
- I spend more than an hour each day feeling trapped by one or more of:

  - Obsessive fears about contamination, resulting in compulsive washing.
  - Obsessive fears about fire/ flood/ theft, resulting in compulsive checking.
  - Anxiety leading to counting, arranging or aligning.
  - Unfounded fears of unwittingly causing harm to or abuse of others.
  - Horrible thoughts that I agonize over but can't get out of my head.

I'm now at the stage at which I need to appeal to you, as a professional, to help me.
OCD is seriously affecting my life. It's stealing my time and my ability to be happy, and:

- I can feel frequently and deeply depressed.
- Life at home can be difficult.
- It can be hard for me to work, study or travel.
- I can have problems making or keeping friendships and relationships.
- My self-confidence and self-esteem have hit an all-time low.

The charity OCD-UK has made me realize that I'm not alone in feeling the way that I do. It has also taught me that help can be found. Please offer me the help that I need to allow me to get my life back.

Notes on thoughts about harming a child

To my health professional:

I think I have obsessive-compulsive disorder (OCD):

- It's hard for me to talk about this.
- My OCD differs from the more well-known perception of OCD.
- I am scared to talk about it.
- It's impacting on my life and my daily functioning.
- I spend more than an hour a day obsessing and fearing my thoughts.

I am now at the stage where I am visiting you to seek help from you, my health provider.

Can I please tell you about some of the thoughts that I am experiencing? They include some, or all of these:

- Distress because I fear I might be attracted to children, despite finding such thoughts abhorrent and against everything I believe in.
- Unwanted thoughts/feelings/urges that cause me immense anxiety that I want to, or may in the future, or might have previously touched a child inappropriately or caused harm to them, even though I don't want to.

- Constant self-questioning whether or not these are wanted thoughts, and what the thoughts may mean or say about me.
- Avoidance of places where children are or might be.

OCD-UK have helped me understand that I am not alone in feeling the way that I do, and that this is a very commonly held belief by those affected by OCD. They have explained to me that these are all thoughts that both men and women can experience with OCD, and that having these thoughts does not place me at any higher risk of acting on these thoughts, or being a danger to children.

Please offer me the help that I need to change the way I deal with these thoughts. OCD-UK have told me that I need to access a form of treatment called Cognitive Behavioural Therapy (CBT), ideally with a therapist that fully understands this aspect of OCD.

Please don't be alarmed by my unwanted obsessive thoughts, these form part of OCD, which are not indicative of any real desire. If you're concerned about my thoughts, OCD-UK ask that you consult an OCD specialist before taking any action, and refer to the paper 'Risk Assessment and Management in Obsessive Compulsive Disorder' by Veale, Freeston, Krebs, Heyman and Salkovskis.